Praise for Brad Warner's *Don't Be a Jerk*

"A delightful blend of irreverent everydayness, precise scholarship, and heartfelt commitment to practice."
— **Stephen Batchelor**, author of *After Buddhism*

"Warner renders the esoteric [Shobogenzo] into a fun, readable text, conveying its spirit with humor and deep respect."
— *Publishers Weekly*

"What's clear in reading Warner's book is his deep respect and lifelong engagement with Dogen.... While Warner's approach to Dogen may be unorthodox, its freshness might be exactly what the doctor ordered for anyone wanting a way in to the old monk's still fresh perspective."
— **Adam Frank**, *13.7: Cosmos & Culture* blog, NPR.org

"Each chapter opens with a passage from the original, which is then carefully and often humorously unpacked.... Although the tone may be irreverent and humorous, the book shows the utmost respect for the monk, who has influenced so many over the centuries."
— *Booklist*

IT CAME FROM BEYOND ZEN!

IT CAME FROM BEYOND ZEN!

More Practical Advice from Dogen, Japan's Greatest Zen Master

Volume 2 of a Radical but Reverent Paraphrasing
of Dogen's *Treasury of the True Dharma Eye*

BRAD WARNER

New World Library
Novato, California

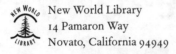 New World Library
14 Pamaron Way
Novato, California 94949

Text design by Tona Pearce Myers

Library of Congress Cataloging-in-Publication data is available.

First printing, October 2017
ISBN 978-1-60868-511-0
Ebook ISBN 978-1-60868-512-7
Printed in Canada on 100% postconsumer-waste recycled paper

 New World Library is proud to be a Gold Certified Environmentally Responsible Publisher. Publisher certification awarded by Green Press Initiative. www.greenpressinitiative.org

10   9   8   7   6   5   4   3   2   1

CONTENTS

Introduction   ix

1. It Came from Beyond Zen! *(It!)*   1

2. Don't Be Half-Assed *(Instructions for the Cook)*   28

3. A Thousand Eyes and Hands of Compassion
   (Compassion)   52

4. Compassion and Zen Buddhist Ethics   68

5. Four Good Ways to Treat People Right
   (Four All-Embracing Virtues)   83

6. Eating Cornflakes and Doing the Dishes *(Everyday Life)*   103

7. Garbage In, Garbage Out
   (Deep Belief in Cause and Effect)   117

8. Wait! What Was the Deal with Cause and Effect Again?
   (Great Practice)   136

9. Buddhist Superpowers *(Mystical Power)*   164

10. He Not Busy Being Born Is Busy Dying
    (Living and Dying)   189

11. Does Life Exist? 203

12. A Willingness to See the Truth *(The Will to the Truth)* 213

13. A Needle in the Butt of Zazen *(A Needle for Zazen)* 226

14. Talking to the Trees about Reality
(The Insentient Preach the Dharma) 265

15. It's All in the Mind, or Is It?
(The Three Worlds Are Only the Mind) 286

16. All You Have to Do Is Dream
(Explaining a Dream within a Dream) 305

17. In Conclusion 329

Bibliography 337
About the Author 343

INTRODUCTION

WE CAME VERY close to losing Dogen.* When I first heard that Dogen was a Japanese Buddhist monk and writer who lived eight hundred years ago, I just sort of assumed that for the past eight hundred years Dogen's teachings were part of the philosophical underpinnings of Japanese society and that we in the West were just now learning about him.

Not so. For the first seven hundred or so years of their existence, Dogen's writings were barely known, outside of a few dedicated monks at monasteries scattered throughout Japan. The general

---

* Maybe you're used to seeing his name as Dōgen. In this book I've decided not to use any diacritics. In Japanese, diacritics are those little marks over certain vowels that show which ones are to be held longer. When speaking Japanese it makes a big difference if certain vowels are held longer than others. For example, the Japanese word for *granny* is *obaa-san* (with a long *a*), and the Japanese word for *aunty* is *oba-san* (with a shorter *a* sound). Sometimes Japanese people address women they don't know as *aunty* as a form of polite familiarity. Foreigners often hold the *a* sound a little too long when they try to do this and end up saying, "Hey, granny" when they mean to say, "Excuse me, ma'am." Since this book is not intended for studying Japanese, I've decided these differences don't matter that much in this context. Diacritics are just confusing for people who don't know what they mean and redundant for those who do. So I left them out. Just be careful when speaking to Japanese people about things you've read in this book!

populace did not read them. They weren't taught anywhere. The copies that existed mostly sat in the backs of temples, slowly rotting away, unloved and neglected, food for mice and moths.

In the eighteenth century there was a small revival of interest in Dogen among Japanese scholars. But it took the Meiji Restoration of the late nineteenth century to get folks really looking into his work. History could easily have gone very differently. If Japan had not been forced to open itself to trade with the Americans, someone else — or even the Americans themselves — could have come into that tiny, unimportant, technologically backward island nation with modern weapons of war and taken it over by force. It would've been a piece of cake! They could have demolished a great deal of Japan's culture. So few copies of Dogen's writings existed at that time that it would have been easy to destroy all or at least most of his work, and it would have been gone forever.

Even with the way history actually went, it never fails to amaze me that it took centuries before the world was ready for what Dogen was writing. It must have been lonely work for Dogen, spending so much time and effort on a huge-ass book that he knew most of his contemporaries would not understand, one that he could not have been certain would last long enough for the rest of the world to catch up to it.

I've always been a fan of so-called cult artists. I have an affinity for people who were unknown in their time. But something like, let's say, *Pet Sounds*, the Beach Boys album that waited twenty years to finally be discovered by hipsters, can't compare to a book that took centuries before it was ever even read by the wider public. At least *Pet Sounds* made the bottom of the music charts when it was new, before it sank into obscurity for a couple of decades. Dogen's writings were unknown to anyone except his students during his lifetime.

Did twenty people read *Shobogenzo* when Dogen was alive? Fifty? Maybe. *Mayyyyybe* fifty. More than that? It's very doubtful.*
And we are still only at the very beginning of a wider international rediscovery of Dogen. The first English translations only began to appear in the seventies. Hell, I was already in the fifth grade when the first English translations of Dogen started to show up at a few little Zen centers out on the West Coast, a long, long way from Wadsworth, Ohio, where I lived. By the time I was old enough to appreciate them, though, copies of those translations were already nearly impossible to come by, at any price. I was there when my own teacher's complete English translation of *Shobogenzo* first came off the printing presses in Tokyo. The book you're reading represents one of the first attempts by anyone outside Japan to create a book about Dogen aimed at an audience other than scholars and devout Buddhist converts.

When I think about what a doofus I am and how completely unqualified I am to even attempt to understand Dogen, I realize I have somehow accidentally become part of something incredibly significant. That's a funny feeling.

I don't claim to be the final word on Dogen. Far from it. Throughout this book I constantly encourage you to look beyond what I'm giving you here. Please find the more orthodox translations and check them out for yourself. Dogen's writing contains a depth and a beauty that this book barely even hints at. But I also have to warn you: if you think the stuff you'll be reading *here* is a brain twister, you should see the more reliable translations.

With this book and some of my others, I am hoping to bring Dogen's ideas to a broader audience than they've ever enjoyed

---

* Some of Dogen's sayings from his lectures were preserved more carefully than his writings and were taught at certain Zen temples through the centuries. But it's really in his extensive and detailed written work where Dogen shines, and most of that stuff was put away and more or less forgotten not too long after he died.

before. His philosophy shouldn't just be something that a few academics and religious nuts jealously guard for themselves. Commentaries on them shouldn't be buried in so many brainiac buzzwords that you have to stop and consult a dictionary every third page. His stuff is much too important for that. It needs to be exposed.

Dogen shows us a new and better way to understand ourselves and the world we live in. He shows us, in fact, that the way we've been thinking about stuff for centuries borders on insanity. He's showing us how to get sane.

Eihei Dogen lived and died in Japan almost eight hundred years ago. And just in case you were wondering, Eihei is pronounced like the letter *a* followed by the word *hey*, as in "Hey! Ho! Let's go!" Dogen is pronounced with a hard *g*, as in Godzilla — so it's not *Do-jen*. Don't ever say Do-jen around me! I'll smack you!

His first name wasn't even Eihei, by the way, nor was Dogen his family name. No one knows for certain what name, first or last, he was given when he was born. Dogen was the dharma name bestowed on him when he became a monk at around age twelve, after which he never used his birth name again, as far as we know. Eihei-ji was the name of the temple he founded much later. As the master of that temple he was called Dogen of Eihei-ji, or Eihei Dogen for short.

Dogen was Japanese, meaning he was from a country whose main exports these days are pornographic comic books and toy robots. In Dogen's day, the forerunners of today's porno comics were just beginning to emerge in the form of naughty picture books printed from woodblocks, but toy robots were still a long way off. At the time Dogen lived, Japan was generally regarded as an utterly insignificant island nation populated mostly by ignorant bumpkins who liked to dress up in weird costumes and slice each other up with swords. It was a long way from the economic powerhouse it briefly became in the twentieth century.

Dogen was the founder of the Japanese branch of the Soto school of Zen Buddhism, and for this he has been held in high regard as a famous figure for the past eight hundred years. And yet, as I've said, for most of that time almost nobody read his extensive writings about Zen practice and philosophy.

When I say he wrote a lot, I mean he wrote *a lot a lot*. Most contemporary versions of his masterwork, *Shobogenzo*, or *Treasury of the True Dharma Eye*, consist of ninety-five chapters, some of which are very long. As I said, it's a big-ass book!

Shobogenzo wasn't even the only thing Dogen wrote. He also wrote a number of shorter pieces about monastic rules and practices that were collected centuries later, plus a bunch of poetry. And Dogen's students made notes during the talks he gave that were put together as *Eihei Koroku* (Extensive Record of Eihei) and *Shobogenzo Zuimonki* (Diary of the True Dharma Eye Treasury).

And even though his writings reached only a minuscule audience when he was alive, he wrote as if he was addressing a vast audience. Who was he writing for? The means to publish his written work barely even existed when Dogen was alive. What few copies did exist were made by hand. Yet he wrote anyway.

Dogen was born in 1200 CE. This makes it very easy to figure out exactly how old he was at any given year listed in the dates he gives at the ends of most of his writings. Dogen was the illegitimate son of a nobleman who was assassinated when Dogen was two years old. His mother died when Dogen was seven. He entered monastic practice at age twelve in the Tendai sect of Buddhism because he wanted to find out if there was something more to life than pain and heartbreak.

One question in particular always troubled the young monk. He asked the older monks and teachers, "Buddha said we are all perfect just as we are. So why do we have to do these strange practices like chanting, meditating, wearing robes, and so on?"

No one could answer him. But he heard about a new temple that taught a form of Buddhism called Zen. The temple was called Kennin-ji. It was the first Zen Buddhist temple in Kyoto, where

Dogen lived, and only the second one in Japan. In 1217, at the age you and I were when we were in high school and our only concerns were acne and where to score weed, Dogen went to that temple and became a monk.

The difference between Tendai Buddhism and Zen Buddhism is that Tendai Buddhism tends to emphasize study and ritual, whereas Zen Buddhism focuses on meditation practice.

In 1223 Dogen accompanied the head teacher of that Zen temple, a guy named Myozen, to China to learn about Zen practices there. At first Dogen was disappointed in Chinese Zen. But in 1225 he met a teacher named Tendo Nyojo,* who told him, "To practice the Way singleheartedly is, in itself, enlightenment. There is no gap between practice and enlightenment, or between zazen and daily life." This impressed Dogen, and he became Tendo Nyojo's student.

In 1227 Tendo Nyojo made Dogen one of his dharma heirs. This means he publicly declared that Dogen had an understanding equal to his own and gave him permission to teach independently. Soon after this, Dogen returned to Japan. He then began writing about the practices he had seen in China and the philosophy he had learned from Tendo Nyojo.

In 1233 he founded a temple in the city of Uji, near Kyoto, which was the capital of Japan and the center of Buddhist study. Ten years later he moved to the remote province of Echizen (now called Fukui Prefecture) and started a temple called Eihei-ji. Some say that he moved because the leaders of the older, more established Buddhist temples were jealous of his growing popularity and forced him to leave Kyoto. There are even suggestions that his life would have been in danger if he didn't get out of Dodge.

Dogen continued writing and revising *Shobogenzo* until he died

---

* This is the Japanese pronunciation of his name. When Japanese people read Chinese characters, they pronounce them differently from the way the Chinese do. The Chinese pronunciation is usually written in roman letters as Tiantong Rujing. I prefer the Japanese pronunciations because that's how I learned them.

in 1253 at the age of fifty-three. He never completed *Shobogenzo*, but he produced about eighty-four finished chapters and about eleven other chapters that were nearly finished. Scholars argue about the exact number, and about which ones were intended as part of *Shobogenzo* and which ones were independent pieces. Plus, as late as the 1930s, previously undiscovered writings of Dogen's were found. This raises the possibility that there might be other unknown writings by him still out there or that some pieces he wrote have been lost for all time, having turned to dust in the back room of some temple.

Dogen's students established many temples throughout Japan, and the Soto school of Zen became extremely popular. However, as we know, Dogen's book *Shobogenzo* was not widely read. Dogen was revered as the founder of the sect, but that's about it.

From 1633 until 1865, Japan closed its borders to outsiders. In 1865 the American Commodore Matthew Perry forced Japan to open itself to international trade. If you've seen the film *The Last Samurai*, it's a fairly accurate portrayal of that time. Except Tom Cruise wasn't really there.

Japan suddenly realized it was very much behind the rest of the world and needed to modernize. This led the Japanese people to try to find Japanese things that were as good as similar things in Europe and America. This included philosophy and religion.

In 1925 a scholar named Tetsuro Watsuji published a book called *Shamon Dogen* (The Monk Dogen) in which he presented Dogen as one of Japan's most important philosophers. This led to a widespread rediscovery of Dogen's work. For the first time since Dogen wrote *Shobogenzo* seven hundred years earlier, his book was being read by ordinary people instead of just a few monks.

As I mentioned, the first English translations began to appear in the 1970s. The first translation of the entire thing was by Kosen Nishiyama and John Stevens. The second complete English translation of *Shobogenzo* was made by my teacher Gudo Wafu Nishijima and his student Mike Cross in the 1990s. Since then two more complete

English translations have appeared, one by Kazuaki Tanahashi and the folks at the San Francisco Zen Center, and one by the Reverend Hubert Nearman of Shasta Abbey. Yuho Yokoi of Aichigakuin University in Japan apparently also published a complete English translation, but good luck finding a copy. I have only ever been able to track down one volume of the dozen or so I believe exist. A few books in English have been written since then that have attempted to make Dogen's work accessible to nonscholars. I myself have written two of those, *Sit Down and Shut Up* and *Don't Be a Jerk*. But we are still in the early days of this attempt.

I think one of the reasons it's taken so long to really discover Dogen's work is that he was ahead of his time. He understood aspects of human nature that we take for granted today but for which there weren't even words in his time.

He says amazing stuff constantly. For example, he'll point out that even the things the traditional Buddhist sutras warn us against, like doubt and anger, take place within what the Buddhists call "original enlightenment." Reality isn't some pristine thing far off in outer space where there is no doubt or anger or greed or delusion. Reality is what you are living in at the very moment when you doubt you are living in reality.

But more than that, Dogen takes the basic premise of Buddhism to its ultimate conclusion. And he does so fearlessly. He doesn't accept any doctrine without question. He is the ultimate skeptic — he's skeptical even of himself, his own senses, and his own conclusions. That kind of attitude would paralyze most people. Yet Dogen manages to take that skepticism and turn it into something that's freeing rather than paralyzing. It's also a very contemporary attitude.

As a society we are only now getting close to where Dogen was eight hundred years ago. We are watching all our most basic assumptions about life, the universe, and everything come undone, just like Dogen saw his world fall apart when his parents died.

Religions don't seem to mean much anymore, except maybe to

small groups of fanatics. You can hardly get a full-time job, and even if you do, there's no stability. A college degree means very little. The Internet has leveled things so much that the opinions of the greatest scientists in the world about global climate change are presented as being equal to those of some dude who read part of the Bible and took it literally. The news industry has collapsed so that it's hard to tell a fake headline from a real one. Money isn't money anymore; it's numbers stored in computers. Everything is changing so rapidly that none of us can hope to keep up.

All this uncertainty has a lot of us scrambling for something certain to hang on to. But if you think I'm gonna tell you that Dogen provides us with that certainty, think again. He actually gives us something far more useful. Dogen gives us a way to be okay with uncertainty. This isn't just something Buddhists need; it's something we all need.

We humans can be certainty junkies. We'll believe in the most ridiculous nonsense to avoid the suffering that comes from not knowing something. It's like part of our brain is dedicated to compulsive dot-connecting. I think we're wired to want to be certain. You have to know if that's a rope or a snake, if the guy with the chains all over his chest is a gangster or a fan of bad seventies movies. Being certain means being safe.

The downfall is that we humans think about a lot of stuff that's not actually real. We crave certainty in areas where there can never be any. That's when we start in with believing the crazy stuff.

Dogen is interesting because he tries to cut right to the heart of this. He gets into what is real and what is not. Probably the main reason he's so difficult to read is that Dogen is trying to say things that can't actually be said. So he has to bend language to the point where it almost breaks. He's often using language itself to show the limitations of language. Even the very first readers of his writings must have found them difficult.

Dogen understood both that words always ultimately fail to

xviii   IT CAME FROM BEYOND ZEN!

describe reality and that we human beings must rely on words anyway. So he tried to use words to write about that which is beyond words. This isn't really a discrepancy. You use words, but you remain aware of their limitations. My teacher used to say, "People like explanations." We do. They're comforting. When the explanation is reasonably correct, it's useful.

But there will always be things we can't explain. In fact, our explanations are always provisional. This isn't a problem unless we start to confuse the explanation with the reality it's trying to explain. We have a strong tendency to do that because we like explanations so much.

It's ironic that you have to use words to explain why words are so limited. But it can be done. If you understand exactly why explanations are always limited, you can use explanations in a practical way.

I've studied Dogen's words for more than thirty years, and I've also studied myself for those thirty-some years. Dogen studied himself for forty-some years, and did so much more deeply than most of us have ever attempted. Certainly much more deeply than I have in my thirty-odd years of study. His words are based on his explorations of himself and on his explorations of the words of others who had explored themselves. That's a huge contribution to the philosophical outlook of humanity. Dogen is not just a Japanese philosopher or the representative of some religion. He is a world philosopher, a human philosopher.

One thing that Dogen explores in detail is the Buddhist teaching that mind and matter are not two different things. Rather, they are contrasting aspects of one unified reality that is neither mind nor matter. Even though this insight goes all the way back to the Buddha, 2,500 years ago, it's somehow still startling. I think that's because even Buddhists themselves have often failed to understand it.

I have a theory that our inability to see the unity of mind and matter may have roots in human evolution. We are extraordinarily good at imagining things that are not real. We use this ability to reason abstractly and to help us survive, not only individually but as a species. Perhaps because of this ability we have had to evolve ways of constantly making a clear distinction between what we imagine and what is actually out there in the real world. This leads us to be almost incapable of comprehending that mind and matter are really two aspects of the same thing, which is neither mind nor matter.

Which brings me to my own big question: Does it matter whether or not we have a realistic point of view?

You could argue that it doesn't matter much. A person can have a completely unrealistic outlook and still live a very happy life. For example, I have a high school friend who believes that one day Jesus will return and send evildoers to hell and take him and his family back up to heaven to live with Him in paradise everlasting. This belief brings him comfort and helps him manage the sadder aspects of life. Jesus won't return, but my friend will die happily believing that one day He will.

On an individual level, this can work, to some extent. As I said, this belief makes him happy. But on a collective level, beliefs like that can be tremendously harmful. They lead people like my friend to being negligent about the environment, for example, and to push for political action that damages the world. So, long after my friend is gone, his children and grandchildren, as well as your children and grandchildren, may suffer because of my friend's mistaken belief that Jesus will return before that can happen. A realistic outlook is necessary for our overall survival and well-being.

When I was in Germany earlier this year I met a guy who had recently started keeping bees. He told me that to understand bees you can't just look at them as individual insects. You have to think of the entire hive as if it were a single being.

I think people are the same.

If you study evolution, you'll know that all multicellular creatures evolved from colonies of creatures that banded together as a single organism. This allowed these collective organisms to have specialized structures that cooperated as if they were a single being. So even though we think of ourselves as individuals, we are actually all just hives of beings that had once been individual beings on their own.

Just as our individual bodies are collectives, our societies function as single beings. Ultimately, the whole of humanity is a single being. Perhaps the entire planet Earth can be considered a single living being. It may even go further than that. Dogen certainly believed it did. He believed that we were part of, and intimately connected to, absolutely everything in the universe. He not only believed this; he knew it deeply in ways that you and I can also come to know it.

A lot of the greatest conflicts in our human hive have been clashes between idealistic or religious philosophies, that is, clashes of philosophies that value the mind or spirit, and philosophies that value matter. Religions say that spirit/mind is real while matter is negligible. Materialistic philosophies, such as classical science, say that mind is just an illusion caused by the interactions of material objects and processes.

Contemporary physics is starting to dimly comprehend that this distinction is false, but it will probably take a long time before this view becomes widely accepted.

This is much more than just a dry philosophical debate. People get killed over this stuff. Part of what happened on September 11, 2001, was that people who believed mind or spirit was more important than matter were trying to prove that was true by destroying some of the great emblems of materialism. Of course, there was more to the attacks than that. But this aspect was crucial.

Classical science is based on the materialistic outlook. It seems to work pretty well, but it fails to address a lot of our deepest concerns. We live in greater comfort than ever before, with all sorts of conveniences, yet we're still just as sad and confused as ever. Material prosperity clearly does not lead to happiness. Religious people argue for a return to spirituality, but we can't go back. Buddhism offers a middle way that includes materialistic and idealistic or spiritual aspects but doesn't favor either of these outlooks.

The Buddhist idea is revolutionary because if you take it to its logical conclusion, not only does it overturn all religions and all idealistic philosophies, but it also makes materialism seem ridiculously incomplete and inadequate. That's a scary prospect to a society that's heavily invested in one or the other of these outlooks. But it's a far more realistic way of looking at things. Once we put the Buddhist view into wider use, we'll find that we human beings are capable of things we have never even dreamed of.

If we can find a way as a society to integrate these two opposing outlooks, we'll no longer have to fight about them. Right now we deal with the contradictions between science and religion by allowing them to operate in completely separate arenas. The Buddhist outlook allows us to fully integrate them. I don't think this integration will happen for a few hundred years, at least. By then Buddhism will probably no longer be called "Buddhism" and won't have much connection to ancient Indian cosmology and mythology. But I think future historians will see the connection between Buddhism and a more fully integrated and realistic view of life.

Part of this process will involve understanding Dogen's philosophical outlook. I don't think I can stress enough how important Dogen really is. His philosophy is the key to seeing the world in an absolutely new way that is more realistic than the way you saw things before. Once you get it, you'll never be the same. Once you go Dogen, you never go back.

One of the biggest hurdles in understanding Dogen is the simple fact that he wrote in Japanese eight hundred years ago. Dogen is of a very different cultural background from ours. So not only do you have to translate what he wrote from Japanese into your chosen language, but you also have to translate his worldview. This means that any strictly literal translation of Dogen's writing contains large portions that make very little sense. The cultural references are lost on us. We don't know who the famous historical figures he refers to even are, let alone what they did and why he's writing about them, and we've never heard of the books he quotes from.

So the best Dogen translations, like the Nishijima/Cross version, are filled with cumbersome footnotes and worse yet are written in painfully difficult language in an effort to match Dogen's way of expressing himself. Other translations just leave the obscure references in, and it's up to the reader to puzzle them out. Some translators are so in love with Dogen's beautiful similes and metaphors that they neglect to tell you what the heck they mean. Unless you've got a whole lot of time and patience, there's no way you're gonna get into it.

With this and my other books I have tried to simplify Dogen without dumbing him down. I've removed a lot of that cultural stuff or tried to translate it into more contemporary equivalents. Since I am not even pretending to give you a faithful translation, I have also felt free to edit his often cumbersome, convoluted, and lengthy sentences and paragraphs into something easier to follow. I've also added jokes. This may seem like just a way to spice things up, but Dogen's writing is full of puns and wordplay. I believe a lot of it was intended to be funny, but this never comes across in translation.

For each of Dogen's essays we'll be looking at in this book, I have provided a short introduction, a simplified paraphrase of the essay in question — with requisite jokes — and a commentary. The commentary gives you details about what I've changed in my paraphrase as well as alternative ways of reading certain problematic parts. It will also tell you what I think Dogen means and why I think so.

Let's take a look.

1. IT CAME FROM BEYOND ZEN!
Inmo
It!

IN THE FIRST half of this book, I will be looking at some of Dogen's easier, more straightforward stuff and then I'll transition into the harder, more abstract and philosophical stuff in the second half. But, just to be contrary to myself, I'm going to lead off with one of Dogen's most difficult and deeply philosophical pieces. The main reason for this is that I think this piece lays the groundwork for much of what is to come.

Most translations of *Shobogenzo* give the title of this essay as something along the lines of "Thusness" (Tanahashi), "Suchness" (Nishiyama/Stevens), "That Which Comes Like This" (Shasta Abbey), or some other such fairly pretentious designation. Nishijima and Cross translate the title simply as "It."

The word Dogen actually used is 恁麼, which is pronounced *inmo* in Japanese and *renme* in contemporary Mandarin Chinese. Online Chinese-English dictionaries tend to give "this way" or "what" as the contemporary meaning, though one I consulted also gave me "do you." Do they mean as in "you do you"? I do not know.

Anyhow, in his intro to this chapter in his translation of *Shobogenzo* into contemporary Japanese, Nishijima explains the more ancient meaning as being akin to the Japanese words *ano* or *are*. These words are used to suggest a thing you don't know the name of

1

but that you have to indicate, as in the English phrase "that thingam-ajig over by the whatchamacallit." So the word is kind of a catchall term for something you can't name.

The words *suchness* and *thusness* are very popular among English-speaking Buddhists in general, and not just to be used as the title of this essay. *Suchness* is often used as a translation of the Sanskrit word *tathata*, which is part of the word *tathatagata*, which is one of the nicknames that Buddha gave himself, according to the ancient sutras. This name means something like "that which comes and goes in the same way," or to quote Shasta Abbey, "that which comes like this." It's a weird nickname, to be sure.

By the way, the *h* in the word *tathatagata* is pronounced like a kind of short puff of air, so it's tat-(h)a-gat-a. The *h* does not affect the *t* that comes before it and make it into the sound that begins words like *thistle* or *thwack*. It's the same with the *th* in *Siddhartha* and in *Theravada*, by the way. It always annoys me when people who should know better mangle those words, pronouncing *Theravada* kind of like they'd pronounce Thera-Flu®.

Anyway, the problem with translating the title of this chapter as "suchness" or "thusness" is that 恁麼 (*inmo*) is not the character combination Chinese and Japanese Buddhists use for *tathata*. The character combo they use is 真如, which is pronounced *shinyo* in Japanese. For *tathatagata* they use 如来, which is pronounced *nyorai*. So Dogen doesn't seem to me to be specifically trying to draw a connection to the Buddha's ancient nickname, the way a lot of English translators tend to.

Having said that, there is some justification for making a connection. In his English intro to the chapter Nishijima says, "The word *inmo* was used to indicate the truth, or reality, which in Buddhist philosophy is originally ineffable." Shasta Abbey's introduction to the chapter says of the word *inmo*, "It was used by the Chinese Zen Masters to designate 'That Which Is,' the Ultimate Reality which goes beyond any words we can employ to describe It." The weird capitalization is theirs. Perhaps the Buddha also chose his nick-name to indicate that he was the voice of that ineffable something. Could be.

Maybe that's why translators like froufrou-sounding words like *suchness* and *thusness* when titling this chapter. So, okay, suchness or thusness. Fine. Personally, I prefer *It* because it reminds me of fifties science fiction films like *It Came from Beneath the Sea*; *It: The Terror from Beyond Space*; and the Roger Corman classic, *It Conquered the World*. These are films in which the big, ugly, gross, tentacle-y thing in question could not be named. Even though Dogen was not writing cheap science fiction, I feel that he was going for the same sort of feeling that's evoked by these film titles.

In a lecture he gave in 1969, Shunryu Suzuki, founder of the San Francisco Zen Center and author of the book *Zen Mind, Beginner's Mind*, explained the meaning of the word *inmo* like this: "In English you say, 'It is hot.' That 'it' has the same meaning as when you say, 'It is nine o'clock,' or, 'It is half-past eight.' We are also 'it,' but we don't say 'it.' Instead we say 'he' or 'she,' or 'me' or 'I.' But actually we mean 'it.' Everything can be 'it.' It's the same as using a question mark. When I say 'it,' you don't know exactly what I mean, so you may say, 'What is it?'"*

Dogen used the word *inmo* a whole lot in his writings, as we shall soon see. He uses the word four times in one of his most famous essays, "Fukanzazengi" (Universal Guide to the Standard Method of Zazen). Two of those usages occur in the closing sentence. English translations usually split that sentence into two sentences that go something like, "If you practice the *state like this* for a long time, you will surely become the *state like this* itself. The treasure-house will open naturally, and you will be free to receive and to use [its contents] as you like" (Nishijima/Cross) or "If you practice *suchness*

---

* I have taken the liberty of editing the verbatim transcript of this lecture, which can be found in the San Francisco Zen Center's library, for clarity. It's the lecture from Monday September 1, 1969.

continuously, you will be *suchness*. The treasure-house will open of itself, and you will be able to use it at will" (Shohaku Okumura). The italicized words are their translations of the word *inmo*.

As far as Dogen was concerned, zazen wasn't intended to induce some special mental state. Rather, it was a practice in which you try to experience clearly the state you're already in. You can't understand that state, no matter what it is. So it's ineffable, unnameable; it's *it* because you can't call it much else.

To me, this use of the word *inmo* is Dogen's way of indicating something like the Western concept of God. I don't mean the concept of God as a giant guy with a white beard who smites the Peloponnesians with lightning bolts for carving unto themselves a graven image of a horned beast. I mean a subtler idea of God. It's more akin to what the Irish philosopher and poet Johannes Scotus Eriugena, who lived 815–77 CE (four hundred years before Dogen), talked about when he said, "Every visible and invisible creature is an appearance of God" and "We do not know what God is. God Himself does not know what He is because He is not anything. Literally God is not, because He transcends being." Or, to put it in more Buddhist-friendly terms, this *it* that Dogen refers to is the ineffable something that pervades the universe with what we humans perceive as meaning, order, and intelligence.

Let's see what Dogen has to say about *it*.

Master Ungo Doyo (Ch. Yunju Daoying, d. 902 CE) said, "If you want to get it, you gotta be it, since you already are it, why worry about it?"

That means if you want to experience the unnameable, you need to be a person who is the unnameable. Since you already are a person who is the unnameable, why worry about the unnameable?

I'm using the word *it* to describe directing yourself toward the supreme truth. The whole universe in every direction is just a teeny-weeny bit of the supreme truth. Maybe the supreme truth* is bigger than everything there ever is, was, or could be.

We ourselves are just tools it uses to experience itself. How do we know this indescribable something I'm calling "it" exists? Because even your own body and your own mind aren't really you.

Your body is obviously not the real you. Days and nights race by. We can't stop time, even for a split second. Where did the snot-faced little kid you once were go? Look all you want, but you'll never find him or her. Think about it. So much stuff has happened that'll never happen again. If you look at it honestly, you have to admit that even your raw mind doesn't stick around, either. It appears and vanishes from one moment to the next.

The truth exists. It just isn't likely to hang out with the likes of you. Thus† within the limitless universe, something establishes the will to the truth.

Once you establish a willingness to align with what is true, you put aside all the other crap you've been messing around with. You hope to hear what you've never heard before and experience what you've never experienced before. This isn't something you do yourself. It happens because you are a person who is *it*.

You might ask, How do I know I'm a person who is *it*? You know you're a person who is *it* because you want to understand what *it* is and align yourself with *it*. You have the face and the eyes of an *it* person, so you don't have to worry about the ever-present *it*. Heck, even

---

* The word I'm giving as "supreme truth" is 菩提, which is pronounced *bodai*. It's the Japanese way of pronouncing the Sanskrit word *bodhi*. I'll talk about this in my commentary.

† In the Nishijima/Cross version there's a nice footnote about how Dogen uses the word *inmo* in a variety of ways in this chapter. It can function as an adjective, adverb, or even as a pronoun. In this case it's used something like the word *thus* in English: "This frequent usage has the effect of emphasizing the inconspicuous, ever-present, and normal nature of the state Master Dogen is describing." Thus, the word *thus* at the beginning of this sentence is actually *inmo* in the original, and so are a lot of other words I'll be using.

worry itself is part of the great, unknowable *it* that is the universe and is you. So it's beyond worry!

Also, don't be surprised by the *it*-ness of *it*. Even if you're surprised by *it*, *it* is still just as *it* as it ever was.

Buddhas can't understand it. The mind can't understand it. Even the whole universe can't understand it. There's only one way to put it: If you're already a person who is *it*, why worry about the matter of *it*?

The *it*-ness of sensation is *it*, and the *it*-ness of mind and body is also *it*, and even the *it*-ness of Buddha is also *it*.

Look. You fall down and hit the ground. Ouch! But you also use the ground to help yourself get up. You can't get up any other way. The ground you fall on is *it*. The ground you use to help yourself up is *it*, too. Buddha's attainment of the truth is just like someone using the ground to get up off the ground. That's the way it's always been for every Buddha there ever was. That's the way it is for us, too.

Even so, there's another side to it. The Indian Buddhists never said this, and nobody else did, either. But even if you tried for a million-zillion years to get up off the ground by using the ground, you could never, ever do it. There's just one way to do it. Those who fall down on the ground get up by using the sky. Those who fall to the sky get up by using the ground. That's what all the Buddhas and ancestors did.

Maybe somebody might ask, "How far apart are the sky and the ground?" You can tell them, "They're exactly 108,000 miles apart!" You can only get up off the ground by using the sky. You can only get up off the sky by using the ground. If you can't understand this, you'll never understand Buddhism at all.

There's an old story that relates to this stuff. A guy named Samghanandi* had a student named Geyashata.† Some bells were ringing and Samghanandi, the teacher, asked his student Geyashata, "Is that the sound of the wind ringing or the sound of the bells ringing?"

---

* Dates unknown.

† Dates unknown, but since he was the eighth Indian patriarch of Buddhism, that would put him somewhere around 200–100 BCE.

Geyashata must have been used to being asked weird questions, so he said, "It ain't the wind or the bells! It's my mind ringing!"

Samghanandi said, "Then what's the mind?"

Geyashata said, "The reason it's ringing is 'cuz it's still and serene."

Samghanandi said, "Good answer! Who else but you could've said that?"

This state of the wind not ringing is the study of "my mind is ringing." The time when the bells aren't ringing is studied as "my mind is ringing." "My mind ringing" is *it*. And all is still and serene.

This story has been around for ages, and lots of people think it expresses some great truth, but most people have misunderstood it. They think that whole deal of Geyashata saying, "It ain't the wind or the bells! It's my mind ringing!" means that at the moment of hearing the bells, a state of mindfulness occurs. This state of mindfulness is called "the mind." If there wasn't a state of mindfulness, then how could you recognize you were hearing bells? The root of hearing, then, is the mind, they say. It's all in the mind, they say.

That's totally not the way this story should be understood.

Here's the real deal. If one thing is still and serene, then everything is still and serene. It's a metaphor. In the story we have an agent — either the wind or the bells or the mind, take your pick — and an action, the ringing. In reality agent and action are not separated. That's what it means to say everything is still and serene. Another way to say the same thing is, "Why worry about it — the unnameable?" How can the unnameable be related to something with a name?

One other time, two monks were watching a flag waving and arguing about it. One said, "The flag is moving." The other said, "The wind is moving."

Daikan Eno (Ch. Dajian Huineng, 638–713 CE), their teacher, heard this and told them, "You knuckleheads! It's not the flag and it's not the wind. You are the mind moving. Now get back to work!" The monks agreed with the teacher and went back to what they were supposed to be doing.

Daikan Eno was saying that the wind, the flag, and the movement all exist not *in* the mind but *as* the mind. Even nowadays most people get this wrong. If you think these words mean, "Your mind is moving," you don't know dip about Daikan Eno's teachings. You could just cut to the chase and say, "You are moving." That's because moving is moving, and you are you. You are *it*. You are the indescribable something that is the all-inclusive universe. There's no separation between you and the universe, just as there's no separation between wind and flag and movement.

Daikan Eno started out as a woodcutter. He didn't know anything about Buddhism. He couldn't even read the sutras. His dad died when he was young so he had to work hard and look after his mom. He had no idea he had a precious jewel of wisdom hidden under his woodcutter's coat.

Then one day he heard a monk chanting the Diamond Sutra, and he knew what he had to do. He made sure his mom would be okay, and then he just up and left his life as a woodcutter to study in a temple. That must have been a huge deal to him, to leave his mom like that. Nobody takes such obligations lightly. But, like the Lotus Sutra says, "Those with wisdom understand the truth from the first moment they hear it."

You don't get wisdom from somebody else, and you don't make it yourself. It's not intentional or unintentional. It's not conscious or unconscious. You can't talk in terms of delusion and realization. None of that stuff applies.

Daikan Eno didn't even know Buddhism existed, so there was no way he could have aspired to understand it. But as soon as he heard that sutra — blammo! — he got it. These kinds of things happen because the body and mind of someone endowed with real wisdom is not their own. Nobody knows how many times somebody has to be born and die while possessing wisdom they don't even know they have. Imagine a rock that has a jewel inside it. The rock doesn't know there's a jewel in it, and the jewel doesn't know it's inside a rock. It's kinda like that.

But when they finally get it, they grab it. You could say that the person and the wisdom don't even know each other. Yet somehow the wisdom discovers the truth. It's not even like you *have* wisdom or *lack* wisdom. Yet wisdom is there, just like the trees and flowers are there.

When wisdom appears as being without wisdom, everything is

unknown, everything is doubt and wonder. All things are lost forever at this moment, and all things are real action. Words that ought to be heard, and things that ought to be understood, are totally doubt and wonder.

The entire universe is not me. There's no place to hide. Yet there is nobody else. It's a single unified thing, like an iron rail ten thousand miles long.

The entire universe exists in having wisdom and in not having wisdom, just like daylight and darkness are part of the same day. That's an example of how the universe is the unnameable *it* I've been talking about.

Anyway, I was telling you about Daikan Eno. Once he realized he had this wisdom stuff in him, he went to a Zen master named Daiman Konin (Ch. Hongren, 601–674 CE) who lived in a monastery up on Obai-zan Mountain. They put Daikan Eno in charge of rice pounding. He did this for eight months, which is not really that long, considering what happened next.

One night the master came in while Daikan Eno was pounding some rice. The master said, "Did you get all the hulls off the rice yet?"

Daikan Eno said, "It's white but not sifted."

The master pounded the rice three times. Then Daikan Eno sifted it three times. That was the moment when teacher and student truly connected. You'd had to have been there to really understand. When a teacher transmits the dharma to a student, not even the teacher or the student himself knows it. And yet it totally happens at just that precise moment.

Master Yakusan Igen (Ch. Yaoshan Weiyan, 745–827 CE) was a lecturer. He studied all there was to study about Buddhism. One time Yakusan said to Master Sekito Kisen (Ch. Shitou Xiqian, 700–790 CE), "I've studied lots of Buddhist theory and I pretty much get it. But I've heard that way down south where you're from they have this way of directly realizing the true nature of mind and becoming a Buddha. Can you teach me about that?"

Sekito Kisen replied, "The unnameable can't be grasped. The unnameable can't *not* be grasped. To grasp it or not grasp it, both are impossible. What do you make of that?"

This answer isn't about words being limited or anything like that.

We should learn the great unnameable *it* as impossibility itself. We should really look into this matter of impossibleness. It's not like this great indefinable *it* and impossibleness are something only Buddhas can understand. Understanding is ungraspable. Realization is ungraspable.

One day Daikan Eno was talking to his successor, Nangaku Ejo (Ch. Nanyue Huairang, 677–744 CE). Daikan Eno said, "There is something that comes like this." The word he used for "something" is 什麼物, pronounced *shimobutsu*. It means "something" or "what." So the phrase could also be a question: "What is it that comes like this?" The word he used for "like this" was *inmo*, the great indefinable *it* we've been discussing.

Daikan Eno was saying that this *something*, this *what*, this unnameable place we're living in right now, these unnameable things we're doing right now; he was saying *this* is beyond doubt and beyond understanding. Everything is *something*. Everything is *what*. The unnameable *it* that is the universe is *us* right here and right now. This isn't open to doubt. This is this. This whole universe is *what*.

— Preached to the assembly at
Kannon-dori-kosho-horin-ji Temple on March 26, 1242

I like this particular essay so much that I wrote a whole book inspired by it called *There Is No God and He Is Always with You.* In that book I took the stance that the word *God* might not be quite as awful as our current crop of neoatheists say it is. Once you stop imagining the word *God* to indicate a big white man with a long beard who lives in the sky, you can start to work with it and make something useful out of it. Some readers reacted by stating that *God* is too loaded of a word to ever be of much use anymore. Dogen may have agreed. It's hard to tell.

The notion of God in the Judeo-Christian-Islamic sense was unknown in Japan in Dogen's time. However, it's possible he may have known about the similar Indian idea of Brahman, a kind of abstract version of the Supreme Being.

The idea of Brahman — and the idea of God — are not part

of Buddhism. So it's fair enough to say that Buddhists don't believe in God. Yet this does not mean that Buddhists believe in an essentially dead universe governed only by random chance, in which life is just a by-product of chemical interactions. Which isn't to say that Buddhists don't accept science. Most of us do. It's just that we don't believe in a dead universe. Even by-products of chemical interactions governed by the laws of chance are part of the great unfathomable *it* that Dogen is talking about.

But maybe you have a hard time believing that such a something even exists at all, no matter what we call it. In this essay Dogen expresses why he believes this *it* exists. He feels that our very presence is, itself, evidence. This isn't just a matter of someone having some kind of faith in what he's learned from others.

In fact, this whole chapter might represent a bit of a break from established Buddhist tradition, at least in terms of the way Dogen expresses it. The Buddha did not accept the existence of the supernatural. He didn't think the universe was created by an all-powerful being. Dogen, too, talks about having deep belief in cause and effect and never accepting the idea that things can happen without cause or by the intercession of supernatural entities.

In a sense, then, Buddhism could be called atheistic. But that doesn't mean Buddhists take the kind of mechanistic view of the universe often favored by atheists today.

Dogen uses the term *bodai* (菩提) to express his view on the matter. This is the Japanese pronunciation of the Sanskrit word *bodhi*. *Bodhi* is often translated as "enlightenment" or "realization." Lots of people these days tend to view *bodhi*, or enlightenment, as a kind of psychological state of ultimate with-it-ness attained by certain special people. But reading this chapter, you can see very clearly that Dogen views *bodhi* much more broadly. Even the entire universe is not big enough to contain *bodhi*. That's definitely not a reference to a mere psychological state, no matter how profound.

So let's talk about what Dogen says in this essay. One of

my favorite lines is the one I've paraphrased as, "We ourselves are just tools it uses to experience itself." In the original it is: われらも、かの尽十方界のなかにあらゆる調度なり, which is pronounced *warera mo, kano jinjuppokai no naka ni arayuru chodo nari*. The word I'm paraphrasing as "tools" is 調度 (*chodo*). Jim Breen's online Japanese-English dictionary says this word means "supplies, furniture, or fixtures." Kaz Tanahashi translates this word as "accouterments," which is fine — if you're a French fashion designer. Shasta Abbey uses "accessories," which is fine — if you're working at the jewelry counter at a Macy's department store. Nishijima/Cross has, "We ourselves are tools which it possesses within this Universe in ten directions." "Tools" is a far better translation than the others. Deal with it.

My paraphrase is a little interpretive. Dogen only says that we ourselves are tools that this great unnameable *it* possesses. I added that *it* uses these tools — uses us — to experience itself. I think this follows from Dogen's statement. But he actually only says that the unnameable *it* possesses us as tools. He doesn't say what those tools — us — are used for.

The word I translated a little after this as "raw mind" is *sekishin* (赤心). It literally means "red mind." *Red* in this case means raw, like raw hamburger. Or raw like sushi, if you're a Neneh Cherry fan. It means the unadorned mind or heart, just as it is. *Mind* and *heart* are represented by the same Chinese character, by the way.

The line I've given as, "The truth exists. It just isn't likely to hang out with the likes of you" has been translated a variety of ways. Nishijima/Cross have, "Although the state of sincerity does exist, it is not something that lingers in the vicinity of the personal self." Shasta Abbey's version is similar: "We may say that there is truth in this sincere heart, but it is not something that lingers behind within the vicinity of a personal self." Tanahashi's version is, "Even if there is truth it does not stay within the boundary of yourself."

This line has been important to me for a long time. It goes back to the Buddhist idea of non-self. We all have a notion of self. Dogen also had one, and so did the Buddha. You can't get through life without some kind of sense of self.

Some folks seem to think that the Buddhist idea of non-self says that all the aspects of reality we tend to include within the idea of "self" don't exist. That's not right. You have your own likes and dislikes, your own history, your unique take on the meaning of the shower scene in the movie *Heathers*, and so on. The concept of self is a convenient shorthand so that you can talk about all this stuff as a single unit, without having to explain each individual component.

It's like a circle you've drawn with a crayon around a few inter-related things so that you can conceive of them as one. Or it's like the recyclable bag you take to the grocery store so you can carry your organic bean sprouts, your cage-free eggs, and your Nacho Cheese Doritos as if they're a single thing. But we all have plenty of moments when we transcend these arbitrary boundaries. We have moments of deep friendship and love in which the boundaries between ourselves and another melt into nothing. We take long walks through the woods during which we feel no separation between ourselves and the nature that surrounds and embraces us.

We tend to look on these moments as anomalies, interruptions in what we take to be the solidity of our individual existence. We assume separation is the reality and oneness is some kind of an illusion. Or we think oneness is some kind of special state that we have to work hard to achieve.

Dogen saw it differently. Over and over he emphasized the idea that oneness and separation are both illusions. In reality we are neither separate from the universe nor at one with it. What we really are transcends those distinctions.

Moving along. In the original Japanese, the phrase "will to the truth" that I used a little ways after this in my paraphrase is the word *hasshin* (発心). This word is generally translated as "spiritual awakening," to quote once again from Jim Breen's very useful online

Japanese-English dictionary. Nishijima Roshi often used the phrase "will to the truth" as a way of expressing this word and related words, such as 菩提心 (*bodaishin*), which Breen translates as "aspiration to Buddhahood." "Aspiration to Buddhahood" sounds to me more like a desire to become a famous religious figure with statues made of you and cities named after you. I feel like "will to the truth" is far better. Later we'll encounter another term for this idea, the word 道心 (*doshin*). I'll talk about that one some more when we get there.

I like "will to the truth" better than the other English renderings, even though it sort of makes me think of Leni Riefenstahl's 1935 propaganda film about Adolf Hitler, *Triumph of the Will*, as well as some other fascistic uses of the word *will*. It's unfortunate that the word has such a checkered history, because it's so useful. In the sense I'm using it, it means something more like "willingness" than any kind of pigheaded determination. But it has aspects of both. You have to be both deeply determined to experience the truth and humbly willing to accept the truth once you discover it, since invariably the actual truth will be different from anything you could possibly imagine it would be.

Next up, we come to a part where Dogen gets really twisty. He starts in with all that stuff about "don't be surprised by the *it*-ness of *it*. Even if you're surprised by *it*, *it* is still just as *it* as it ever was." Odd sounding as it is, my paraphrase is actually fairly close to most of the standard translations, so I'll let you look those up yourself.

This phrase reminds me of something my first Zen teacher said about enlightenment. He said, "It's more you than you could ever be." The first time I heard him say that, I didn't know what to make of it. But it stuck with me, and eventually I understood what he meant. Here's what I think he meant and what I think Dogen meant.

Life, the universe, and everything are exactly what they are. When we think we're trying to understand them, what we usually end up doing instead is trying to find foolproof ways to *describe* them to ourselves rather than just fully experiencing them. We try to make symbolic representations of them in our brains. But it doesn't work because the representation is never the thing it represents.

Dogen and other Buddhist teachers suggest, instead, allowing the mind to be like a mirror that reflects clearly the world it encounters without trying to reduce it into something else. If you can do this, you start to see that the division you think exists between yourself and the rest of the universe is really just a trick of thought. It has some usefulness for communication purposes, so that you can describe that one small unit of the universe you imagine yourself to be. But it's not real. The universe is more you than the "you" that you've created could ever be.

Maybe that sounds just as weird as what Dogen is saying, but that's my take on it. Or *it*. Ha!

The part I paraphrased as, "The *it*-ness of sensation is *it*, and the *it*-ness of mind and body is also *it*, and even the *it*-ness of Buddha is also *it*" in the original is このゆゑに声色の恁麼は恁麼なるべし、身心の恁麼は恁麼なるべし、諸仏の恁麼は恁麼なるべきなり (*kono yue ni kowairo no inmo wa inmo naru beshi, shinjin no inmo wa inmo naru beshi, shobutsu no inmo wa inmo naru beki nari*). Nishijima/Cross have, "Thus, the 'suchness' of sound and form may be 'it'; the 'suchness' of body-and-mind may be 'it'; and the "'suchness' of the buddhas may be 'it.'" Tanahashi has, "This being so, thusness of form is thus; thusness of body and mind is thus; thusness of all buddhas is thus." Shasta Abbey's version is, "So, the True Nature of sound, color, and form is That Which Is, the True Nature of body and mind is That Which Is, and the True Nature of Buddhas is That Which Is." Again, all the weird capitalization is theirs. Don't ask me why.

The question I know I'd be asking if I were reading this book instead of writing it is: What the holy heck is that supposed to mean? Let me see if I can answer.

For one thing, the English language forces all of us who've tried to translate this to stick that suffix -*ness* in there, which doesn't exist in the original. He just says "the *inmo* of sound and form is *inmo*, etc." So we're back to this idea of an unnameable, unfathomable something that permeates all reality. The phrase means that everything is a manifestation of the one, unnameable *something* that is you and that is the universe.

This "it" is so unfathomable that Dogen says, "Buddhas can't understand it. The mind can't understand it. Even the whole universe can't understand it." The word I've paraphrased as "understand" in this sentence is *ryo* (量), which means "to measure." That's the way most translators translate it. However, the kind of measuring Dogen is referring to here is the way we measure things in our mind by comparing them to other things, or, to be more precise, by comparing our *ideas about* a thing to our *ideas about* other things. What Dogen is talking about here when he talks about "it" is something that is beyond our ability to measure it against anything else.

That's precisely the point of the whole essay. Any description of anything involves this kind of mental measurement. But no possible description of this *something* — this *it* — will ever suffice, because there's literally nothing else to compare it to. That's why Dogen uses the vague word *inmo*.

A bit later we come to a section about falling down on the ground and using the ground to help you get up. Here I squeezed a long rant by Dogen into just a few short sentences. It's clear that this idea was very important to Dogen, so he goes on at great length to make sure his readers know that there's no way to get up off the ground except by using the ground.

The metaphor is pretty obvious, I think. We use our delusions (ground) as a way to free ourselves from delusions. In his essay "Genjo Koan" (which I wrote about in my book *Don't Be a Jerk*), Dogen says, "Those who greatly realize delusion are buddhas. Those who are greatly deluded about realization are ordinary beings."

We don't seek to change our deluded state into an enlightened one. Rather, we try to penetrate deeply into delusion itself, since even delusion is part of the supreme truth of *bodhi*. This is why the style of meditation Dogen taught is called *shikantaza* or "just sitting." We don't try to do anything at all except directly experience the state we already have.

But right after he spends a page or so (in the original) telling us this, he says the exact opposite. He says that you *can't* get up off the ground by relying on the ground. You have to use the sky. The word Dogen actually uses here can be pronounced either *ku* or *sora* (空). When it's pronounced *ku*, it means "emptiness," and when it's pronounced *sora*, it means "sky."

Since the word can be read either way, we can't be entirely certain which pronunciation Dogen was going for. But I'm voting for *sora*. Let me tell you why.

Nishijima/Cross, Nishiyama/Stevens, and Shasta Abbey all apparently read it as *ku*. As I said, when it's pronounced *ku*, the word translates as "emptiness" (Nishijima/Cross) or "the void" (Nishiyama/Stevens) or "Empty Space" (Shasta Abbey; they capitalized it, but I wouldn't).

I prefer Kaz Tanahashi's translation in this case. He reads the Chinese character as *sora*, which means "sky." So his version reads, "One who falls to the ground uses the sky to stand up." This is a much more colloquial usage of the Chinese character used by Dogen.

It's hard to say if Dogen's intended audience would be more likely to read it as *sora* (sky) or *ku* (emptiness). However, in either case they would certainly have been aware of the dual meaning. I like reading it as "sky" in English because it completes the metaphor, and I think that's what Dogen was going for. Ground and sky are a pair, but ground and void/emptiness? Not so much.

As I said, though, Dogen's audience would also know that this Chinese character has the more philosophical Buddhist meaning of "emptiness" as well. Since the English word *sky* does not have that philosophical connotation, most translators tend to use words that have fancier meanings.

I take this line as a reference to the Heart Sutra, which says "form (ground) is emptiness (sky), emptiness (sky) is form (ground)."* Form and emptiness are two aspects of the same thing, which is neither purely form nor purely emptiness. Matter and the nonmaterial aspects of real experience are also the same.

Most philosophical systems and religions draw a very sharp distinction between mind/spirit (emptiness or sky) and matter (form or ground). Idealistic philosophies regard mind as primary, while materialistic philosophies regard matter as primary. Buddhism doesn't regard either one as primary. The *it* that Dogen refers to is neither mind nor matter, neither spiritual nor physical, neither emptiness nor form, neither sky nor ground. It's both and, because it's both, it's neither.

Next up we have that weird story about bells, and the part where Dogen criticizes the common understanding of that old story about whether it's the bells ringing or the wind ringing or the mind ringing. This needs some explanation.

In my version, as in the Nishijima/Cross translation, I have Dogen saying that the misunderstanding involves the idea that there is something called "mindfulness," which folks confuse with the more basic thing Dogen calls "the mind."

The Nishijima/Cross translation is the only one that uses the word *mindfulness* here, so it's the only one in which Dogen can be seen as criticizing the concept of mindfulness. Since Nishijima Roshi had a bit of a beef with the use of the word *mindfulness*, I thought I'd better look at Dogen's original to be sure he wasn't just inserting his personal prejudice into Dogen's work. It turns out that the Japanese word Dogen actually uses here is *nen* (念). In current usage this word has a variety of meanings, such as "sense," "feeling," "attention," "thought," and even "desire" in some contexts. The Chinese

---

* Hey, Buddha nerds! I know the word usually translated as "form" in the Heart Sutra is *iro* (色) and that it literally means "color," not "ground." I'm just trying to highlight the metaphor. So settle down.

character is a combination of the character *ima* (今), meaning "now," on top, and the character *kokoro* or *shin* (心), meaning "mind," on the bottom.

The specific Chinese character that Dogen uses here is also the one that ancient translators of Buddhists texts into Chinese chose to represent the concept known as *sati* in Pali, the language of the oldest Buddhist sutras, or *smriti*, as it was known in Sanskrit. The standard English translation of this Pali/Sanskrit word is "mindfulness." So it's clear Dogen actually *is* criticizing the idea of mindfulness, or at least some people's versions of that concept.

As I'm sure most folks who would be inclined to read a book like this already know, the term *mindfulness* is just about the biggest money-spinner there is in contemporary Buddhist-influenced popular psychology. I'm genuinely surprised that nobody has trademarked the word yet.

According to a paper entitled "Mindfulness Training as a Clinical Intervention: A Conceptual and Empirical Review" by Ruth A. Baer of the University of Kentucky, "Mindfulness involves intentionally bringing one's attention to the internal and external experiences occurring in the present moment, and is often taught through a variety of meditation exercises."* This is pretty much the standard definition of mindfulness for our time.

Obviously Dogen comes from a different time and place. In his day mindfulness had not yet become an industry. So as much as I'd like to make my version of Dogen take a few potshots at that industry, it would be inappropriate to do so. Still, it's evident from this passage that the common understanding of mindfulness hasn't changed a whole lot, eight hundred years later and half a world away. Ms. Baer's definition seems very close to the way lots of people in Dogen's day also thought of mindfulness. I think Dogen would take exception to this definition. To him, mind (as opposed to

* Published in *Clinical Psychology: Science and Practice* 10, no. 2 (summer 2003).

mindfulness) is much more than intentionally bringing one's intention to the present moment.

But allow me to step away from Dogen studies for a second and
do a little ranting.

I don't think mindfulness as it's being taught and used in clinics,
schools, and workplaces these days is necessarily a bad thing. It's an
improvement over not teaching and using it. I fully understand that
in America and Europe it's very problematic to introduce anything
that seems the least bit religious into such places, what with the separation of church and state and all that. I know that removing mindfulness from its Buddhist context enables clinicians, teachers, and
others to enjoy the benefits of meditation practice without having to
deal with people getting their panties in a bunch because somebody
else's religion is being forced on their innocent children, or whoever
they're getting all worked up about. I get that.

The main problem is that there are some very solid reasons mindfulness was never traditionally taught as a single practice divorced
from the rest of Buddhism. And these reasons have nothing at all
to do with indoctrination into any particular religion or belief system. Most Buddhists couldn't care less about what anyone believes,
especially in terms of metaphysical stuff like the nature of God, the
origin of the world, or what happens to people after they die.

However, Buddhist practitioners throughout the ages have
worked with this mindfulness stuff a whole lot longer than our current crop of popular psychologists have. They've seen the kinds of
difficulties that arise when people get deeply into meditative practices and they've worked out and refined a lot of ways to deal with
these difficulties. They borrowed a lot of their solutions from practices that are often associated these days with what we in the West
define as "religion." But they've also tried to avoid turning these
solutions into matters of doctrine, belief, or dogma.

For example, back in the olden days, just like now, most people who got into meditation figured it was a good way to make

themselves feel more balanced and serene. And, just like nowadays, that's usually what happened, at least in the early stages. However, as you get deeper into your own mind, you start to find some troubling stuff in there. Everyone does. Even Buddha did.

Getting through these rough patches requires some skill. Because these rough patches don't only show up as scary or alarming stuff. Sometimes the roughest things that happen for meditators is when their meditation delivers exactly what the ads in the backs of the meditation magazines promise — bliss, tranquillity, cosmic awareness, and even enlightenment.

My first Zen teacher's teacher was a guy named Kobun Chino. Someone once asked Kobun what the worst part of working with a Zen student was. Kobun said, "Right after they've had their first enlightenment experience."

Most of us would imagine that would be the best part. After all, isn't enlightenment what it's all about? Wouldn't that be a time of high fives and woo-hoos all around? Not really, as it turns out. The ego is an amazing thing. It can even turn the knowledge of its own unreality into something it can use to aggrandize itself. *Hey, you losers! Look at me! I've realized I don't exist! Isn't that cool of me? Don't you wish you could do that, too?*

Not only that, but there's also nothing intrinsic in the meditative experience that helps a person incorporate what she or he discovers into their overall sense of themselves. Only someone with previous experience in the practice can help with that. What's even better is if you have a whole tradition of people with meditative experiences to draw on, as well as a community of people helping others deal with this kind of stuff as it comes up.

We call Buddhism a religion because it resembles one, but I don't think it belongs in that category. I don't think my point of view is ever going to gain wide acceptance, though. So we're stuck being lumped in with religions.

I think it would be a shame to toss out 2,500 years of research and development in the area of meditation just because the traditional Buddhist ways of dealing with the problems that come up seem religious to Westerners. I think our contemporary mindfulness teachers will end up with their own versions of a lot of the same solutions the Buddhists have been using for centuries. Maybe that's how this stuff will have to progress. End of rant. We now return to our regularly scheduled Dogen commentary.

A bit later in the paraphrase I have Dogen say the following: "Here's the real deal. If one thing is still and serene, then everything is still and serene. It's a metaphor. In the story we have an agent — either the wind or the bells or the mind, take your pick — and an action, the ringing. In reality agent and action are not separated." This is not what he actually wrote, but I think it's what he means. He actually says some stuff about how wind ringing and bells ringing and mind ringing are beyond wind ringing and bells ringing and mind ringing. If you want to know what he really says, just read one of the standard translations. They're all pretty close in this passage. Then he says, "It's the wind ringing, the blowing ringing, and the ringing ringing." It's beautiful and poetic, but I think it's pretty confusing to the average reader these days, so I kind of threw out what Dogen really said and stuck in my own explanation of what I think he meant. You're welcome.

A bit further down we come to a line I paraphrased as, "How can the unnameable be related to something with a name?" My paraphrase is based on the Nishijima/Cross translation. Others translate the key word here, kan (関), which I've paraphrased as "be related to," as "pursue" (Tanahashi) or "get stuck on" (Shasta Abbey). Thus, Tanahashi has Dogen ask, "Why pursue thusness?"

I can sorta understand why these translations came out the way they did. But the Japanese word Dogen uses is pretty unambiguously about being related to things, not pursuing or getting stuck on them. So once again I have to give it to Nishijima/Cross.* I added the "to something with a name" part myself, though. Dogen's implication is that the indefinable "it" can't be related to anything else. It's all-inclusive. To put it in Christian terms, God can't stand apart from his creation because it's all created out of himself.

The story that shows up after this, about the monks arguing about the flag waving, has always bugged me. I know it's meant as an illustration of a philosophical point and not as a description of something that actually happened. But I also know that if either of my Zen teachers had come across me having that kind of argument with someone else at a retreat or something, they'd have told us to knock it off and get back to what we were supposed to be doing. So I added that to the story. It's not there in the original.

The teacher's answer, "You are the mind moving," is from the Nishijima/Cross translation. Tanahashi has him say, "It is your mind that is flapping," while Nishiyama/Stevens have, "Your minds are moving." Those are the standard English readings of the phrase *jin sha shin do* (仁者心動). Nishijima/Cross add a footnote that explains why they deviated from the standard interpretation. It says, "In Master Dogen's interpretation, these characters mean 'You are the mind moving' — a description of the reality which is the mind. The alternative interpretation is that [it] means 'Your minds are moving' — a criticism of the monks." The original phrase is ambiguous and could be taken either way. I prefer Nishijima/Cross's more mystical-sounding reading.

The lines after that, which I've rendered as, "That's because moving is moving, and you are you. You are *it*. You are the

---

* I honestly wish I could award some more "wins" in these arguments to the other translators. It would make me seem like less of a slavish devotee to my teacher. And I swear I'm not. I try my best to look at his translation as critically as I look at the others. It's just that whenever I go back to the original text, the Nishijima/Cross translation is almost always the one that most closely resembles Dogen's Japanese.

indescribable something that is the all-inclusive universe" are much
shorter and more poetic in the original. Most translators try to give
you some sense of that poetic brevity. I don't think I've changed the
meaning. But I encourage you to check out the more standard translations and see for yourself.

A little bit after this we come to a line I've paraphrased as,
"When wisdom appears as being without wisdom, everything is
unknown, everything is doubt and wonder." This is a tricky section,
so let's look at it more closely.

I paraphrased one part as "everything is doubt and wonder." In
the Nishijima/Cross translation there's a footnote explaining how
Dogen changed a quotation from the Lotus Sutra from a character
combination meaning "doubt and grief" (疑悔, pronounced *gike*) to
one meaning "doubt and wonder" (疑怪, also pronounce *gike*; the
second character is a favorite of mine because it also appears as the
first character in the word 怪獣, *kaiju*, meaning "monster," as in a
Godzilla-type monster, or literally "wondrous beast").

Wisdom appearing as being without wisdom might mean a lot
of things. To me it means wisdom that doesn't boldly announce itself
as wisdom. A lot of people these days make a lot of money by letting
the world know just how wise they are. Often these folks invest a lot
more effort in *appearing* to be wise than in actually *being* wise.

To folks like this, wisdom usually means having very definite
ideas about how things are and being able to explain and defend
those ideas with great skill. But Dogen dismisses that sort of thing
by saying that doubt and wonder are part of true wisdom.

In my paraphrase I have Dogen say next, "All things are lost
forever at this moment, and all things are real action." Often this
phrase is taken as a negative, as in Tanahashi's translation, "At that
moment one is lost forever." But the phrase Dogen uses is *yo shitsu
soku i* (永失即為) and means "forever lost is action." It's Dogen's
own reworking of a phrase from the Lotus Sutra, and it's ambiguous

as to whether it's meant as a positive or negative thing. I tried to preserve the poetic ambiguity by saying it both ways.

I love the lines that follow, which I paraphrased as, "The entire universe is not me. There's no place to hide. Yet there is nobody else. It's a single unified thing, like an iron rail ten thousand miles long." I think I'm sticking pretty close to the original here. Other translators say more or less the same thing.

To paraphrase my first teacher, the universe is more you than you could ever be. There is nothing in this universe that isn't you. So there is no place you can ever hide from you.

I also want to point out that Dogen lived and died around six hundred years before the invention of the railroad. Yet he uses that metaphor of a super-long iron rail here, as well as a few other times. Who knows what he was imagining?

The line a little after this that I paraphrase as, "That's an example of how the universe is the unnameable *it* I've been talking about" mashes together a much longer poetic digression about flowers and leaves and the dharma world. Please, go look it up in one of the standard translations. It's quite beautiful.

Next up, we get to that weird story about Daikan Eno's teacher helping him pound some rice. That's an important story, even though it probably just sounds strange. Dogen points out that at the moment of dharma transmission, neither the student nor the teacher knows it's happening.

So it's not like the teacher sits there being all enlightened and stuff, then confers a bunch of knowledge and wonderment upon the student, then tests the student to see if he or she's absorbed the info, and then finally gives the student a dharma diploma. That's not the way it works. It's more like a deep, personal connection. It's like being in love. There's probably one moment in any couple's time together where the relationship changes from just going out and having fun on the weekends to truly being in love. That moment doesn't generally announce itself. Later on, the couple may or may not be able to pinpoint when it happened. But at that exact moment they usually don't even know it themselves. This isn't an exact metaphor, but I think it's a similar kind of thing.

A bit later I have Dogen saying, "We should learn the great unnameable *it* as impossibility itself." The word I have variously paraphrased as "impossible," "impossibleness," and "ungraspable" in this section is *futoku* (不得). This is the same word that I paraphrased as "ungrabbable" in the chapter "Stop Trying to Grab My Mind" from my other book of Dogen mutilations, *Don't Be a Jerk*.

Dogen returns to this theme a whole bunch of times in his writings. Buddhist enlightenment or realization — or *satori* or *kensho* if you prefer pretentious-sounding Japanese words — is usually envisioned as a state of ultimate knowing. Like suddenly you transition from being a know-nothing dweeb into being a Fully Awakened Being Who Knows All and Sees All.

It's not like that. The very state of unknowing itself, which you probably feel like you're in right now if you're anything like me, this know-nothing dweebified state *is* enlightenment. If you can fully experience your own state of not being the least bit enlightened, *that* is enlightenment. Hell, you don't even have to try to fully experience it. You can't help but fully experience it. And yet, as Dogen also liked to point out, some kind of training is necessary.

Shunryu Suzuki, author of *Zen Mind, Beginner's Mind*, said, "You're perfect just as you are, but you could use a little improvement." It sounds contradictory, but it's really not. Just do a little bit of meditating, and you'll start to understand that this is just how it is.

I took tons of liberties with the final paragraph. It's way more poetic in the original. Kaz Tanahashi's translation is the most poetic. It goes, "Study thoroughly his statement that all things are invariably *what*, as *what* is beyond doubt, beyond understanding, but, just *what*. Study thoroughly that the one thing is just *what*. *What* is not to be doubted. *What* thus comes." The word Tanahashi translates as *what* is our old friend *inmo*, the subject of this essay.

Here Dogen is trying to get us into what the contemporary Korean Zen master Sung Sahn called "don't-know mind." No matter how much knowledge we acquire about the universe, it will forever remain unknowable. We can learn a lot of specifics about the spin of quarks, or the distance of the farthest galaxies, or evolution, or a million other aspects of the universe. This information is useful, practical, and fun to learn. There is absolutely nothing wrong with it. Dogen is not one of those guys who tries to get people to shun scientific inquiry in favor of religious mythology or tries to say, "Why bother studying? It's all unknowable anyhow!"

But he does try to get us to recognize that the unknowableness of the universe may be one its most important characteristics. The human mind can't grasp it, he says. But he goes even further, saying that no one can really understand it. Even the entire universe itself can't understand it. Even *it* can't understand *it*. You could even say that God cannot understand himself. Yet we can directly experience it, we can directly experience ourselves. And that real experience is a kind of profound wisdom.

And so he calls this understanding "it" and he calls the unnameable thing that one understands "it" as well. In fact, there can be no understanding in the usual sense because understanding usually implies subject and object. Since you are the universe, you can't possibly step outside it and understand it as an object. As the contemporary Zen teacher Joshu Sasaki said, "The God who is standing in front of you as an object says, 'I am your God,' but he is not. Even if that God has great power he is not the real God."

I hope this chapter wasn't too much of a brain twister. I think it says a lot of useful things about God, the universe, and everything. Rejoice and be glad, though; the next few chapters will be easier.

2. DON'T BE HALF-ASSED

Tenzo Kyokun

Instructions for the Cook

PHEW! AFTER ALL that heavy philosophizing, maybe it's time to change gears. This one is just a little essay about cooking. What could be simpler?

"Tenzo Kyokun" (典座教訓) or "Instructions for the Cook" is not part of *Shobogenzo*, the long work from which the other essays in this collection are drawn. Originally it was supposed to be exactly what its title suggests, a set of instructions for the person who held the position of *tenzo*, or chief cook, in the temple Dogen established.

Although it is mainly a set of guidelines for making food at Zen temples, it's also chock-full of nuggets of wisdom — so much so that it has become one of the most popular pieces of Dogen's writing both in Japan and elsewhere. I know of at least four English translations, one by Taigen Dan Leighton and Shohaku Okumura, one by Griffith Foulk, one by Thomas Wright, and one by Shohei Ichimura. I have used all these except for Ichimura's, which is impossible to find, as well as the original version (see below for what I mean by the "original version") to prepare this paraphrase. I've also referred to Bernie Glassman's book *Instructions to the Cook*, which is not a translation but a book about Dogen's instructions.

My teacher, Gudo Nishijima, never translated "Instructions for the Cook" into English. He was more interested in finishing

Shobogenzo. He had planned to translate all of Dogen's other writings, but by the time *Shobogenzo* was done he was pretty old and the work was getting more difficult for him.

So I worked on this paraphrase without his guidance from beyond the grave. This is the only Dogen piece I've worked on without being able to refer to a translation by my teacher. However, Nishijima Roshi used to mention "Instructions for the Cook" sometimes in his talks, so I've drawn on what I can recall from those talks and from what I learned from him about Dogen in general. Not having a translation by my teacher to work with made this one pretty tough, though.

Another reason this piece was more difficult than the others in this book is that Dogen wrote "Instructions for the Cook" in Chinese rather than Japanese. In Dogen's day, educated Japanese people generally could read at least some Chinese. It functioned a bit like Latin did in Europe at around the same time period. It was the language of educated discourse and formal documents. In fact, Dogen's *Shobogenzo* is often cited as the first major philosophical work produced in Japan to be written in Japanese rather than Chinese.

The fact that this essay was written in Chinese made it a bit harder for me since I don't read Chinese. However, there is a Japanese version of the text that's become accepted as standard in Japan, and I used that as well as the Chinese version. Even with my severely limited Chinese ability, I can tell that the Japanese version stays pretty close to the Chinese original. I've also heard that Dogen's Chinese was actually pretty bad. It's Chinese written by a Japanese person for other Japanese people, so it's a bit closer to medieval Japanese than to standard Chinese.

"Instructions for the Cook" is part of a group of similar writings that are usually collected together these days and called *Eihei Shingi*, which means "Rules for Eihei-ji Monastery." That's the monastery Dogen established near the end of his life. But calling it part of *Eihei Shingi* is actually totally wrong for a few reasons.

"Instructions for the Cook" was actually written before Dogen established Eihei-ji in 1237, when he was running a temple in Uji, near Kyoto. Furthermore, Dogen himself didn't group the writings now included in *Eihei Shingi*. The first time that was done was a few hundred years after Dogen died. So *Eihei Shingi* is sorta like one of those fake Jimi Hendrix albums that came out thirty years after he died claiming to be his supposed "lost follow-up to *Electric Ladyland*." I think there are like half a dozen versions of that album.

Remember how I said that much of Dogen's writings were neglected after he died? That goes double — no, triple! — for "Instructions for the Cook." Kosho Chido, the thirteenth abbot of Eihei-ji, the guy who first published the compilation of essays that included "Instructions for the Cook" in 1667, wrote an afterword to that edition that'll tell you a little about how Dogen's writings were treated.

In this afterword he says that "Instructions for the Cook," along with some similar writings about monastic practice, was "sealed up in the dust and hidden in the mists" and that it was rare for anyone to read it. He said he found these writings in a "worm-eaten container." He mentions that "Instructions for the Cook," along with the other similar writings he found with it, were full of mistakes and incomplete phrases. Dogen's original is lost, and Kosho Chido had to work with these mistake-filled copies. It's reasonable to guess that Dogen never considered "Instructions for the Cook" to be finished and probably would have rewritten it if he'd lived longer. It's pretty amazing it's even available for us to talk about. What's even more amazing is how incredible "Instructions for the Cook" is, and yet for hundreds of years nobody even cared.

While some of Dogen's original works in his own handwriting still exist, no one has yet found a copy of "Instructions for the Cook" in Dogen's writing. Nonetheless, even though it's in Chinese, no scholar seriously doubts that it was written by Dogen, since it's very characteristic of his other writings.

Plus, he talks about a lot more than just cooking in this little essay. Let's have a look!

There are six administrators in charge of different aspects of life and practice at Buddhist monasteries. There's the director, the assistant director, the treasurer, the monks' supervisor, the work leader, and the cook. They're all disciples of Buddha and carry out Buddha work. The cook's job is to oversee meals for everybody at the monastery. Since way long ago, only really awakened people got to be the cook. If you don't have the right mind-set you can't help anyone.

When I was in China, I talked to a bunch of monastery cooks, and they told me what it takes to do the job. First off, you have to study the ancient monastic rules. After that you have to talk to people who've actually done the job.

The cook's working day officially begins right after lunch.* That's when you consult with the director and assistant director about what you'll need for the next day. After you get all the veggies and stuff together, the ancient rules say you gotta protect them like they were your own eyeballs. Respect the temple food like it was food for the emperor.

Next, all the administrators meet up and decide the next day's meals. Once you work that out, you post menus by the abbot's room and in the study hall.

After that you can start working on making stuff for the next day. Select and prepare the veggies and rice with your own hands. Don't multitask. Even one little speck of good makes a mountain of goodness that much bigger, so don't neglect to do your job well.

Examine the rice for sand and examine the sand for rice. One time when a cook in China was sifting rice, his teacher asked him, "Are you sifting rice and throwing away the sand or sifting sand and throwing away the rice?"

The monk said, "I'm throwing away both rice and sand!"

---

* The earliest Buddhist monks ate only breakfast and lunch and weren't supposed to have food after noon. This tradition persists in some areas. But a different custom developed in China and Japan of having an informal meal of leftovers in the evening. It isn't clear whether Dogen's monks did that.

His master said, "Then what's everyone gonna eat?"

The monk spilled out the whole bowl.

His master said, "You better get another teacher." The monk had to clean up the mess he made.

That's how the ancients did things. When you make a mistake you gotta fix it yourself. Cooks enact the Buddhist Way by rolling up their sleeves and getting to work.

Don't waste the water you use to wash the rice. In China they use that water to boil gruel the next morning. Pay attention to your cooking pot. Don't let mice fall in, and don't let some lazy sod come along and poke around in it.

After lunch is done, wash all your utensils and put them away. It's important to treat all your stuff with equal respect.

Then get your utensils ready for the next day's lunch. While the chief cook works on lunch, the assistant cook chants a sutra dedicated to the god of the kitchen.

Next, get the ingredients for lunch from the person in charge of food storage. Don't complain about the amount or the quality of what they give you. Just do your best with what you have to work with.

All day and all night stuff will come through your mind, and you'll deal with it. Just keep your attention on what you're doing, and don't get distracted.

After breakfast, do the dishes and get everything ready to make lunch. The chief cook needs to be at the sink when the rice gets washed and the water gets measured. Don't leave this to somebody else, even if you're in one of those big monasteries where they assign assistants to be in charge of different parts of the meal. Even then you should do your work with the same spirit as in the days when the chief cook had to take care of everything. Back in the day they said, "Think of the pot like it was your own head and the water like it was your own blood."

Don't get all picky about the ingredients. Remember that even the most mundane and boring things can be a means to enter into the Buddhist Way. Don't take cheap ingredients lightly or get all excited when you get to work with some good stuff. Don't be like people who change their whole personality according to who they're talking to.

You should try to take the same seventy-five cents* your grandma used to buy some cheap-ass soup greens and use them to make a bowl of the finest cream of mushroom soup right now. And that ain't easy. How can you ever measure up to what your ancestors did? Still, if you really work at it with the right attitude, you can do it.

You don't understand this because your mind's going crazy and your emotions are running around like a bunch of monkeys. If you can, just once, make those monkeys turn the light around and shine it inward. You'll naturally become one with whatever you do. That's when you start to make stuff happen, even while stuff is happening to you that you can't do anything about.

Treat even a piece of lettuce like you're the Buddha himself and now you've got to make somebody a sandwich. That's real divine power. It benefits everybody.

When you're done cooking and putting stuff away and all that, join the other monks and do the rest of your training without fail.

When you get back to your room, close your eyes and envision how many people you have to feed the next day. If you're not sure you got it right, ask somebody. Then calculate what you're going to need to get the food ready for tomorrow. Recheck your calculations until you're absolutely sure.

When someone donates money for a feast or gives the monastery some stuff, all of the administrators have to get together to decide what to do with it. Don't step on anybody's toes by getting involved in something that's someone else's responsibility when it comes to making these kinds of decisions.

Once lunch is ready to be served, the chief cook puts on robes, faces the hall where the monks eat, and does nine prostrations. After that's done, the food can be sent out.

Don't waste any time during the day. What you do right now becomes the seeds for raising up the next crop of wise people. Putting everyone at ease by doing your job well is how you transform yourself and everybody else.

Buddhism came to Japan a long time ago. But nobody here in

---

* Literally "three coins"; I decided to make them quarters.

Japan has ever written about the proper procedure for preparing meals in a temple. We need to learn this stuff.

When I was in China at the monastery on Mount Tendo, the chief cook there was a guy named Yong. One day after lunch, I happened to see him outside, laying some mushrooms out to dry. It was hot out and he was all sweaty. He was an old guy with big white eyebrows, all bent over doing this hard work with a bamboo cane to support him and no hat to keep the sun from burning his bald head.

I asked him how old he was. He said he was sixty-eight. I was, like, "How come you don't get someone else to do this work?"

He said, "Other people aren't me."

I said, "It's blazing hot out now. Why not wait and do this later?"

He said, "What time should I wait for?"

I left him to do his work. But I immediately felt the real significance of the job of chief cook.

I first arrived in China in 1223 when I was twenty-three. But I was stuck on the ship for a while because of some immigration problems. While I was hanging out there, an old monk of about sixty showed up to buy some Japanese mushrooms. I offered him some tea and asked where he'd come from.

He said he'd walked about twelve miles to get to the ship from his temple. He said he'd trained at a bunch of temples over the years. He was the chief cook, and he wanted to make something special for the following day since it was supposed to be a feast day. He figured he'd serve up some nice exotic mushroom soup with noodles.

I told him I was really happy to be able to meet someone with his experience and that I'd like to talk some more. I offered to treat him to dinner and let him spend the night on the ship so we could talk more.

He declined, saying he had to get back to his temple right after he got the mushrooms so he could get to work on the big meal. He said the food wouldn't turn out right unless he oversaw the cooking.

"Can't your assistants take care of it?" I asked.

He said, "How could I hand my job over to someone else? Besides, I didn't get permission to be out overnight."

I said, "You're a venerable old monk. How come you don't just spend your days meditating and reading scriptures? Being chief cook sounds like a big pain in the ass. Why would you do that?"

He chuckled and said, "Listen, you're a nice young fellow from a foreign country, but you don't know much about the Buddhist Way."

I felt kind of ashamed and said, "What is the practice of the Way?"

He said, "If you work real hard and don't fool yourself, one of these days you'll understand." He could see I was still confused, so he said, "Come visit me at my temple sometime and we'll talk more." Then he said he had to get going because it was getting late.

A few months later I was at the monastery at Mount Tendo. That same old cook heard I was there and paid me a visit. I just about jumped for joy! He told me that by studying words you start to understand the purpose of words. And he said that if I wanted to understand the Buddhist Way I had to actually practice it.

I asked what the words were. He said, "One, two, three, four, five." I asked what the practice of the Way was. He said, "Nothing in the whole world is hidden."

The old cook told me a lot more that night, which I won't bore you with here. Most of what I learned about being a chief cook, I learned from my conversation with that guy.

Later on I came across a Chinese poem meant to instruct Zen monks. It went like this:

One letter, seven letters, three letters, five
The truth can't be grasped by anyone alive
Late in the night the moon sets into the sea
Looking at the waves, not one moon but many

I hope those of you reading my words after I'm gone pay attention to this message. Don't get all hung up on the words used to express the truth. They don't really matter that much. Try to figure out the meaning behind the words. Learn how to see *this* in *that*, and *that* in *this*.

If you make this kind of effort, you'll get the true meaning of Zen. If you don't, you'll just get all mixed up between various opinions and views. Then how are you ever gonna be a decent cook?

This attitude is the key to everything. Food prepared with

expensive ingredients isn't necessarily better, nor is food prepared with cheap ingredients necessarily worse. When you prepare food with the right attitude, that makes all the difference.

It's the same with people who study Zen. It doesn't matter if you're brilliant or stupid. As long as you have the right attitude, it'll be fine.

In old China they say, "A monk's mouth is like a fireplace." Whatever you put in the fireplace burns, whether it's wood or incense or cow dung. Just eat whatever is given to you and use the fuel to continue your practice. The same attitude applies to whatever you are given in life. Just accept it and make it part of your practice.

Don't worry about your fellow monks, like who is better or worse. You don't even know your own strengths and weaknesses. How can you know about anyone else's? You might project your own shortcomings on other people. What good would that do?

Maybe there are differences between advanced monks and newbies, but who really cares? All members of the sangha are the same in the end. What was true in the past isn't necessarily true right now. The old rules for Zen monks say that we should accept everyone without distinction.

When I came back to Japan from my study in China, I lived in Kennin-ji Monastery. They had a chief cook there, but he was just a CINO, a cook-in-name-only. He let his assistants do all the work while he stayed in his office and goofed off. What a waste! Here he was given a golden opportunity to practice the true ancient Way, and he squandered it. He could've been a great practitioner if he'd only put in just a little bit of real effort.

When I was in China I encountered a number of chief cooks in temples. They all had three things in common. They tried to benefit others, knowing that was the best way to benefit oneself. They maintained the high standards of the monasteries they served. And they tried their best to be equal to the practitioners of the past.

There's another old poem that goes like this:

Two-thirds of your life has already passed
But your spiritual progress is, at best, half-assed
You've wasted so many nights and days
If you're called into action, what'll you say?

Unless you meet a good teacher, you're likely to get caught up in your own emotions. You'll be like the child of a wealthy family who ends up squandering the family fortune and being a garbage collector.

Some of the greatest ancient Buddhist masters have held the job of chief cook. It's an important position that shouldn't be taken lightly.

You need three kinds of mind to be the chief cook: joyful mind, nurturing mind, and magnanimous mind. A joyful mind is a mind of happiness. Think about it. If you'd been born in one of the heavenly realms from the old legends, you'd have been so distracted by pleasure you'd never have been able to study the Way. Then you'd never have had the opportunity to cook meals for true practitioners. The ancient texts say the community of practitioners is more precious than anything else in the whole world.

If, on the other hand, you'd been born in one of the legendary hell realms or as an animal, your life would have been too difficult for you to have any opportunity to practice, even if you'd wanted to. And still, you couldn't have cooked for the community of practitioners.

Be glad you were born where you were and that you have this fine opportunity to serve good food to some cool people. They say it's incredibly difficult just to be born as a human being, and even more difficult to encounter the true Way. It's like you're concentrating a million, billion years of good work into this job of being the chief cook. The merit won't wear off for a very long time. If you think about it this way, you can't help but pursue cooking with a joyful mind.

Nurturing mind is like the mind of a parent of an only child who gives every bit of love they have to their kid. Think about the community the way a parent thinks of a child. No matter if the child is weak or strong, beautiful or ugly, a parent loves them just the same. You need to look at the community like that.

Shakyamuni Buddha loved his students so much that it is said he gave up an extra twenty years that he might have lived just to be a better teacher to them. Someone like that can't do anything just for the sake of gaining something for himself.

Magnanimous mind is a mind like a mountain or like the sea. It's stable and impartial. It tolerates anything and everything and keeps a broad perspective. A magnanimous mind isn't prejudiced and doesn't take sides.

All the great teachers of the past have had this joyful mind, nurturing mind, and magnanimous mind. They knew what it meant to be joyful, nurturing, and magnanimous, and they practiced accordingly. People of today should try their best to be like them.

— Written in the spring of 1237 as instructions for practitioners of the Way by Dogen, abbot of Kannon-dori-kosho-horin-ji Temple

First off, coming up with English equivalents for that list of six administrators was kind of a nightmare. Dogen doesn't list the positions in the original text, but they can be found elsewhere in his writings. I figured I couldn't just say there were six administrators including the cook without saying what the other five were. But none of the sources I checked agreed what the proper English translations of the Japanese names for these administrative positions were. Or worse, they translated them with words like *comptroller*. What the hell is a comptroller? Even Microsoft Word's dictionary function doesn't know. It tells me the word means "[the] same as controller." Which is not helpful. Other dictionaries were similarly vague.

The important thing to take away is that Zen monasteries have administrators and that the cook is considered one of them. Therefore, being the cook is an important job, not just an undesirable task you hand off to some flunky. Also, the fact that there are administrators in Zen temples sometimes comes as a surprise to people who imagine Zen monasteries must be sort of like anarchist hippie communes where everybody, like, does their own thing, man. They're actually pretty disciplined places with clear hierarchies and divisions of labor.

Some people like to complain endlessly over the supposed militarism of Zen. What they're talking about is stuff like the fact that Zen temples have hierarchies of administrators. It is true that there have been instances of Zen monks taking this administrative stuff far too seriously, to the detriment of real practice, and of junior monks getting beaten up by seniors. But those are the exceptions, not the norm.

Zen monasteries are intended to be places where individuals can engage in the very personal practice of deep introspection in a communal setting. So rather than going off alone to a cave where no one will bother you, you instead get real introspective in a little building surrounded by other people doing the same thing.

This is a nice idea. It's less lonely; you don't have to do every little thing yourself; if you have an accident or get sick there are people around to help; and so on. But in order for the deep personal introspection part to work, you need to have some very strict ground rules. Everybody's really got to be on the same page about who is supposed to do what, and when and how they're supposed to do those things, or else the whole deal collapses.

Therefore, you need administrators and you need a hierarchy. However, the tradition is to keep these hierarchies very loose. Jobs are rotated often so that nobody gets too set in any one position.

A little further along in my paraphrase I used the word *multitask*, a word that, of course, didn't exist in Dogen's day. Here are some more standard translations of what he does say: "Put your whole attention to the work" (Thomas Wright), "You should not attend to some things and be slack in others" (Taigen Dan Leighton / Shohaku Okumura), and "[Work with] close attention, vigorous exertion, and a sincere mind" (Griffith Foulk). In other words, don't multitask.

I like the line I paraphrased as, "Even one little speck of good makes a mountain of goodness that much bigger, so don't neglect to do your job well." The original is 善根山上一塵亦可積歟, which is very old Chinese and I can't tell you how to pronounce it. In Japanese it's *zenkonsan-jo, ichijin mo matatsumu beki ka* (善根山上、一塵も亦積むべきか), which is something like, "Shouldn't you add one speck of dust on top of a mountain of merit?" I also cut out a similar metaphor that appears after this and goes something like, "In the ocean of merit, don't waste a single drop."

This is kind of a corollary to something I had Dogen say in my other book of paraphrasings, *Don't Be a Jerk*: "Even if the whole world is nothing but a bunch of jerks doing jerk-type things, there is still liberation in simply not being a jerk." Even if all you can do is one little good thing, it still counts. And even if nobody else is doing good stuff, it still matters that you do the right thing.

Then we get a story in which a monk is asked whether he's sifting out the sand or the rice and he ends up spilling the bowl. Most commentators say that the master thought the monk's action was overdramatic. He's trying so hard to demonstrate his nondual understanding — or whatever — that he ruins a whole bowl of perfectly good rice.

I reordered a couple of lines here. Originally the line about rolling up your sleeves came before the one about fixing your own mistakes, and there was no line about the monk having to clean up his mess. But any monk who did such a thing would have to pick all that rice up and do the whole process again, which is a waste of effort and would probably make dinner late for everyone. I think that's implied, but I also think we in the West might miss that implication. So I added a few words to make it clear.

But the story has a happy ending. The monk in question did go on to find another master and later became a revered teacher in his own right.

After this story we get a line that says, "Don't let mice fall in, and don't let some lazy sod come along and poke around in it." The word I paraphrased as "lazy sod" is *himajin* (暇人), meaning someone who has a lot of free time on their hands. Just in case you wondered.

A bit after this it says the assistant cook should chant a sutra dedicated to the god of the kitchen. The word *god* is my rendition of the Japanese word *kami* (神). A *kami* is more like one of the ancient Roman or Greek gods who had a specific and limited domain, rather than the Hebrew God who rules over everything. Sometimes this chanting is still done, even in America, where very few people believe in kitchen gods. You don't have to believe there really is a kitchen god. I don't. The chant itself helps you focus on the work at hand and consider its importance.

Moving right along, a few sentences later in my paraphrase I have Dogen say, "All day and all night stuff will come through your mind, and you'll deal with it. Just keep your attention on what you're doing, and don't get distracted."

Taigen Dan Leighton's version of this is, "All day and all night things come to mind and the mind attends to them; at one with them all, diligently carry on the Way." The Griffith Foulk version has, "During the day and through the night, whether things come and dwell in your mind or your mind turns and dwells on things, put your mind on a par with them and diligently engage in the Way." Thomas Wright translates it as, "Allow your mind and all things to function together as a whole." In Chinese it is, 竟日通夜、物來在心、心歸在物、一等與他精勤辨道, just in case you needed to know.

It's an important phrase, so let's talk about it. People ask me all the time about doing "meditation off the cushion." Meditation isn't just something you do for thirty minutes on a zafu. It's something you carry into the rest of your life and work. In a way, that's kind of what this entire essay is about. Of course, sitting silently is a special form of meditation. Dogen insisted that zazen was a necessary practice for anyone following the Buddhist Way.

Yet in another sense, everything you do is a kind of meditation, whether or not you know it. Once you notice that everything is meditation, you can start to give everything your full attention. No special state of concentration is necessary to transform cooking up a nice pot of mac and cheese into meditation. But giving whatever you do your full attention makes whatever you do that much better.

I like the phrase Griffith Foulk uses in his version, "put your mind on a par with them." That means you're not being "unmindful" if you happen to get distracted now and then. There's a difference between your mind's natural tendency to wander and getting lost in the wanderings of your mind. Most of us don't notice the difference, but there is one. Let me see if I can explain.

In his book *The Wholehearted Way*, a commentary on Dogen's essay "Bendowa" (A Talk about Pursuing the Truth), Kosho Uchiyama says that thoughts are just the secretions of our brains the same way that stomach acid is the secretion of our stomachs. We're accustomed to ignoring our stomach and letting it get on with what it needs to do, without trying to force it into doing what we think it should do.

If you could somehow make your stomach digest that delicious Twinkie you had for dessert before dealing with the yucky broccoli, or something like that, it wouldn't be healthy. Yet when it comes to the contents of our brains, we feel like we must control what goes on. This is especially true for lots of people who get into meditation. Zennies sometimes think it's their job to completely shut down the higher functions of the brain. But this is also unhealthy.

When your mind wanders, that's fine. Just keep paying attention to what you're doing. You don't have to force some heightened state of hyperawareness on the situation at hand. It doesn't need to be like that. Just diligently carry on, leaving the brain to do what it needs to do. As Dogen says, "Cooks enact the Buddhist Way by rolling up their sleeves and getting to work."

However, this doesn't mean you just space out during zazen. Okay. Maybe you will. We all do. But if you find yourself doing that, just come back to where you really are. Zazen is a curious blend of tension and relaxation. You allow what is actually happening to happen without trying to control it. And yet you try to maintain full awareness of all of it. Work on this for a while, and you'll get the hang of it. Or you won't. Which is also okay. Just keep doing it anyhow.

A few paragraphs further along I have Dogen saying, "You

don't understand this because your mind's going crazy and your emotions are running around like a bunch of monkeys. If you can, just once, make those monkeys turn the light around and shine it inward. You'll naturally become one with whatever you do."

There were a few oddities in the different translations. None of the standard translations just say "monkeys" here; some mention *birds* and monkeys, while others mention *horses* and monkeys. The Chinese character for *bird*, 鳥, and the Chinese character for *horse*, 馬, look very similar. This is one of the mistakes that the guy who first compiled these related essays back in the 1600s wrote about. Even though there are discrepancies between the translations that say "birds" and those that say "horses," all of them say "monkeys," so I just dropped the birds/horses reference from my paraphrase.

And all of them also have some variation on the idea of making those mental monkeys (and birds/horses) turn the light within. This is important. When I started meditating I thought the idea was to get rid of the monkeys in my mind, or to subdue my "monkey mind." That's not what Dogen says. He says it's those monkeys of the mind themselves that make meditation happen.

Furthermore, he doesn't say you have to make this happen all the time. I led a retreat a little while back in Seattle in which one of the participants asked about how to get your mind to settle down 24/7 like the ancient masters did.

I told her I didn't think any of the so-called masters, ancient or modern, were ever able to keep their monkey minds in check around the clock every day of the year. The Buddha spoke about encountering the "temptations of Mara" even after doing meditation practice for decades. The "temptations of Mara" is just another way of referring to the monkey mind. Mara is a mythological figure, something like Satan in the Bible, who makes people do bad things. Buddha didn't believe some disembodied spirit of evil was responsible for his temptations. He just used the terms that were familiar to the people of his time. The point is, even he had to deal with his own shit after becoming arguably the greatest meditator that ever lived. And if he did, so will you.

It's not that you have to somehow squash all that stuff down, or flatten those mind monkeys like you were playing Whac-A-Mole. You actually use all that shit to become truly yourself. Your own shit, when used wisely, becomes the fertilizer of your enlightenment. That's what Dogen means when he tells us to make those monkeys turn the light around and shine it inward.

After this monkey business, the next line in my version goes, "That's when you start to make stuff happen, even while stuff is happening to you that you can't do anything about." Thomas Wright's translation is more literal. It says, "Doing so is the means whereby we turn things even while simultaneously being turned by them." He notes that Dogen here echoes a passage in another work of his, "Gakudo Yojinshu" (Practical Advice on Pursuing Buddhist Truth). Wright gives that passage as, "The dharma turns the self and the self turns the dharma. When we influence dharma, dharma is weak and we are strong. When dharma influences us, dharma is strong and we are weak. Both of these principles have always been part of the teachings of Buddhadharma."

My teacher, Nishijima Roshi, translated the same passage as, "The Universe turns us and we turn the Universe. When we can turn the Universe, we are strong and the Universe is weak. When the Universe turns us back, the Universe is strong and we are weak. The Buddhist teachings have always had these two factors, but no one other than true successor has ever known it."

Dogen says some similar things in the *Shobogenzo* chapter usually titled something like "The Flower of Dharma Turns the Flower of Dharma." (In my book *Don't Be a Jerk* I paraphrased the title as "Twirly Flowers Twirl Twirly Flowers.") Here he also talks about the dharma turning you and you turning the dharma.

It's hard to find a lot of commentary relating to this idea, but let me give you my take. In the West we often argue about free will versus predestination. We think it has to be one or the other. But Dogen doesn't go for those kinds of either-or arguments. He likes to have it both ways.

When the universe turns you, you are at the mercy of whatever events you are embroiled in — you have no free will. When you turn the universe, you are taking action as an individual and influencing what happens next — you have free will. These days, loudmouthed motivational speakers make boatloads of money selling the idea that you turning the universe is the best thing that can happen. I don't think that's true.

The truth is that the individual and the universal are two aspects of the same thing. The back-and-forth of the universe turning you and you turning the universe is the natural way. Keeping both sides in balance is better than either struggling to force your will on the universe or just rolling over and letting things happen. In this passage Dogen is saying that even in the simple act of cooking up some food, this universal back-and-forth is still taking place.

The next bit starts with, "Treat even a piece of lettuce like you're the Buddha himself and now you've got to make somebody a sandwich." Of course there's no sandwich in the original. In Chinese this is, 拈一莖菜作丈六金身。請丈六金身作一莖菜。 Griffith Foulk translates this as, "Lifting a single piece of vegetable, make [yourself into] a six-foot body [i.e., Buddha] and ask that six-foot body to prepare a single piece of vegetable."

Thomas Wright adds a line after this that doesn't appear in other translations or in the original, but I like it. His version says, "This is a power which you cannot grasp with your rational mind. It operates freely, according to the situation, in a most natural way." He's riffing on what Dogen actually writes, which is shorter and more like my line, "That's real divine power."

The two stories that follow soon after this about the two chief cooks and mushrooms are my personal favorite parts of "Instructions for the Cook." They're not that hard to understand. In both cases the old and experienced monks are doing manual labor instead of resting on their laurels like people tend to do in normal society once they reach a certain age, if they're able to. These monks could be doing that, too, but they choose to work instead because they feel like their work is the best way of studying the dharma. That part doesn't need much explaining.

The parts that hang people up come at the end of the stories when Dogen asks one of the old cooks what the words are and the cook responds by just counting at him, and the punch line to the whole thing goes, "Nothing in the whole world is hidden." This line is so significant that one of the translations I consulted comes from a book called *Nothing Is Hidden: Essays on Zen Master Dōgen's Instructions for the Cook*. In the original, the line is 界不會藏, and it means, "Nothing in the whole world is hidden." The various translations are all pretty consistent.

Zengan Hashimoto addresses the meaning of the cook counting at Dogen in his essay "Mendicant Practice in Buddha's World" from the book *Nothing Is Hidden*. According to Hashimoto, the cook is telling Dogen to just do things one by one — or not to multitask, to put it in contemporary terms. "The essence expressed in the sayings of ancient Zen masters is nothing other than each and every action in daily monastic life," Hashimoto says.

I think that's a good explanation. I also like the idea that the old cook is just giving Dogen a concrete example of words and that there might not be any other significance to it. That's how I always read it. But, then again, I'm kind of a dim bulb and that's how I take a lot of things — just at face value without even bothering to look for hidden subtext. I find this to be a useful practice. That way, whenever someone is saying something in a roundabout or ambiguous way, you force them to be more direct. You're less likely to get things wrong because of a misunderstanding.

As for nothing being hidden, that to me is kind of the crux of Buddhist philosophy, when it comes to defining the world we live in. Most religions go the opposite way. They tell you that there are hidden things that are incredibly important. You can't see heaven or hell or God, and you can't know what happens after you die, but these religions tell you that after you die you'll be judged by God and sent to heaven or hell forever. So the most important things in life are completely hidden. There are a lot of different variations on this idea of hidden things being super-significant. But most religions seem to have that basic idea as their starting point.

In Buddhism nothing is hidden. Everything you need to know is as plain as day. That doesn't mean that the way you conceive of the things you encounter all day long every day is correct. It doesn't even mean your perceptions are right. But it does mean that all the big answers to the important questions about life, the universe, and everything are right there staring you in the face.

This is hard to accept. So the phrase "Nothing is hidden" comes off sounding absurd. Of course things are hidden! There are all kinds of important things going on right this very minute that you and I know nothing about. Politicians keep secrets that affect our lives. The Internet screams about how things you eat all the time, thinking they're just delicious snacks, are giving you cancer. The whole universe seems like one giant puzzle that nobody can ever hope to figure out.

Yet in the face of all that, Dogen insists that nothing is hidden.

As I've continued doing the practice that Dogen recommended in my own half-assed way over these many years, I feel more and more like he's right. Nothing is hidden. The problem is getting honest enough with myself to see what's been right there in front of me all along.

Following this part of the essay, Dogen gives us a little poem about the moon reflecting on waves. As I did in *Don't Be a Jerk*, I decided to make my version rhyme. Still, if you check other books, I think you'll find that my version agrees with the standard translations.

Dogen frequently uses the metaphor of the moon reflected in

water to express that the truth is always one but that this one truth has many facets. Kazuaki Tanahashi even titled one of his many books about Dogen *Moon in a Dewdrop*. There is only one moon, but as it sets into the sea, each wave reflects it a little differently. It's the same way with us human beings and the truth. "The truth is only one," as Nishijima Roshi used to say. But each of us reflects that truth a bit differently.

A little later, when Dogen tells his future students to try to see the meaning behind the words used to express the truth, I have him say, "If you make this kind of effort, you'll get the true meaning of Zen. If you don't, you'll just get all mixed up between various opinions and views."

In the original, what I've paraphrased as "the true meaning of Zen" is more like "one-flavor Zen" (一味禪). What I paraphrased as "various opinions and views" is more like "five-flavor Zen" (五味禪). So I'm being a little interpretive here. But I thought if I said "one-flavor Zen" and "five-flavor Zen" readers might miss the point of what Dogen is saying and instead just get lost in the beautiful Orientalness of it all. You're welcome.

A bit further along I have Dogen saying, "It doesn't matter if you're brilliant or stupid. As long as you have the right attitude, it'll be fine." Sometimes people read statements like this only as assurances to dumb people that they'll be as okay as smart people. But often smart people actually have it worse, I think. They get so lost in their cleverness that they can't see the real world outside their own heads. So the proper attitude is just as important for the smarties as it is for the dummies.

I left a longish passage out of this section that involves stories about an ancient Indian king attaining the truth after being given a crab apple to eat, and the Buddha accepting the sincere offer of some scummy water to drink. If you want to read them, they're in all the standard translations. I just thought the point was already made without those stories and that they tend to be distracting to contemporary readers.

The line I paraphrased a little further down as "a monk's mouth is like a fireplace" is usually translated something like "a monk's mouth is like an oven" or "like a stove." I never got those metaphors myself because I think of ovens and stoves as things you cook stuff in. But Dogen is actually referring to the part of an ancient oven where you put the wood in to burn and not to the other part where the cooking happens. So I changed it to a fireplace and then added some descriptive explanations (some of which come from the footnotes to the book *How to Cook Your Life*) to try to make the metaphor clearer.

A bit later I have Dogen saying something about the child of a wealthy family squandering the family fortune and ending up being a garbage collector. In the original it's a reference to an ancient Buddhist story that Dogen's original audience would have known but that we wouldn't. But in the original version, the kid does end up as a garbage collector. I didn't change that part.

After that I have Dogen say, "Some of the greatest ancient Buddhist masters have held the job of chief cook." In the original this section is much longer, with Dogen giving some specific examples. Since I'm assuming that most of the audience for this book wouldn't know any of those people (I sure don't!), I just left all that out. You can consult a standard translation if you're just dying to know who he mentioned.

In the next bit, Dogen talks about the three kinds of mind a chief cook needs. I give these as "joyful mind, nurturing mind, and magnanimous mind." I took that straight out of Taigen Dan Leighton's translation, which appears in the book *Dōgen's Pure Standards for the Zen Community*. Griffith Foulk's translation is "a joyful mind, an elder's mind, and a great mind." Thomas Wright's translation splits it into two instead of three and says you need the "spirit of joy and magnanimity, along with the caring attitude of a parent."

In the original it's 喜心 (pronounced either *kigokoro* or *kishin* in Japanese), 老心 (pronounced either *rokokoro* or *roshin* in Japanese), and 大心 (pronounced either *okokoro* or *daishin* in Japanese). The second character in each compound is *kokoro* (心), which means "mind," "heart," or "spirit." *Ki* (喜) means "joy." *Ro* (老) means "elder." And *o* or *dai*, depending on the context (大), means "great" or "big." I think Leighton's translation is as close as you're gonna get in English, so I just stole it from him outright. I hope he doesn't get mad.

Occasionally *rokokoro* (老心), which Leighton translates as "nurturing mind," gets translated as "grandmotherly mind." Dogen once used a similar word, *robashin* (老婆心), literally "old woman mind," which could also be translated as "grandmotherly mind," when he was talking about his student Gikai. He said Gikai hadn't properly developed this "grandmotherly mind." So even though he used a gender-neutral word in "Instructions for the Cook," another way of expressing the same idea could be "grandmotherly mind." I went with "nurturing mind" to preserve the original's gender neutrality.

I think Dogen does a pretty good job of explaining what he means by these three types of mind. I left that part pretty much like it is in the original and in most translations.

All the stuff in this section about being born in heavenly or hell realms and about concentrating millions of years of good karma into this lifetime doesn't need to be taken literally. Honestly, I don't know whether Dogen believed in that stuff literally. I devoted a chapter of *Don't Be a Jerk* to the question of whether he did or did not believe in reincarnation or rebirth. I concluded that he probably did but that he definitely did not think it was important for his audience to have any specific belief about what happened to them after they died. Personally, sometimes I take all the rebirth stuff as metaphor, and sometimes I wonder if it might be true. But in either case, it doesn't make a whole lot of difference. To me what Dogen is mainly doing here is giving words of encouragement to the cooks he was trying to train.

I liked Thomas Wright's translation of the part where Dogen describes what *magnanimous mind* means, so I borrowed liberally from him in that section. My apologies. The original has a lot of stuff about thinking of things that are light and things that are heavy as the same and about not getting caught up in the colors of spring and autumn. It's all very beautiful, but you can get lost in that beautiful stuff. Wright's translation adds some words that make Dogen's meaning more down-to-earth, so I used a lot of the same words he used.

Then the whole essay just sort of ends abruptly. Perhaps this is because Dogen never really finished it.

The general message of "Instructions for the Cook" applies to everyone who tries to practice, not just to the chief cooks at temples. It's all about what some people like to call "wholehearted practice." Whatever you do, put your entire body and mind into it. Don't be half-assed. Whatever work you're doing is important work.

Dogen focused on temple cooks because he saw that in Japan, the position of temple cook was looked down on as a lowly service position. But Dogen didn't allow for such distinctions as lower and higher. As I said at the outset, there are hierarchies in temples. This requires people in certain positions to answer to people in other positions. But this doesn't mean those positions are any better or any worse. People just have roles to perform, and who answers to whom is merely a part of what a given job entails, not an indication of some kind of status.

The world would probably run a lot more smoothly if more people started seeing things that way.

3. A THOUSAND EYES AND HANDS OF COMPASSION

Kannon

Compassion

EVERYBODY LOVES COMPASSION. It's gotta be the number one buzzword wherever Buddhism or other kooky Eastern philosophies are sold. But most people have no idea what compassion actually is.

And that is a problem.

If you run around trying to be compassionate without any real understanding of what compassion is, you can end up doing more harm than good. Your image of what compassion ought to look like gets in the way of real compassion. Dogen addresses that problem here.

In the original, this essay is beautifully poetic, rich with metaphor and imagery. But when you read it in translation, most of that just goes over your head. Or at least that's what it does with *my* head.

I had to read and study this essay a lot before I felt I could even begin to comprehend it. I've tried my best to make the paraphrase straightforward without tossing away all the poetry. Reading it back again, I think I failed pretty badly. Yet I think what you get in my paraphrase will probably have a better chance of making sense than what you'd get if you read even the best translations available.

I don't mean to sound arrogant here. A translator has a different job from what I'm trying to do here. A translator is trying to give you an insight into what the document in question actually would say if you could read it in its original language. Good translators try to avoid putting their own interpretation into what they translate any more than is absolutely necessary. In this book, I feel like my job is almost the total opposite of that. I'm supposed to tell you what I think Dogen means rather than present you with what he really said.

Anyway, I hope that if there are difficult bits in the paraphrase the commentary at the end will make things a little more comprehensible. Then you can go back and reread my paraphrase — or, better yet, read one of the legitimate translations — and have a clearer understanding of what Dogen is getting at.

Master Ungan Donjo (Ch. Yunyan Tansheng, 780-841 CE) asked Master Dogo Enchi (Ch. Daowu Yuanzhi, 769-835 CE), "What does Kannon, the Bodhisattva of Compassion, do with all her bazillions of hands and eyes?"

Dogo said, "She's like someone reaching for a pillow in the middle of the night."

Ungan said, "Right on. I get that."

Dogo said, "How do you get it?"

Ungan said, "The entire body is hands and eyes."

Dogo said, "Not bad. I'd give that answer a B-plus."

Ungan said, "That's my take on it. What's yours, bro?"

Dogo said, "No matter where you go it's all hands and eyes."

Lots of people have tried expressing what compassion really is, but nobody has ever equaled Ungan and Dogo. If you really want to know about compassion you should study their words.

Along with Kannon, the Bodhisattva of Compassion has a lot of other names, too. Sometimes she's called "the One Who Hears the Sounds of the World" and sometimes she's called "the One Who Perceives Everything." Don't think of Kannon as one of the lesser Buddhist deities. She is the mother and the father of all the Buddhas. She's a pretty big deal, actually.

So let's take a look at what Ungan says when he says, "What does the Kannon, the Bodhisattva of Compassion, do with all her bazillions of hands and eyes?"

Some schools of Buddhism are all about Kannon, and in others she's never even mentioned. Ungan was from one of the schools that are all about Kannon. You could even say that Kannon was part of Ungan and part of Dogo, too. And not even just one Kannon either — like a hundred thousand Kannons.

Kannon is really only Kannon in the lineage of Ungan. Which is to say, compassion is only really compassion in that lineage. Only Ungan could express the truth about Kannon. Other people just like the *idea* of Kannon, the *idea* of compassion. But their ideas about compassion are way too limited. They don't understand what real compassion actually is.

We can tell Ungan's ideas are better because he asks about Kannon's "bazillions of hands and eyes," which is a way of saying they're limitless in number. So it's not just eighty-four thousand or whatever. Her hands and eyes are beyond any measure or restriction. That's another way of saying that compassion is unrestricted.

Ungan and Dogo were close friends who practiced together for something like forty years under their teacher Yakusan Igen (Ch. Yaoshan Weiyan, 745-827 CE). So by the time they had this conversation they had already hashed out a whole lot of stuff together. They knew each other well and they knew what was what.

When Ungan says "bazillions of hands and eyes" and Dogo doesn't disagree, we know they're on to something. So don't just pass by that part of the story.

Notice that Ungan asks Dogo what Kannon does with all those hands and eyes. This question itself is a manifestation of Kannon's compassionate hands and eyes. When Ungan asks what Kannon *does with them*, this is an expression of the truth. Compassion means doing things.

Dogo says that Kannon is like someone reaching back to adjust a pillow in the night. That means groping around in total darkness. Let's look at that statement closely. There's a difference between nighttime as conceived of by a person during the day and the reality of the darkness on an actual night. You should also look into times that aren't quite day but aren't quite night, either. If you catch my drift.

When someone gropes around for a pillow at night they might

not understand that they're acting like the Bodhisattva of Compassion. But there's no denying they are.

The person groping for the pillow may not be just any sort of person. Maybe it's you. Even pillows have their own specific shapes and sizes. They're not all the same. Furthermore, nighttime isn't just of one kind. Also make note that we're not talking about grabbing the pillow or pushing it away.

Dogo talks about reaching for a pillow. Don't disregard that eyes see the night. The hand he's talking about hasn't actually touched the pillow yet. If it's important to reach back with the hand, it might also be important to reach back with the eyes.

We need to be clear about what nighttime really is. Maybe it's the world of hands and eyes. Is it hands and eyes alone flying around at lightning speed? Do these hands and eyes always do the right thing? Maybe hands and eyes are being used, but just who is this Bodhisattva of Compassion that supposedly uses them?

Maybe we should talk about a Bodhisattva of Hands and Eyes? Maybe we should ask what the Bodhisattva of Hands and Eyes does with all her bazillions of acts of compassion?

Hands and eyes don't get in each other's way. They just do what they do. What they do is something we can't ever express in words — even though it has never been hidden. Nor are these hands and eyes waiting for someone to come along and explain them. They are not you. They are not the sun or the moon. And they are not "Mind here and now is Buddha."

Ungan says, "Right on. I get that." But he isn't saying he understood Dogo's words. He's using the real hands and real eyes of unnameable reality, of actual experience. He then expresses the truth of that experience.

This is freedom to enter the place where he is. This is freedom to be exactly in today.

When Dogo asks, "How do you get it?" that's another way of saying, "Right on. I get that." But Dogo says it his own way, which is to ask, "How do you get it?"

How could "How do you get it?" be anything other than "Right on. I get that"? How could it be anything but eyes getting it and hands getting it? Is it understanding that you've understood, or is it not understanding that you've understood?

Maybe *I* got it. But it was *you* who were asked if you got it. Get it?

Dogo said, "She's like someone reaching for a pillow in the middle of the night." And Ungan said, "The entire body is hands and eyes." He's not saying that her "hands and eyes" are an "entire body" that is everywhere.

Being everywhere would mean being the whole universe. But your real hands and real eyes at this real moment aren't everywhere. Even if there were bodies, hands, and eyes that could be everywhere all at once, they wouldn't be hands and eyes that could shoplift a shirt from an American Apparel store. Such hands and eyes don't know rightness from wrongness.

Remember how I said that when Ungan said "bazillions" he meant that Kannon's hands and eyes were beyond number? This doesn't just go for her hands and eyes. Every instance of doing the right thing is also limitless. That's how we make this world a better place. We ought to take care never to get in the way of doing what's right, whether that means actively doing something or refraining from doing something.

Dogo said, "Not bad. I'd give that answer a B-plus." He's saying that it's "not bad" to speak the truth. He's saying that Ungan said all that needed to be said. If he didn't mean that, he wouldn't have said, "Not bad." He'd just have said, "I'd give that answer a B-plus."

Ungan's words aren't less than perfect. They are a completely perfect B-plus answer. Ungan is so super-cool that he could express himself with A-plus clarity if he wanted to. Yet he chooses instead a B-plus answer. If Buddhism always had to be expressed in an A-plus way, there would be no Buddhism at all today.

Ungan said, "That's my take on it. What's yours, bro?" He says this because he wants to hear Dogo's take on what Dogo has just called a B-plus answer. Ungan doesn't mean to say that his own expression was imperfect.

Dogo said, "No matter where you go it's all hands and eyes." He's describing the way that using hands and eyes is the same as "no matter where you go."

If somebody asks *what* Kannon does with her bazillions of hands and eyes, then "No matter where you go it's all hands and eyes" might be the right answer. It might be a way of expressing that Kannon's hands and eyes are doing *what*, or in other words how they are doing unnameable work.

Furthermore, it's useless to compare Ungan's answer to Dogo's. Both are expressions of Kannon's bazillions of hands and eyes. Both are expressions of real compassion.

The number of Kannon's eyes and hands of compassion are beyond too many and too few. When you learn this in experience, you learn the real meaning of compassion present in every moment. There are many Buddhist writings that express this truth. The story about Ungan and Dogo is just one of them.

— Preached to the assembly on April 26, 1242

This one starts off with one of those weird Zen stories. It needs a little explaining since it's really hard to translate.

The first part of the story is fairly straightforward and there aren't any big variations in the translations. And just FYI, Ungan really does call Dogo "bro" in the original. Or at least he calls him "brother." Also where I have him say, "I'd give that answer a B-plus," he actually says something like, "You've expressed 80 or 90 percent of the truth." That was a B-plus when I went to school. Or maybe a B? It's been a long time.

The tough part is when we get to the bit at the end where they start saying the entire body is hands and eyes and everywhere you go it's all just hands and eyes.

As you'll recall, first Ungan gives an answer, then Dogo says it's a B-plus answer, then Ungan asks what Dogo's answer would be, then Dogo gives his answer.

The Nishijima/Cross translation has Ungan say, "The whole body is hands and eyes." In their version, after Dogo tells Ungan that his answer is just 80 or 90 percent of realization Dogo says, "The thoroughly realized body is hands and eyes."

In the Tanahashi translation, Ungan says, "All over the body are hands and eyes." And Dogo's answer goes, "Wherever the body reaches, it is hands and eyes."

The Nishiyama/Stevens translation calls the Bodhisattva of Compassion Daihi. Their version has Ungan asking, "Does Daihi have hands and eyes all over its body?" To which Dogo replies, "The entire body of Daihi is hands and eyes."

The Shasta Abbey translation makes the Bodhisattva male — he or she can be either. In their version Ungan says, "His whole body is hands and eyes." And Dogo says, "His whole being, through and through, is hands and eyes."

I know, right? It's nutty, I tell ya!

The key words we're all struggling with are *henshin* (編身) and *tsushin* (通身). Ungan says it's the first one, and Dogo says it's the second. You'll note that the second character, *shin* (身), which means "body," is the same in both answers.

Hen (編) in this case means "entire." I became very familiar with that character, when I worked in the film industry in Japan, as part of the word *henshu* (編集), which means "to edit," as in editing film. The English word for "editing film" implies taking things out. But what you're really doing is compiling it all together, which is what the Japanese word indicates, to compile or assemble pieces into a whole. So "entire body" seems like a good enough translation for Ungan's statement. That's the easy(ish) part.

Tsu (通), which is part of Dogo's answer to Ungan, means "to pass through." When you combine this with the character for *body*, what you get is no more comprehensible in Japanese than it is in English. Which is why everybody has such a hard time with it.

Luckily, Dogen gives us some words of explanation.

One of the first things Dogen tells us is that only Ungan really understands what compassion is all about. I have him saying, "Other people just like the *idea* of Kannon, the *idea* of compassion. But their ideas about compassion are way too limited. They don't understand what real compassion actually is."

In the original Dogen actually says something more like, "The Kannon expressed by other buddhas is only twelve faces" (Nishijima / Cross translation). In a footnote, Nishijima and Cross say, "Statues of Bodhisattva Avalokitesvara [Kannon] sometimes have eleven small faces carved around the head. The Kannon of twelve faces suggests the idealistic image of Kannon." Dogen uses this poetic image to suggest the *idea* or *image* of compassion, as opposed to true compassion. So I just did away with the poetry and had my version of Dogen say it the way someone of our time would say it.

Then Dogen says some stuff about how other lineages think Kannon has just eighty-four thousand hands and eyes but that Ungan isn't like that — meaning that Ungan's idea of compassion isn't as limited as other teachers' ideas.

Next up, Dogen does one of those things he likes to do. He dissects the dialogue in ridiculous detail. Some of what he does involves breaking down the Chinese characters in the original dialogue. That's nearly impossible to convey in English. I'm going to spare you most of the details. I think my paraphrasing here follows the standard line of thinking of most Dogen scholars. But I'll go into some of what I changed and why I did so.

A little ways into this dissection of the dialogue, I have Dogen say, "There's a difference between nighttime as conceived of by a person during the day and the reality of the darkness on an actual night. You should also look into times that aren't quite day but aren't quite night, either. If you catch my drift."

That's pretty close to the original, even though he doesn't really say "if you catch my drift" at the end. I put it in there for people who might be like me and miss the metaphor.

Here's what I think the metaphor means. We're talking about compassion here, remember. So *day* means times when it's easy to see what the compassionate thing to do is. Like when you see a turtle on its back. The compassionate thing to do is turn it over. Easy.

Night in this case would mean times when you have no idea

what the best thing to do is. I'm sure all of us can think of our own examples. In my case, what springs to mind is when a close relative of mine got involved with someone who was clearly abusing him emotionally and financially. My relative steadfastly refused to acknowledge this and would react with anger and defensiveness at any attempt the rest of us in the family made to intervene. None of us who loved him had any idea how to break through. That's an example of "night" when it comes to compassionate action. There was no clear-cut, easily identifiable way to be compassionate.

Then there are times that are neither day nor night. That means times when you might kinda sorta see what you ought to do but also might not know which among several options is really the best.

When Dogen says "nighttime as conceived of by a person during the day," I believe he's talking about the kinds of things where folks think they can see what somebody else ought to have done in a certain situation. One specific example of this has come up a lot among people who studied Zen in the West with Japanese teachers who came to America and Europe in the fifties through the seventies.

These teachers all seemed like decent enough people. But pretty soon their students learned that not all of them had reacted in what they (the students) thought of as the "right way" when Japan was fighting World War II. Some of these teachers even served in the Japanese Imperial Army, one of the most universally vilified fighting forces outside of the Nazis. My teacher, Nishijima Roshi, for example, answered the call when he was drafted in the 1940s.

Nishijima got lucky. He was sent to a remote outpost and never saw any real action. Knowing the kind of guy he was, though, I think if he'd been called on to fire at the enemy, he probably would have done his duty. Other people who later became Zen teachers who were placed into such positions did just that.

This sort of thing made some Western students of Japanese Zen teachers of that age very queasy. It would have been nice for us if all those teachers had steadfastly refused to participate in the war. But the truth is, many of them did not refuse.

It's easy for those of us in the "daylight" of a world at peace (at least our corner of it) to speculate about what those in the dark night of war ought to have done or what we would have done if we were there. But we weren't there. So we have no idea what we would have done. In fact, our assumption that we know what we'd do in such a situation is the height of ignorance and arrogance.

It's totally pointless to claim moral superiority in these kinds of speculative matters. It's better to listen to what people who were actually in those situations have to say about it. Sure. Sometimes some people make lame attempts to justify themselves. But sometimes you can learn a lot by listening, even if you don't necessarily believe everything you're hearing.

There is a big difference between real night and night as imagined by someone during the day.

A little further down I have Dogen say, "The person groping for the pillow may not be just any sort of person. Maybe it's you." In the original he doesn't come flat out and say, "Maybe it's you." He says something more like, "Do not take it as merely someone" (Tanahashi translation) and says it's not an ordinary person. To me that sounds like he's trying to get his readers to put themselves in the place of the fictional person in the story, so that's what I had him say. It could also mean the person in question is an exceptional person. So you can try going back and reading it that way if you like.

After this I have Dogen say that eyes see the night. That's a pretty standard translation. In a footnote to that, Nishijima and Cross say, "In other words, eyes (mental function) and night (objective fact) are one reality." Then, after the part where Dogen says it's important to reach back with the eyes as well as the hands, Nishijima and Cross have a footnote that says, "Master Dogen's question encourages consideration of the relation between body and mind."

The paragraphs right after this one are full of weird stuff. If you think my paraphrase is hard, just be glad you're not trying to deal with one of the standard translations. For example, Nishijima/ Cross say, in part, "Hands and eyes do not hinder each other; at the same time, their use is doing what is the ineffable functioning and is the use of the ineffable. When the ineffable expresses the truth we should not expect to be able to express the whole of hands and eyes — although the whole of hands and eyes has never been hidden — as 'the whole of hands and eyes.' Unhidden hands...are not the self, they are not the mountains and oceans, they are not the face of the sun and the face of the moon, and they are not the mind here and now as buddha." Other translations are pretty much the same in terms of difficulty and convolutedness.

It could drive you batty. But maybe it's not as difficult as it seems. Let me see if I can break it down a little.

After the part of this paragraph that I paraphrased as, "Hands and eyes don't get in each other's way," Nishijima and Cross add a footnote that says, "Hands and eyes not hindering each other suggests the state in which physical actions and mental processes are harmonized."

The stuff in this paragraph about the actions of hands and eyes never being explainable in words is my attempt to deal with yet another instance of Dogen using that word *inmo* (恁麼). You'll recall that this word literally means "what." Nishijima/Cross usually translate *inmo* as "the ineffable." Dogen uses this word as a way to refer to the mystical, inexpressible *something* that is ourselves and is the universe.

So real compassion is the functioning of the universe using *us* as its hands and its eyes. At the same time, it's not ourselves. Not in the way we think of ourselves, anyhow. Even sayings of Buddhist philosophy such as "mind here and now is Buddha" can't really express it.

After this Dogen says that when Ungan said, "Right on. I get that," this didn't mean he understood Dogo's words. When I looked that up in the original Japanese I was kind of surprised.

All the translations — including Nishijima's translation into contemporary Japanese — agree that Dogen said Ungan's reply didn't mean he understood Dogo's *words*. Only that's not what Dogen says. He doesn't say words (言葉, *kotoba*) here, he says "way" (道, *michi* or *do*). I've deferred to the experts and left "words" in my paraphrase. But I think maybe Dogen is getting a little deeper here. Maybe he means that Ungan isn't saying he understood Dogo's way of expressing the truth. You tell me. Even if this is just a colloquial expression of Dogen's time that usually meant "words," it's still intriguing.

Moving right along. Right after this I have Dogen say, "He's using the real hands and real eyes of unnameable reality." Yet again, Dogen here uses the word *inmo*, which is what I paraphrased as "unnameable reality."

Then I have Dogen say, "This is freedom to enter the place where he is. This is freedom to be exactly in today." That's more or less the Nishijima/Cross translation ("This might be freedom in using this place, and might be freedom in having to get into today").

The Nishiyama/Stevens version is, "We should strive to actualize this spirit in our everyday life." Tanahashi's version says, "Daowo [a.k.a. Dogo] used his words boundlessly just like this. He entered that day boundlessly just like this." I'm not sure why Tanahashi attributes this to Dogo. Dogen does not do so in the original, and neither do Nishijima/Cross and Nishiyama/Stevens.

The word Nishijima/Cross translate as "freedom" and Tanahashi translates as "boundless" is *mutan* (無端). This is not a standard word in contemporary Japanese, but it's easy enough to figure out. *Mu* (無) means "without," and *tan* (端) means "edge," "end," or "boundary." So it means something like "without edges" or "without end." Dogen talks about using this boundlessness or this freedom to "enter today."

It's great poetry and evokes something when you read it in the original that's hard to reproduce in English. We often don't really enter the present moment because we're too bound up with ideas about...well, about a whole bunch of things. We're stuck in our concepts *about* what's going on and we miss what's *actually* going on. Dogen feels that Ungan's response indicates he wasn't bound up that way. He expresses the real freedom to be right where he is.

Then we get that crazy paragraph that begins, "When Dogo asks 'How do you get it?' that's another way of saying, 'Right on. I get that.'" I'll let you go back and read that part again in case you forgot. Don't worry. I'll wait here.

Pretty weird, right? The other translations of this section are, if anything, even stranger than what I gave you. For example, the Nishijima/Cross version says, in part, "The understanding described by 'I understand' is the 'I' itself; at the same time we should consider its existence as 'you' in 'How do you understand?'" You can look up the other translations for yourself.

In order to understand this, you have to remember that one of the core ideas in Buddhist philosophy is that subject and object are one. Or, as John Lennon said in "I Am the Walrus," "I am he as you are he, as you are me, and we are all together." That's actually a very coherent Buddhist statement. The Rutles' parody of this song ("Piggy in the Middle") begins, "I know you know what you know, but you should know by now that you're not me." This is also straight-up Buddhism. I'm not kidding.

So Ungan and Dogo are two people. But they are also both manifestations of one underlying reality. Sometimes when two people become very intimate, like when they do zazen together for forty years as these two guys did, they start to be able to manifest this. What's happening in this conversation is not two people challenging each other, but two people arriving at a common understanding through dialogue.

Then we get another weird paragraph that begins, "Being everywhere would mean being the whole universe."

Once again, the standard translations are even more confusing than my paraphrase. Here's a taste of the Nishijima/Cross version: "Even if there is, in the body-hands and body-eyes, the virtue of being everywhere, they cannot be hands and eyes that would rob from a street market." That's the bit I made into a line about shoplifting from an American Apparel store. I was in a movie once in which the character I played did that. It was called *Shoplifting from American Apparel*, of course.

My take on this is that we're again looking at the Buddhist point of view of universal oneness. But, as the Rutles' parody of the Beatles suggests, even if things are all one, "you should know by now that you're not me." The idea of universal oneness doesn't imply that everybody everywhere is the same.

So, yes, the compassionate hands and eyes of the Bodhisattva of Compassion are everywhere and eternal. And yet wrong things still happen. On the individual level, we have the ability to do what's right or to refuse to do what's right. Compassion manifests when we make the correct choice. It is our sacred duty to make that happen wherever and whenever we possibly can.

I took some liberties with the line "Every instance of doing the right thing is also limitless. That's how we make this world a better place." The Nishijima/Cross translation of this line is, "Saving the living and preaching the Dharma may be like this, and the radiance of national lands may be like this." Tanahashi has, "*All over the body are hands and eyes* [is] also for expounding dharma to awaken sentient beings and for causing the land to radiate light." The italics are in the original to indicate that Dogen is quoting the story.

This is another place where I think Dogen's poetry is wonderful, but any attempt to translate it directly tends to obscure what he's getting at. To me it's simply that any little good thing you do is worthwhile because it makes the whole world that much better. You'll recall that he also says something like this in "Instructions for the Cook."

Then we get all that stuff about Ungan giving a B-plus answer.

In the original this section is much longer and very convoluted. I'll let you check out the standard translations on your own. But what it boils down to, to me at least, is that it's not always necessary to hear *the most incredibly excellent teachings that ever existed in the whole wide world of ever.*

In fact, sometimes you're better off not hearing that kind of stuff because you'd probably just tune it out. It's like theoretical physics. Sure, if you understand all the math, you have a much better grasp of it if you hear physics explained with all the fancy science words and stuff. But sometimes it's enough to see Neil deGrasse Tyson boil it down to the basics in a YouTube video. That's also how scientific understanding gets transmitted. Same with Buddhism.

There's a footnote in the Nishijima/Cross translation after the bit I've paraphrased as, "It might be a way of expressing that Kannon's hands and eyes are doing *what*, or in other words how they are doing unnameable work." Their footnote says, "In other words, the question might be interpreted, 'Is there any real meaning in all the human activity going on in the world?' And the answer is, 'The real meaning is in the activity itself.'"

I like that footnote. We always look for meaning outside of what we do. But the real meaning of anything we do, or anything we are, is not something imposed from outside. It's not an explanation. The meaning *is* the thing itself.

At the very end I have Dogen say, "There are many Buddhist writings that express this truth. The story about Ungan and Dogo is just one of them." This is actually a condensation of a long addendum at the end of the piece in which Dogen cites a bunch of specific examples of dialogues that express this same idea. You can look that up if you like and even go track down the stories themselves if you're so inclined.

To me the basic idea of this whole essay is that compassion is intuitive. You can assess a given situation and think about how to deal with it compassionately. And you might even come up with the right answer that way. But in actual moment-by-moment interactions, compassion isn't a matter decided by thought. You have to be able to see your instantaneous intuitive response and then do it.

This is hard. One of the reasons we practice meditation is to help us see our intuitive responses more clearly. We all have a lot of very strong habits, of both action and thought. Even though the right intuitive response comes up instantly, our habitual responses follow very close behind. Once that happens, it's hard to know your intuition from your habitual responses. When that's the case, it's usually best to remember the Buddhist precepts. These represent the right things to do in most ordinary situations.

Since compassion is very much related to ethics, I'd like to take a short break from studying Dogen to look at that relationship a bit.

4. Compassion and Zen Buddhist Ethics

Compassion is very closely related to ethics. To relate with people, animals, and objects ethically is to be compassionate, and vice versa. So let's talk about Buddhist ethics.

Let's look first at what Buddhist ethics is not. The British newspaper *The Guardian* published an article entitled "Anders Behring Breivik Used Meditation to Kill — He's Not the First."[*] Anders Behring Breivik, you may recall, was the guy who, in 2011, planted bombs in government buildings in Oslo, Norway, that killed eight people, and then he gunned down sixty-nine more at a youth camp on the Norwegian island of Utøya. According to the article, Breivik "told psychiatrists that he used meditation to 'numb the full spectrum of human emotion — happiness to sorrow, despair, hopelessness, and fear.'"

The article also says, "Japanese Buddhists rejoiced that the Pearl Harbor attacks had occurred on 8 December, the day when they mark the Buddha's enlightenment; and leaders insisted that fighting was a patriotic and a Buddhist duty." This is not an entirely incorrect statement as far as it goes. But it's a bit like saying that German Christians rejoiced when the Nazis invaded Poland. Sure, some Germans who identified as Christian did rejoice at the Nazis' triumphs, but not all

---

[*] Written by Vishvapani Blomfield and published on May 22, 2012.

of them. Many German Christians were outraged and horrified. And the fact that Nazi leaders sometimes invoked Christian doctrine to justify their crimes doesn't mean that Christianity itself condones mass murder or Nazism. The same goes for Buddhism.

It's important to say this because many of us in the West imagine that Buddhism is one unified, coherent thing that everyone agrees on. Just think about it for a second, and you'll see how absurd that idea is. I've already pointed this out, but I'll say it again, for good measure. Buddhism has been around five hundred years longer than Christianity and has had five hundred more years to diverge into different forms. Tarring all of Buddhism — or even all of *Japanese* Buddhism — with the same brush in the way this article does is unfair and, frankly, kind of dumb. Yet it is extremely common.

Lots of people believe that Buddhism, particularly Japanese Zen Buddhism, has no ethical content. According to that *Guardian* article, "Mahayana Buddhism, from which Zen evolved, teaches that all phenomena are mysterious and ungraspable — empty of any fixed essence. So what should we relate to everyday reality in which, the Buddha stressed, actions have consequences and ethical considerations apply? The various Mahayana schools have different answers, but Zen teaches that the ultimate perspective should inform everything." The writer then concludes that "Zen's non-dual philosophy obscured Buddhism's ethical teachings."

This is simply not true. Zen Buddhism is very much concerned with ethics.

However, I will admit that it is entirely possible to misconstrue Zen's nondualistic philosophy this way, so we need to be very careful.

Of course, all religions and philosophies contain elements that can be taken as endorsing violence. The Islamic idea of jihad is frequently used to endorse violence, as are many ideas found in Christian scriptures. But there are also very different ways of interpreting these ideas, ways that do not endorse violence. Still, we're looking at Zen Buddhism here, so we can leave it to authors of books about those religions to discuss those doctrines.

The idea that Zen Buddhism is special in its lack of any ethical component is pretty pervasive, but it is entirely incorrect. I've met a lot of Zen teachers in my time, and never once have I encountered one who did not stress ethics as crucial to the practice.

This strong attitude toward ethics as crucial to Zen practice is borne out by two important ceremonies conducted regularly at most Zen Buddhist institutions: *jukai* or Taking the Buddhist Precepts and *ryaku fusatsu* or the Full Moon Ceremony, which is held once a month at most Zen temples in Japan and many in the West.*

When you officially enter into an apprentice relationship with a Zen teacher, the first thing you're usually required to do is to publicly declare your intention to follow the Ten Grave Buddhist Precepts and the Three Pure Precepts, and to announce your allegiance to the Three Treasures. This is accomplished in the very ancient ceremony of *jukai*. The *jukai* ceremony is usually done either for an individual or for several people who take their vows at the same time. Once a month the entire community comes together on the night of the full moon to go through pretty much the same ceremony as a group, and that's the Full Moon Ceremony.

The first thing you do in both ceremonies is to publicly declare the following, "All my ancient twisted karma, from beginningless greed, hate, and delusion, born of body, speech, and mind, I now fully avow." To avow means to confess to something. So we start off by acknowledging that we have committed wrongs in the past. We plead guilty. That's the first step.

My first Zen teacher's teacher, Kobun Chino Roshi, said it like this, "Recognition and acknowledgment of one's own personal, individual faults, mistakes, or dissatisfactions, if this occurs in reality, is a universal occasion because it is revealed in the universal scene. This

---

* *Ryaku* actually means "abbreviated" and refers to the fact that the monthly ceremony done at most Japanese temples is a shorter version of a much longer ceremony. If you ever saw the "short" ceremony — which goes on and on and on — you're probably okay with skipping the long one!

reverse recognition appears in each individual's life. So this word *repentance* is personal, and it is also universal."

In a sense what we're confessing to resembles the Christian idea of original sin. We acknowledge our wrongdoings and take responsibility for them. But we also acknowledge that our wrongs were "born of beginningless greed, hate, and delusion." We're not saying this stuff is beyond our control. Quite the contrary! In the later parts of the ceremony we vow not to do such things anymore. However, we admit that in a very real sense our wrongdoings come from a place far older and more elemental than our current individual body, speech, and mind. As Kobun says, it is universal.

In Buddhist cosmology, greed, hate, and delusion exist before we come into being and embody them. Yet we also have the understanding that greed, hate, and delusion are not separate from the greedy, hateful, and delusional actions we take.

Like many aspects of Zen philosophy, it's a paradox. But one of the key aspects of Zen philosophy is the understanding that things in the real world are often paradoxical, that the human mind cannot always make rational sense of what actually exists. I wonder if the mystery of original sin might have been conceived of this way, not as something we ought to feel guilty about, even though it wasn't us who ate the forbidden fruit, but as an allegorical acknowledgment of the way things just *are*.

In the next part of these ceremonies, we announce our devotion to Buddha, dharma, and sangha. This is the part of the ceremony that feels most religious. Sangha is the community of fellow Buddhists, dharma is the Buddha's teaching, and Buddha is the old man himself who taught that stuff and established the first Buddhist community 2,500 years ago.

Overtly it almost sounds like you're acknowledging the historical Buddha as a god or at least as a God-like being. You're not. Let me try to show you why.

First let's see why it feels like we're acknowledging Buddha as a god. In every other part of the ceremony we repeat each vow three times in the exact same words. But in this section it goes as follows:

> *Respectful devotion to Buddha, Respectful devotion to Dharma, Respectful devotion to Sangha.*
> *Devotion to Buddha, the Supreme One; Devotion to Dharma, the Supreme Purity; Devotion to Sangha, the Supreme Community.*
> *Perfect devotion to Buddha, Perfect devotion to Dharma, Perfect devotion to Sangha.*

Saying "Buddha, the Supreme One" sounds very much like calling Buddha God. In fact, isn't "Supreme One" just a synonym for God? Calling his words "the Supreme Purity" and his church "the Supreme Community" also feels kind of like you're surrendering to the Buddhist Church and its doctrine. To lots of us rational Westerners, that sounds like the first step down a slippery slope that usually ends in disaster.

I'll admit that the standard formula kind of made my skin crawl when I first said it at my own precept-taking ceremony all those years ago, and it still kind of makes me feel icky when I perform the ceremony for others today. The way I deal with that is to view it a bit abstractly. Let me explain.

I don't think of the historical Buddha as a God-like savior, nor do I believe that Buddha exists somewhere up in the sky judging all of us from his position as Supreme Being. Yet I acknowledge the power of conceiving of Buddha, his teachings, and his community this way in the abstract. Which probably sounds weird, so let me try to unpack what I mean.

It's kind of like the folks who put those "What Would Jesus Do?" bumper stickers on their cars. Jesus, to them, represents a perfect person. They guide their actions by imagining what such a person might do when faced with whatever situations they themselves face. It doesn't matter if the actual historical Jesus was just as flawed as the rest of us. They're not necessarily invoking him but an ideal they've identified with him. Even if some of them do think of the historical Jesus as being literally perfect, it doesn't really make much difference if it helps them to act a little more ethically.

I tend to look at the whole "Supreme One/Purity/Community" thing that way. Of course the Buddhist community is made up of flawed individuals who often collectively fail to understand the dharma they've vowed to uphold. But the very fact that they vow to uphold the dharma at all is something truly special. And naturally, not everything that gets filed under the heading of Buddhist doctrine is right. But the fundamentals are very good. That, too, is something truly special and worth dedicating oneself to, in my opinion.

Next come the so-called Pure Precepts. My teacher, Nishijima Roshi, called these the Universal Precepts because he believed they applied to pretty much everyone, Buddhists and non-Buddhists alike, acknowledging them as part of just being a decent human being. They are:

1. To observe the rules of society.
2. To observe the moral rule of the universe.
3. To work for the salvation of living beings.

There are different versions of these precepts, as there are variations in all versions of the Buddhist precepts. The most common version is (1) To do no evil or to renounce evil, (2) To practice good, and (3) To save all beings.

Nishijima Roshi felt it was important for his students to obey the common rules of society. He thought we should obey the law and behave in ways that were acceptable to the society in which we lived. Like all the precepts, this one is designed to make our lives easier. Of course, if we find ourselves in a society whose rules are unjust — for example a society that has racist or sexist laws — we ought to work to change those rules. But we should do so within the established structure of that society's rules. It's a challenge.

Changing the usual version of the second Pure Precept from "practice good" to "observe the moral rule of the universe" is a very Nishijima-like way of putting things. It's hard for many of us to believe there is a moral or ethical rule to the universe. After all, we see some people get away with doing terrible things while other people die young even though they're always nice. Yet one of the core beliefs within all forms of Buddhism is that there is a moral/ethical law of the universe and that going against that law is as difficult as defying the physical laws of the universe, like gravity.

Historically, Buddhists have relied on the ideas of karma and rebirth or reincarnation to account for how people sometimes seem to get away with murder, or worse. They postulate that maybe these folks don't suffer the reaction of their actions in this life but that in the next one they will. The problem for most of us Western people these days is that we tend not to believe in rebirth. The evidence for it is just not very convincing. It certainly isn't convincing to me! Other religions hold that evildoers are punished by being sent to hell after they die. But there's not a lot of convincing evidence of this either, as far as I've seen.

Nishijima Roshi didn't like the idea of reincarnation or rebirth very much. He said it was a non-Buddhist notion that got grafted onto Buddhism after Buddha was dead and couldn't argue about it. Others insist that it goes back to Buddha's original teachings. I'd like to tell you about my own experience with this.

Nishijima Roshi said we didn't need faith in any kind of life after death to see how the moral rule of the universe worked. He said we could see it in our own lives here and now, if we just learned how to look for it. By practicing meditation, we learn to observe our own lives more clearly. In doing so, we see the workings of the ethical law of the universe in action in our real lives.

Once I had been doing zazen regularly for a few years, I started to see it, too. It became so clear that it now feels kind of stupid to deny there is an ethical law of the universe that's just as real as the law of gravity. It's hard to explain this intellectually. The intellect has ways of twisting around what we experience and making those experiences mean whatever it wants them to mean. When you stop looking at reality through the lens of the intellect, the stuff your own mind invents starts to seem kind of irrelevant.

Jared Piazza, a University of Pennsylvania postdoctoral fellow who studies the interrelation of psychology and faith, told the *Philadelphia Weekly*,

> Azim Shariff [an assistant professor of religion, morality, cultural, and evolutionary psychology at the University of Oregon] and Ara Norenzayan [a social psychologist at the University of British Columbia, Vancouver] have found that how people view God — whether they view God as primarily punitive and exacting or benevolent and forgiving — does influence how people behave. In particular, in one experiment, they found that people are less likely to cheat if they view God as punishing, but more likely if they view God as forgiving. Likewise, they found that countries with populations that tended to believe in hell had lower crime rates than countries with populations that tended to believe only in heaven.[*]

This makes a lot of sense to me and helps explain why religions that believe in punitive gods and hell have been so successful. They help make societies more stable. Survival of the fittest dictates that stable societies last longer than unstable ones. But what happens when a society can no longer believe in its old gods and starts to doubt the existence of hell? This seems to be the case in our Western societies today and may have been the case in India in Buddha's time. In those days, Indian culture was beginning to accept a materialistic and scientific outlook, leading to great skepticism about its older religions.

The belief in a moral/ethical law of the universe may be a good way to replace the older fear of punishment by supernatural forces

---

[*] April 23–30, 2014, issue.

with something that makes sense according to our emerging world-view. I also happen to believe it's true and observable, if only you learn to quiet your brain enough to see it. The debate about this can never be resolved. So I'm not going to try to resolve it. Let's just keep on moving along.

The final of the Three Pure Precepts is the same in Nishijima Roshi's formulation as in the standard version. One makes a vow to work for the salvation of all beings.

At first this seems utterly impossible. When I first heard it, I thought of an old Superman comic I'd once read. This particular installment was a kind of comedy-relief episode depicting a day in the life of Superman. In it, whenever someone is in trouble Superman has to come to the rescue, even if he's got plenty of work to do already as mild-mannered Clark Kent, reporter for the *Daily Planet* newspaper. In one scene someone's in a jam way over in China, and Superman has to burrow all the way through the center of the Earth to go put things right. At the end of the day the poor guy is completely exhausted!

Of course this is absurd. Not even Superman could respond to everyone who needs his help. So why do Buddhists take a vow to do something even Superman couldn't accomplish?

My friend Rob Robbins put it this way: "I vow to save all beings ...from myself." I think that's the best way to understand this vow. We may not be able to rescue everyone in the world who needs rescuing. But we can work on ourselves and make ourselves into the kind of person no one needs to be rescued from. That may not seem like much. But if everyone did it, think how spectacular this world would be. I sincerely believe that someday the world will be a place of peace and plenty because all human beings will have learned to save the world from themselves.

Then we have what are usually called the Ten Grave Precepts. In my other books I've given the version of these precepts that I received from Gudo Nishijima. This time I'd like to look at the version taught by Kobun Chino Roshi:

1. No killing life
2. No stealing
3. No attaching to fulfillment
4. No using illusory words
5. No selling the wine of delusion
6. No dwelling on past mistakes
7. No praising or blaming
8. No hoarding materials or teachings
9. No being angry
10. No abusing the Triple Treasure: Buddha, dharma, and sangha

That's a lot of nos! But don't worry. There's a positive side to each of these precepts as well.

Kobun explains the origin of these precepts by saying, "The Ten Grave Precepts were brought by Bodhidharma from India to China. Before they became ten, there were hundreds of rules of order for Buddhist life. These ten are like ten beads of light, coming from the center and taking different textures and colors, and if they become very radiant, they appear as one white light."

When the Buddha first established his community there were no rules. But as various things happened and conflicts arose, Buddha made judgments about specific conduct. Eventually there were hundreds of such judgments, which became hundreds of rules. On his deathbed, the Buddha said that his monks should keep the major rules but that they could let the minor rules slide. Unfortunately, he never said which rules were major and which were minor.

But that's not really a problem. Because Buddha never regarded himself as a god whose judgment was flawless. So he left it up to his successors to figure out which rules were important. The Ten Grave Precepts represent a winnowing down of those hundreds of rules into the most general and essential ones.

By following these precepts, we express our true original nature. I know it might sometimes seem like our original nature lacks any sense of ethics. But that's a mistake. We feel like shit when we act against our ethical sense. We can shout down that feeling or numb it with drink, drugs, and the intoxication of words. But that doesn't make it go away.

Here's how Kobun put it: "When you say to yourself, 'This feels right, so I will do it,' you are not relying on how something looks. Sometimes you think, 'That looks fine but something is wrong.' Awareness of the Precepts provides a pretty straightforward standard. If someone blames you for something, and you are doing right and fine, the blaming is like a cool wind. But if you start to get confused and wonder, 'Did I do something wrong?' you feel the blame before it comes. The knowledge came to you already, from outside or inside."

The first precept, no killing of life, is, of course, impossible to keep. Even the strictest vegan in the world kills hundreds of thousands of life-forms in order to stay alive. That's the nature of things.

To quote Kobun Chino again,

> Dōgen Zenji expresses this Precept, "Do not kill. Do not let other people kill. Beyond that, flourish our Buddha seeds." He covers the ethics of our life and the deeper meaning, what this life is all about. We eat living food. Through our food we learn constantly how to live on this earth. We are constantly supported by all phenomenal currents of life; we are lived by all beings. That is the truth. We are lived by whom and whatever we take, by their teachings that guide us. One way to live is to show all of their natures through our existence. It is different from our usual way of continuously exploring our capacities for what we really want to do.

The precept of no stealing seems pretty easy on the surface. But the meaning is much deeper than simply saying you shouldn't take candy bars from the store without paying for them. Bodhidharma explained this precept by saying, "Self nature is mysteriously profound. Unattainable dharma. Not to raise the mind of something being attainable is called 'No stealing or robbing.'" So even to believe you can attain or possess anything is a kind of stealing.

Let's look again at what Kobun had to say.

The ordinary meaning of stealing is to take something from others, make another's thing your own. Together with this meaning, we can observe what the whole thing is about. Something happened, and we appeared on this earth as a very small drop of life, which grew up as matter. A little circle of energy appeared in your mother's circle of energy, and when the time came, it started to separate. It looks like two, but, as you know, mother and child cannot be separated. Even if the mother passes away, that mother is the mother of this child, always. Yet we think this human being is an individual existence. Because this human shape is dynamic, and moves among many things, we do not question that it has a separate existence.

He also said, "This individual existence is a universal thing, in itself. A life of activity becomes a creative art form for you. So study becomes important, research becomes important, also communication. All are necessary. Yet this individual existence is inseparable from this universe."

Ultimately, there is nothing to steal and no one to steal from. Yet conventionally there is stealing and there are people. So we accept that conventional understanding and refrain from stealing.

The third precept is given by Kobun as no attaching to fulfillment. Nishijima Roshi used to give this precept as, "Don't desire too much." But the far more common version in the West these days is, "Do not misuse sexuality." Sometimes it's also given as, "Don't commit adultery."

Here's what Kobun says about this:

There is only you and Absolute Being, so there is basic confusion in having two objects as the Absolute. Yet, the ethical meaning of this Precept is quite obvious. Adultery is a confused state. It causes separation from relating with whom you really wish to relate. That is a kind of chasing after many rabbits and not being able to catch one. The basic problem is not objective, but, rather, subjective. The Absolute has many symbolic forms and images, which actually represent what you were born as, and whom you are serving. The Absolute is this one, it is who we are. This is why we keep following the life of no identity, in order to cleanse our life. It is continually important to have an appreciation for who and what formed you, which is watching your life.

The next precept is no using illusory words. In other words, "Don't lie." Of course you can't always be completely truthful and ethical at the same time. If someone asks, "Do I look fat in this dress?" the ethical answer may not be the same as the truthful one. In that case, ethics may be more important than a hurtful kind of honesty. Still, such occurrences are exceptions. Most of the time we know when we're lying and when we're not.

The next precept is no selling the wine of delusion. In the old days this was a more basic precept about not taking intoxicants or selling them. But I like the more philosophical version better. In the short term, it might seem like we can gain an edge over someone by selling them some delusion or by spreading our own delusions. But no one ever really benefits that way. A lie will always come back to bite the liar in the ass. So we need to be careful.

My favorite among Kobun's version of the precepts is the next one, no dwelling on past mistakes. The normal version of this is, "Do not discuss the failures of Buddhist priests and laypeople." That version of this precept always leaves me cold. At its worst it allows certain people to do terrible stuff and avoid criticism because they're Buddhist priests. There have been plenty of cases of Buddhist clergy who ought to be pointing out the wrongdoings of those among them but who don't out of a misguidedly literal interpretation of this precept.

COMPASSION AND ZEN BUDDHIST ETHICS   81

No dwelling on past mistakes is much more universal, and, of course, much, much more difficult. Who doesn't dwell on their past mistakes? If acknowledging my own wrongdoing helps me not do the same thing in the future, okay. But once that's established, there really isn't any use in dwelling on it. When I find myself doing so anyhow, I try to take a step back and just observe what's happening in my head without judging it.

The next precept is no praising or blaming. The normal version of this is, "Don't praise yourself or berate others." I like Kobun's version because it includes not only praising yourself and blaming others but also praising others and blaming yourself.

Kobun's comment on this one is, "Once it arises, [the sense of comparing things] inexhaustibly continues because it is a relative concept and has no place to rest. It always moves. It gives no satisfaction. Even one who has become the most famous man in the world is still afraid, 'Someone will become more famous than me.' Right behind love of fame there is a shame, too. This is how the comparative sense works. To go beyond this sense or mind attitude is what this Seventh Precept is pointing to."

The next precept is no hoarding materials or teachings. In his commentary on this precept Kobun says, "When I say, 'Everything is given to you,' it sounds like everything belongs to you, and you may feel really good. But when I say, 'Nothing belongs to you,' you may feel bad. Even yourself doesn't belong to you! You are everything. This means you actually have no self to limit. Knowing this Precept is having this deep understanding."

After that we get the precept no being angry. This was always a tough one for me. Anger arises very easily for me. To say, "Don't be angry" to someone like me feels like you're saying to me, "Don't breathe." It can't be done.

Bodhidharma's version of this precept is, "In the midst of selfless truth, truth of selflessness, no measuring of oneself is called the Precept of No Being Angry."

About this, Kobun says, "If you become angry, you don't stop being Buddha. Anger appears, that's all. At that time, you don't say to yourself that you shouldn't be getting angry. When you get close to fire, you don't say, 'It should be cold!'" When you're angry you're reaffirming your sense of self. This is especially true when you know your anger is justified.

Of course there are situations in which it is justifiable to be angry. But the emotion of anger always gets in the way. It clouds our judgment and makes us more likely to act in stupid ways. So when anger arises, I find it's best to allow it to be what it is and wait for it to pass before I take any important action. When the emotion subsides, you can address the problem that made you angry in a more sensible way.

The final precept is no abusing the Triple Treasure: Buddha, dharma, and sangha. About this precept Kobun says, "To think of the Triple Treasure somewhere outside of you is the beginning of abusing, departing, from it. You are keeping yourself from it. If you understand Buddha and sentient beings as different beings, you are misunderstanding Triple Treasure and making the biggest mistake. You are cutting the Buddha's body and looking at his blood running!"

The Buddha, dharma, and sangha are not outside you. They are you. You refrain from abusing them when you allow them to manifest in yourself. You then act as Buddha, whether or not you feel Buddha-like. You follow the truth of the universe, whether or not you have memorized every book of the dharma. And you enact the spirit of community whether or not you like the people you're thrown in with.

Those are the Zen Buddhist precepts, the ethical foundation of our practice. Next time anyone says that Zen Buddhism has no ethical basis, you can set them straight!

Next up, let's look at Dogen's advice about how to put this ethical stuff into real action.

5. Four Good Ways
to Treat People Right
Shishobo
Four All-Embracing Virtues

As I said earlier, human beings are like bees or ants. We need a community to survive. If you heard about a panther or a bear surviving for a year on its own in the forest, you'd just yawn. But when a human does it, it's newsworthy. Because we are communal creatures, it's vital to our survival to know how to conduct ourselves so as to maintain our connection with the community. We need to support the community so that it supports us.

In the close-knit community of a Zen monastery this becomes even more critical. Everyone is in each other's business so much that no single person can afford to be lax about this stuff, or else it endangers the entire group.

This is Dogen's essay about four good ways to ensure that people treat each other right. It applies not only to people in monasteries but to the wider human community as well. I'll get a little technical in this introduction and in the notes afterward because that's the kind of book this is. But it's really important not to get so enchanted by all the technicalities that we lose sight of what Dogen is actually telling us.

All human societies — no matter where they are, no matter their race or ethnicity, no matter what languages they speak, no matter what books they consider holy, or any of that other superficial junk — have to find some way of living together.

There are codes of law that ensure that the worst breaches of conduct are punished and that those who really mess things up are removed from society. But some of us are looking to do better than just obey the rules. We want to fundamentally change the way society operates so that it gets better for everybody. We see the potential for what human beings might be able to do, if we can just learn not to mess with each other's shit so much.

In Buddhist terms, we call someone who is really serious about this a bodhisattva.

There is a lot of history behind the word *bodhisattva*, and there are a lot of ways to define it. Some of that stuff gets very weird and mystical. But when it comes right down to it, all it really means is someone who is serious about individual and social transformation, someone who doesn't just talk about it but is willing to work on making it happen. Even if that means that she or he has to fundamentally change her- or himself.

Nishijima and Cross entitle their translation of this essay "Four Elements of a Bodhisattva's Social Relations." Tanahashi entitles his version "The Bodhisattva's Four Methods of Guidance." Nishiyama and Stevens title theirs "The Four Ways a Bodhisattva Acts to Benefit Human Beings." Shasta Abbey calls theirs "On the Four Exemplary Acts of a Bodhisattva."

According to Nishijima's translation of *Shobogenzo* into contemporary Japanese, the word Dogen uses as the title of this essay, *shishobo* (四摂法, sometimes pronounced *shishoho*), is his translation of the Sanskrit term *catuh-samgraha-vastu*, which is often translated as "Four All-Embracing Virtues."

In this essay Dogen lays out the traditional four categories of virtuous actions that a bodhisattva should undertake and tells us what he thinks they mean. Let's watch.

There are four main ways to treat people right. The first is free giving. The second is kind speech. The third is being helpful. And number four is cooperation.

FOUR GOOD WAYS TO TREAT PEOPLE RIGHT   85

Free giving means not being a tight-ass. It also means not kissing up to anyone. Even if you're a king or whatever, it's important not to be a greedy bastard. You have to be the complete opposite of greedy. Give away whatever stuff you don't need to people who do need it, especially if you don't know them personally. Whether what you give is a material object or something nonmaterial, either way it's still free giving.

According to Buddhist philosophy, nothing ever really belongs to you. Even so, you can still give stuff away. Just be careful when you do that, because if you start giving away things that belong to somebody else, you're gonna make them mad!

It doesn't matter if what you give is really expensive or not. It's the giving that counts.

When you just let the truth be itself, you get the truth. When you get the truth, the truth continues to be left to itself. When you let your own stuff be your own stuff, your own stuff becomes gifts. You give yourself to yourself, and you give everyone else to everyone else. The influence of this kind of giving reaches everyone everywhere. Everybody feels its effects.

The reason this happens is simple. When you become a receiver and a giver at the same time, subject and object are connected. That's why, in the Agama Sutra, the Buddha said, "When a giving person shows up, everybody admires that person." The mind of a person like that is understood by everybody. Everybody can hang out with somebody like that.

So if you give even a little bit of the true teaching, it's the sort of thing that will come back to you later as good stuff. Even if you give a few pennies or whatever, that's like planting good seeds that will bear fruit later on.

The dharma can be like treasure, and even material goods can become a way of teaching the dharma. It's all about how it's given and how it's received.

A hipster once shaved off his epic beard so that a friend who had lost her hair could use it to make a wig. And once a little kid gave some sand to Buddha and a few lifetimes later he was reborn as the great king Asoka, who spread Buddhism all over India. People who give this way don't expect anything in return. They just share whatever they have.

Being alive and dying, these, too, are examples of free giving.

And dig this one. Doing a regular old job somewhere just to earn a living is also originally an example of free giving.

It's important not only to put our energy into doing what we know to be good stuff but also not to overlook any small opportunity to give something. It is precisely because we are able to give freely that we are even alive right now.

The Buddha said you should give to yourself and to your family. It's pretty clear that doing meditation practice is a way to give. When you give even the smallest thing, you can be glad you did because that's the authentic Buddhist practice and the way of the bodhisattvas.

It's hard to change anyone else's mind. But by giving to others we are doing our own little bit to help them learn giving. That's why free giving is number one on the list of things a bodhisattva does. You can never measure the value of anything you give, whether it's big or small. But there are times when minds do change for the better, and free giving is always a part of that change.

The next thing on the list is kind speech.

Kind speech means being compassionate with everyone you meet and talking nicely to them. There aren't any rude or bad words. Regular people use phrases like "Take care of yourself" and monks ask each other, "How's it hanging?" It's good to use that kind of normal polite speech.

Those who have virtue deserve a pat on the back. Those who don't can only be pitied. By using kind speech yourself, you create more opportunities for others to speak kindly. When you speak kindly, kind speech that might not have existed otherwise comes into being. So don't ever stop using kind speech.

Whether you want to promote harmony or defeat an adversary, kind speech is the way to do it. When you hear someone speak kindly you feel happy.

Kind speech comes from a mind that's kind. It plants the seeds for compassionate action. It's not just a way to praise someone's abilities or whatever. It has the power to turn the heavens.

Next up is being helpful.

Being helpful means using your mad skills to benefit others, no matter who or what they are. It means finding ways to help them in the immediate future or in the distant future.

When you help a turtle that's gotten turned over on its back or you nurse a wild bird back to health, you don't expect any reward from the turtle or the bird. You just see a being in need of help, and you do something.

Dumb-bums think that if you help someone else you might somehow fail to benefit yourself. That's bullshit. Being helpful is the whole point of Buddhist philosophy. It helps others and it benefits you.

There's an old story from China about a king who would do whatever was necessary to honor anyone who came to his palace. If he was taking a bath when they arrived, he'd jump right out and put on his clothes to go greet them. If he was eating when they showed up, he'd put away his food and go say hi. He did this even though he was a king and everybody should have had to wait for him. He didn't care if the people he met were from other countries and he didn't know them from Adam. He just did the helpful thing.

We should learn to be like that, being helpful to friends and enemies alike. That's how we help others and help ourselves. You should even help dipshits who seem like they can't be helped at all.

The fourth element of a bodhisattva's conduct is cooperation.

This means to work for a common purpose and not to be contrary to others or even to yourself. It means to avoid differentiating yourself from others.

Remember that the Buddha himself took birth in the human world. He did this because he identified with humanity. Since he did this for us humans, he probably did the same thing for beings in other realms.

When we cooperate, the distinction between ourselves and others disappears.

Guitars, songs, and beer make friends with people and make friends with gods and spirits. And people make friends with guitars, songs, and beer. And guitars, songs, and beer make friends with guitars, songs, and beer. And people make friends with people.

And gods and spirits make friends with gods and spirits. That's what cooperation is all about. Everything is interrelated!

The real action of cooperation means actual, concrete behavior, dignity, and the real situation in which cooperation occurs. You identify with others, and in turn they identify with you. There are limitless ways that people and other beings can identify with one another.

There's an old saying from China that goes, "The sea never refuses any water. That's why it's so big. A mountain never refuses any dirt. That's why it's so tall. Enlightened rulers don't hate anyone. That's why they have so many subjects."

The way the sea doesn't refuse water is an example of cooperation. But remember that the water doesn't refuse the sea, either. That's how it all comes together. Because the sea doesn't refuse the sea, it realizes itself as the sea. Because mountains don't refuse mountains, they are mountains, and they're really tall.

As for enlightened rulers not hating people, that doesn't mean they never reward or punish anyone. When an enlightened ruler hands out rewards and punishments, he or she doesn't do so out of hatred or greedy favoritism. Way back even before there were nations that had laws, there were still rewards and punishments. They were just handled very differently.

Even today there are people who seek the truth without expecting to be rewarded for it. But stupid people never think that way. So when stupid people look for an enlightened ruler, they don't even understand what that means. They're just glad the ruler doesn't hate them. So there can even be cooperation between an enlightened ruler and the dumbest people under his rule. That's why we value cooperation so highly, because it transcends all barriers.

The best way to deal with this stuff is to accept it all with a gentle face.

Each of these four elements of good behavior includes all the others within it. So you could say there are a total of sixteen elements, if you were to add them all together.

— Written on May 5, 1243, by a monk named Dogen,
who brought the dharma to Japan from China

The four virtues Dogen lists in the original Japanese are *fuse* (布施), *aigo* (愛語), *rigyo* (利行), and *doji* (同事). These correspond to the Sanskrit terms *dana*, *priyavacana*, *arthakrtya*, and *samanartharta*. In my version I called these "free giving," "kind speech," "being helpful," and "cooperation." There are, of course, other English translations of these words. We'll get into some of those as we move through this commentary.

Of all these Japanese and Sanskrit terms, the only one you're likely to hear outside a monastery or an advanced university course in Buddhism is *dana*, which is free giving in my version. This has become something of a buzzword among hipsters who define themselves as "into spirituality" these days. So let's talk about that one first.

If you hang around any kind of Buddhist or other spiritual center these days you've almost certainly heard the word *dana*. It's often used as a synonym for donation. The fact that it sounds a little like the word *donation* certainly helps.

But the word *dana* actually means something more like generosity. I've translated it here as "free giving" because I think the word *generosity* is a little inaccurate in the context of this essay. In any case, giving a donation to your local Buddhist center is certainly an example of *dana*. But *dana* doesn't mean "donation." So let's discuss what Dogen says about *dana*, shall we?

Where I have the phrase *tight-ass* most translations give you the word *greedy*, although Nishiyama/Stevens also add *covetous*. Where I have *kiss up* most translations have something like *curry favor* (Nishijima/Cross, Shasta Abbey, and Tanahashi — Hey! I like curry! I favor it all the time!), or *flatter* (Nishiyama/Stevens). Those are all better translations than mine, but they aren't as funny. So I went for the joke in the paraphrase, but I'm letting you know the better translations here.

A little ways down in my version, Dogen says, "According to Buddhist philosophy, nothing ever really belongs to you. Even so, you can still give stuff away." That's all in the original Japanese, more or less. But the line after that about being careful because you might make someone mad is totally my own invention. Let me explain why I added it.

I based my paraphrase of this line on the Nishiyama/Stevens translation, which is, "Although in principle nothing belongs to self we can give alms." Nishijima/Cross have, "There is a Buddhist principle that even if things are not our own, this does not hinder our free giving." To me this seems less clear than the Nishiyama/Stevens version. Although, if you think about it, it's kinda the same thing. Tanahashi's translation just says, "Even if the gift is not your own, there is no reason to abstain from giving." When you put it that way, it just sounds crazy. Of course there's a reason to abstain from giving away stuff that's not your own! It's illegal!

I think it's obvious Dogen doesn't mean to imply that it's okay to give your sister's iPhone to some guy you just met at a bar because Buddhism says to give stuff away freely even if it isn't yours. That sort of thing just makes people mad.

In the original Japanese, the word that Nishijima/Cross and Nishiyama/Stevens are interpreting here as "principle" is *dori* (道理), which means something like "(a) truth (of the) Way (as in the Buddhist Way)." So my guess is that Dogen is saying this for the benefit of people who might get too hung up on a literal interpretation of Buddhist philosophy and might be all like, "Hey! Nothing belongs to anyone! You can't give anything away!" It's kind of pedantic, but I guess there were dweebs like that in Dogen's audience. I added my little caveat for contemporary readers who might think Dogen is saying to give away stuff that isn't even yours to begin with, in the conventional sense.

A bit later my version of Dogen says, "When you just let the truth be itself, you get the truth." The word he actually uses for "truth" is *tokudo* (得道). This often means something like "attaining the Way," which can be used as a euphemism for enlightenment. In that sense you could also read this line as saying that you should leave the idea of attaining enlightenment alone and just carry on doing what you do as best as you can do it.

Then I have Dogen say, "When you let your own stuff be your own stuff, your own stuff becomes gifts." The actual words Dogen used are more like "when you let treasure be treasure" (財のたからにまかせられるとき, *takara no takara ni makasareu toki*). When you do that, Dogen says, your treasure becomes *fuse* (布施), or "free giving" (a.k.a *dana*).

That could sound like a call for selfishness. But perhaps it's not. You can have the things you have in order to be of service to others. If you do that, then your own stuff becomes a kind of gift. It's easy to use this as an excuse to be a hoarder, so it's best to be careful.

For example, I own a ton of books, both about Buddhism and about things like the making of the film *Robot Monster*, a classic of trashy science fiction cinema. Because I own this stuff, I can fulfill my role not only as a Buddhist teacher but also as a bridge between pop culture and Buddhism. However, if I'm not careful, I can also use this idea simply as an excuse to be self-indulgent.

A little further along I have Dogen say, "You give yourself to yourself, and you give everyone else to everyone else." That's pretty close to the original. This is important. If you don't take care of yourself, you can't take care of anyone else. There's no great merit in burning yourself out for the sake of others, since you'll only end up becoming a burden to those who'll have to take care of you after you wreck yourself in the process.

As for giving everyone else to everyone else, this could be seen as saying you need to let people be who they are without trying to change them. For example, lots of people ask me how they can get their friends and relatives to meditate. I usually tell them not to try. I understand the desire to teach others this thing that's been so helpful to you. But the fact is, people have to come to meditation practice on their own. It's the only way that it ever works.

So my recommendation is to just do your own practice. If your friends and relatives ask about it, tell them a little, but don't overwhelm them. Give them a chance to ask questions if they want, but don't answer anything you haven't specifically been asked about. There's no point in doing that. You just end up seeming pushy.

There's also a more philosophical meaning to this sentence. To give yourself to yourself and to give others to others means to maintain a balance between the self and the external world. In Buddhist terms there is no essential difference. There is no hard line between the self and the rest of the universe. They flow into each other seamlessly.

A bit later I have Dogen tell a story about a hipster shaving off his epic beard. Obviously I changed this. It was originally the story of an ancient Chinese king who burned his beard so that one of his retainers could use the ashes as medicine. It's pretty much the same idea, though, I think.

This story and some of the stuff that comes before and after it allude to the theory of karma in the sense that whatever good you do always returns to you. This is a popular idea, and it's clear from this and other pieces of his writing that Dogen believed it was true. I believe it, too. We've talked about this before, but it's worth talking about some more.

As I said, I'm well aware that there's no way in heck to prove this idea that if you do good it comes back to you. And I know that lots of people argue with this idea because the converse of it — that if you do bad stuff, bad things come to you — is highly unappealing.

For one thing, nobody wants their own bad stuff to come back to them. But what's worse is that this idea can be used to blame others for their suffering. Like saying that a starving child born in a war-torn nation must have deserved their fate because they'd obviously done something bad in a previous life.

This excuse is often used in countries that are nominally "Buddhist." Some people in these countries will actually refuse to help folks in trouble because they think it interferes with that person's karma. But thinking that way is total bullshit. Even if it was true that someone in a bad way "deserved it" because of their own bad actions in a previous life, that doesn't mean you shouldn't still do your utmost to help someone who is suffering in such conditions. In fact, if it is true, that means you have even more of a duty to try to help.

Moreover, there's also a Buddhist idea that if you're born into wealth and prosperity, that might also be the result of bad conduct in a previous life. This is because a person born to great wealth is often blinded by their own riches and has greater difficulty realizing the truth than someone born to lesser wealth or even born into poverty. So there.

We keep running into the whole reincarnation thing. To me, reincarnation is one of the least interesting aspects of Buddhist philosophy. Although, sadly, some people never seem to get enough of it.

In my previous book, *Don't Be a Jerk*, I looked at whether Dogen believed in reincarnation or rebirth. This is a subject of some debate since there are places in *Shobogenzo* where he seems to deny it and places where he appears to believe in it. The following words from Shohaku Okumura's book *Realizing Genjō Kōan* may be useful in explaining this contradiction:

> Personally, I don't believe in literal rebirth, yet I don't deny its existence either. I have no basis for either believing in or denying literal rebirth; the only thing I can say about it with surety is "I don't know." ... If rebirth exists, that is all right: I will simply try to continue practicing everything good and refrain from everything bad through my next life. If there is no rebirth, I will have nothing to do after my death and I will have no need to consider my practice. This was my view of rebirth for most of my life as a Buddhist.

When I turned fifty, however, I began to think about rebirth differently....As I enter the latter period of my life, I now find that I do hope I will live another life after this one, since this life has been too short to do all I need to in practicing the Buddha Way. For example, for many years I have been working on the translation of Zen Buddhist texts from Japanese to English. Yet I know that my life will be too short to even fully understand the true, deep meaning of the teachings of Shakyamuni Buddha, Dōgen, and other great teachers, let alone translate them into English. So I actually do hope to be reborn as a Buddhist so I can continue the work I am now doing. I think this wish has arisen because the aging process has shown me my limitations, and I suspect that the Mahayana belief in the bodhisattva's *henyaku-shōji* [transforming life and death] originated in this type of awakening to the limitations of individual life.

I like that. It's an honest statement. I don't think most spiritual teachers have enough guts to be as straight-up as Okumura. I totally agree with what he says here. Even though there have been a few moments when I've seen clearly that the standard ideas most of us have about life and death are completely mistaken, I still have a hard time with the idea of so-called literal rebirth. I feel that what we truly are is, in some senses, eternal and may manifest in many different ways at different times and places. But I don't think that necessarily means I will live forever or that I will be reborn as something else. This probably seems contradictory, but it's the best way I can express my opinion on the matter.

Let's move on. After this stuff, I have Dogen say, "Being alive and dying, these, too, are examples of free giving." In the original it's more like "to accept a body and to give up the body are both giving." That's the Tanahashi translation, but others are pretty much the same. So even our own lives and deaths are our way of giving to others. That's a beautiful idea.

Our life is a gift to others if we use it that way. Even our death is a sort of gift because by dying we get out of the way and let new people have a chance at figuring life and death out for themselves.

Right after this I have Dogen say, "And dig this one. Doing a regular old job somewhere just to earn a living is also originally an example of free giving." In the original Dogen doesn't make as big a point of this line as I do in my paraphrase. I set it off in its own paragraph because that little line helped me immensely through some difficult times.

I first heard the line in the Nishijima/Cross translation, which goes, "Earning a living and doing productive work are originally nothing other than free giving." The phrase Dogen uses that they translate as "earning a living and doing productive work" is *jisei-sangyo* (治生産業). Tanahashi translates this as "making a living and producing things." Nishiyama/Stevens translate it as "to have a position and to act on behalf of society."

When I first heard this line I was earning my living working in Tokyo for a company that made cheap monster movies. Even though I loved working there I also felt really guilty for not doing something better with my life, like, I dunno, saving starving children in the Sudan or whatever. I had a few conversations with Nishijima Roshi in which he assured me that working for that company was a perfectly legitimate way to do good in the world. Those conversations, plus reading this particular line of Dogen's, were immensely helpful.

Originally anything you do to earn a living is a kind of free giving. I use the word *originally* here to indicate the real basis of what we do. We think we're doing our jobs for the paycheck, but Dogen says that's an illusion. The underlying, original reason we work is to give to others. The payment you receive is a kind of karmic payback for the service you give. It just happens to come in the form of a check or a bank deposit. The fact that a bunch of economists have other theories about how and why this happens doesn't really matter.

Right after this I have Dogen say, "It's important not only to put our energy into doing what we know to be good stuff but also not to overlook any small opportunity to give something." To me this means even if all you can do is smile at the clerk at the local Safeway, you should still do that. You never know what benefit that might have. A small, kind gesture can have ripples far beyond anything you can imagine.

Next I have Dogen say, "The Buddha said you should give to yourself and to your family. It's pretty clear that doing meditation practice is a way to give." In the original it says something more like "practice giving to yourself." The Nishijima/Cross translation has, "It is possible to receive and to use [giving] even if the object is oneself, and it is all the easier to give to parents, wives, and children. Clearly, to practice it by oneself is one kind of free giving, and to give to parents, wives, and children may also be free giving."

I take this business about "practicing it by oneself" as a reference to meditation, even though it isn't so specific in the original lines, which are in Chinese and tend to be translated a variety of different ways. It appears to refer back to the practice of giving. But I think that what he's talking about here is the gift of meditation. I admit that's kinda reading things into it. But I like reading it as being about meditating for the sake of self and others. The fact that you're a little more stable because of your practice is something you give to the world.

As we discussed, the first bodhisattva vow is "I vow to save all beings." This doesn't mean you have to be Superman, flying around the world and making it all safe for democracy and free enterprise. Remember what my friend Rob said: "I vow to save all beings... from myself." Meditation is part of that effort. ·

Next we get to the part about kind speech. The word Dogen actually uses is *aigo* (愛語). If you break down the Chinese characters, they mean "love" and "language." I know there's a bunch of new age nonsense out there these days about "love languages," but that's not what Dogen is talking about.

"Kind speech" tends to be the preferred translation, although the Nishiyama/Stevens version says "loving words." Even though that's technically correct, it tends to sound more emotional than what Dogen is getting at.

One of my favorite lines in all of Dogen's writings comes up right at the beginning of this section. I've paraphrased it as, "There aren't any rude or bad words." This is pretty close to the Nishijima/Cross translation, which is the way I first heard it.

On the other hand, there are some other very different ways of translating this line. Tanahashi gives us, "It is contrary to cruel or violent speech." Nishiyama/Stevens give us, "We cannot imagine using coarse speech." Shasta Abbey's translation has, "We do not use language that is harsh or rude."

The original line is *ohoyoso boaku no gengo naki nari* (おほ よそ暴悪の言語なきなり). Nishijima/Cross translate *ohoyoso* as "broadly." *Boaku* is violent or rude. *Gengo* is language. And *naki nari* means something like "there aren't." So the phrase is ambiguous: "Broadly speaking there are no rude/violent words." Shasta Abbey, Tanahashi, and Nishiyama/Stevens all interpret that statement as an admonition not to *use* rude words. But Nishijima/Cross tell you what Dogen actually says, which could mean what those others say it means but could also be seen as a denial that such language even exists.

We can't dig Dogen up and ask him which he meant. But my guess is that Nishijima/Cross have it right. The reason I say so is that Dogen himself uses a lot of words in his writings that many people would consider rude, coarse, or even cruel. Yet when you pay attention to *how* he uses these words, his intentions are never to hurt anyone.

He uses hard language as a way to make strong points. Sometimes that's necessary. That's why I prefer to read him as saying that rude or bad words don't really exist. Even though that seems to be nonsense — anyone who has an Internet connection can easily verify the existence of rude and bad words — what he's saying is that it's not the words themselves but how they are used that matters. At least that's how I read it.

Just after this part I stuck in a thing about monks saying to each other, "How's it hanging?" The original has a polite greeting that means more like "How are you?" But that's not as funny.

Just FYI, for all you fans of reincarnation out there, the line I've given after this as "So don't ever stop using kind speech" actually contains a reference to continuing to use kind speech for "lifetime after lifetime." Folks who are interested in proving that Dogen believed in reincarnation like to tally up these little references as evidence. But I feel like he's just referencing the common ideas of his time when he says stuff like this, not trying to sneak in little product placement–type adverts for reincarnation.

The next section is on being helpful. The word he actually uses here is *rigyo* (利行). The two Chinese characters used to spell the word mean "beneficial" and "conduct."

That story I have Dogen tell about the king getting out of his bath and interrupting his dinner isn't explicitly told in the original. Dogen just makes some weird references to "binding the hair three times" (so the king could get dressed after he got out of the bath) and "spitting out the food three times" (so he could go greet someone when he was supposed to be having dinner). If you don't know the story, like Dogen's audience would have, these lines just sound bizarre. Luckily most translations work the story into the text like I did. Nishijima/Cross adds it to a footnote.

The stuff that appears before this about the turtle and the wild bird is also a reference to old Chinese stories. I just thought it made better sense to skip that part and personalize it by making the person who helps the bird and the turtle you, dear reader, rather than some legendary ancient Chinese person you wouldn't have heard of anyhow.

As for the thing at the end of this section about helping dipshits, the word Dogen actually uses is *gu* (愚), which means "fool" or "stupid." Incidentally, that character is in the dharma name of my teacher Gudo Nishijima. Gudo (愚道) means "the Way of Stupidity." Gudo Nishijima Roshi considered it a great honor to have been given that name.

Next up, Dogen talks about cooperation. The word he uses is *doji* (同事). If you look that word up in a contemporary Japanese-English dictionary it will tell you the word means "the same event." It's also used in stock market reports to indicate that the value of a stock hasn't changed. Obviously the meaning has altered since the thirteenth century.

Tanahashi translates this word as "identity action." Shasta Abbey's translation is "manifesting sympathy." Nishiyama/Stevens leave the Japanese word *doji* untranslated and let Dogen explain its meaning. I got the word *cooperation* from the Nishijima/Cross translation. I think it's close enough. Using made-up words or leaving it in Japanese just adds an unnecessary level of confusion, which there is already plenty of in Dogen's writings.

One of the first things Dogen talks about in this section is how the Buddha took birth in the human world, and then he speculates that he may have done similar things in other realms. Nishiyama/Stevens specify these as animal and hell realms. Dogen doesn't say that directly in the original, but those would be the traditional "other realms" in Buddhism, along with the realms of heavenly devas (or demigods if you prefer) and hungry ghosts.

It's fine to take all that with a grain of salt. I certainly do. I also prefer to think of Buddha here less as an individual person and more as a symbol of a universal principle. So there's not some guy out in the vastness of space who comes down and incarnates as Buddha for us on Earth, and then incarnates as Surak, the father of Vulcan civilization on planet Vulcan, and then as Yoda on planet Dagobah, and so on.

Rather, to me, Dogen is suggesting that the universal principle

Buddha represents manifests in places other than our world, perhaps in the form of a living being, as happened on Earth. I think it's fun to speculate that some of the other realms mentioned in Buddhism could be distant planets with civilizations very different from our own. But that's just my own overwrought imagination at work.

What I paraphrased a little further down as "guitars, songs, and beer" is actually *koto, uta, sake* (琴詩酒), which means *kotos* (a kind of Japanese harp), poems or songs, and, of course, sake, or Japanese rice wine. It's a reference to an old Chinese saying that these three things are a hermit's best friends. So what about that really confusing string of stuff that happens right after guitars, songs, and beer make their appearance? According to a footnote provided by Nishijima and Cross, "Master Dōgen picks up this sentence and uses it to express the principles of mutual agreement between subject and object and identity of subject and object."

This is a formula Dogen uses a lot to express the interrelationship of all things. In the essay I called "Don't Be a Jerk" in my book *Don't Be a Jerk*, Dogen uses the same formula but applied to donkeys looking at wells, wells looking at donkeys, donkeys looking at donkeys, and wells looking at wells. It's the same deal here.

Then we get all that stuff about enlightened rulers. As I wrote the first draft of this paraphrase, the 2016 presidential election was heating up in the United States. So that stuff about ignorant people seeking an enlightened ruler seemed really relevant.

That contentious and crazy election is history now, and many are concerned that our new ruler is not very enlightened. But I think some of the panic I'm seeing right now as I type these words is a little misguided and unnecessary. Let me see if I can explain why.

The United States has never had a truly enlightened leader in the Buddhist sense. But even the worst of our leaders have been far better than most of the leaders Dogen would have been acquainted with. Remember that he lost his own father, a minor aristocrat and public official, to an assassin. That was just politics as usual in those days. Fast-forward a few hundred years, and we are still debating who killed JFK, more than fifty years after the fact. In Dogen's day, political leaders got assassinated so often that obsessing about one that got knocked off fifty-some years earlier would have been absurd.

It's interesting, though, to read Dogen's speculations on what a more stable political system would look like. He understood that societies need laws and that when you have laws, sometimes you need to punish those who disobey them. He was a realist, not a utopian.

I traveled through Germany in 2016 and I'm not sure why, but I kept getting invited to meetings and things there with people who consider themselves to be political activists. Lots of these folks are anarchists who believe in the possibility that people can maintain a stable society without laws and governments. There are many, many different ways of understanding the word *anarchy* and many nuanced views on the subject. I can't follow them all personally, so I'm not the one to try to explain those views.

However, you can see that Dogen was not an anarchist in the contemporary sense. Still, he did believe that all human beings have an inner sense of right and wrong. So my guess is that he would accept that anarchy might be possible in the very far future. But in his time, as in ours, there were far too many people who had no desire to listen to their inner sense of right and wrong, and so anarchy would just devolve into survival of the most powerful. Pretty soon we'd be back to something even worse than what we have now.

So rather than postulating an anarchist society, Dogen envisioned a society with an enlightened ruler who behaved rationally and fairly. Given the times in which he lived — and with his own father having been killed by a political rival — even this probably sounded hopelessly idealistic. Yet we are working toward that in our own societies today. Even as bad as it often gets, we are further along than Dogen could probably have envisioned in his day. I don't know how long it will take to finally get there, but, like Dogen, I believe it is possible.

So there you have Dogen's four good ways to treat people right. Again, we see that the Zen Buddhism Dogen taught valued ethical behavior and compassion. Now let's look at Dogen's views on the normal stuff we do in our everyday lives, like eating cornflakes and doing the dishes.

6. EATING CORNFLAKES AND DOING THE DISHES
Kajo
Everyday Life

THIS IS AN essay about why everyday life is a miracle. I used to get annoyed at people who said stuff like that. It's just so trite and clichéd. I wanted *real* miracles, gosh darn it! Walking on water, raising the dead, or at least the power to turn my enemies into mallard ducks with the wave of my hand. Come on!

But if you sit quietly for long enough and watch your real life unfold naturally, it starts to dawn on you that it actually is a miracle. It is *a-may-ʒing* that we are even here at all. That life even exists on this planet is nothing short of astonishing. If we suddenly downloaded a transmission from another planet, we'd be wowed by watching the most mundane things the multitentacled green beasties did. Their equivalent of going grocery shopping or putting in a new roll of toilet paper would be utterly fascinating. Sometimes I try to look at my own life as if I were an alien observing the ways of planet Earth. When you do that the most inconsequential things we take for granted every moment of the day become tremendously weird and wonderful.

In my paraphrase of this essay I have Dogen say a lot of stuff about eating cornflakes and doing the dishes. The phrase he actually uses is *sahan* (茶飯), which translates as "tea (and) rice." I could have just left it "tea and rice." Everyone else does. But that gives the whole thing an exotic Oriental flavor for those of us who live in places where they don't eat that much rice or drink that much tea.

I lived in Japan for a decade and change, and they serve tea and rice with almost every single meal. So Dogen is trying to reference something his audience would find incredibly boring, mundane, and commonplace. I wanted to try to keep that sense and not give it any exotic feel. I could have gone with burgers and fries, but I'm a vegetarian and that didn't seem right (though I do love me a veggie burger with fries). Besides, it's too specifically American sounding. Eating cornflakes and doing the dishes seems pretty normal to me. So does the stuff about mac and cheese that I put in later. If this stuff doesn't seem normal to you, fill in the things you eat/do all the time.

The life of a Zen master is eating cornflakes and doing the dishes. From the distant past up till today, that's what the masters have all taught.

Master Fuyu Dokai (Ch. Furong Daokai, 1043–1118 CE) asked his teacher Tosu Gisei (Ch. Touzi Yiqing, 1032–1083 CE), "The ancient masters taught eating cornflakes and doing the dishes. Did they teach anything else?"

Tosu Gisei said, "Before the current president makes a speech, does he consult with George Washington or Abraham Lincoln?"

Dokai was about to answer when Tosu Gisei put his hand over Dokai's mouth and said, "By the time you answer I should've already smacked you silly!"

Upon hearing this Dokai had a great realization. He bowed and was about to leave. Just then Tosu Gisei said, "Hey, Dokai!"

Dokai didn't even turn around. Tosu Gisei said, "Are you sure about that?" Dokai covered his ears and kept on walking.

It's clear that the words of the Buddhist masters are their everyday cornflakes and doing the dishes. Plain old cornflakes and doing the dishes in everyday life are the big ideas and deepest insights of Buddhist philosophy. When the great masters pour themselves a nice bowl of cornflakes or do the dishes afterward, that's their true skill. They don't need any other special powers besides this.

Tosu Gisei asked if the current president consulted George

Washington or Abe Lincoln. We need to pay attention to this question. Dokai asked if they taught anything else besides eating cornflakes and doing the dishes. Do you think you'd be able to get into the mind of this question and jump out? Maybe you should try.

Great Master Sekito Kisen (Ch. Shitou Xiqian, 700–790 CE) once said, "I live in a crummy old hut and my wallet's empty. I just ate some mac and cheese. Now I'm looking forward to a nice nap."

Sekito Kisen ate mac and cheese all the time. Every time he ate a bowl, he entered fully into the experience. Not eating mac and cheese means not being satisfied with an experience.

Even so, the truth of just having eaten some mac and cheese is there before he eats, it's there while he's eating, and it's there after he finishes. If you think satisfaction comes only after having an experience, you don't really understand satisfaction.

One day when I was studying with him in China, my teacher said, "When a monk asked Master Hyakujo (Ch. Baizhang Huaihai, 720–814 CE) what a miracle was, Hyakujo said a miracle was sitting alone on top of a mountain, which is what Hyakujo did. He was the master of a temple on a high mountain, where he was often alone. People would say, 'Let that guy kill himself by sitting!' But he still wouldn't budge. If someone were to ask me what a miracle was I'd just ask them how anything could be a miracle. When I want a miracle I just sit down and have a bowl of cornflakes."

The life of a Buddhist master is miracle after miracle. You can call it "sitting alone on top of a mountain" if you want. Even if someone says he's killing himself by sitting, it's still a miracle. And there's something even more miraculous. It's called "sitting down and eating a bowl of cornflakes."

After you finish a bowl of cornflakes, you're satisfied. Eating cornflakes is, in itself, satisfaction. And what's your cereal bowl? Is it just plastic or ceramic? I think it's a bottomless bowlful of crunchy satisfaction!

Another time my teacher was giving a talk, and he said, "When I'm hungry I eat. When I'm tired I sleep. Whatever you really need to bring you to the truth, it's always there."

Getting hungry describes a person who has already eaten. Somebody who has never eaten anything before can never get hungry. So keep in mind that if you experience hunger every day, you're a person who has eaten already.

Getting tired is what happens when you're already tired. It has leaped free of the concept of getting tired and become actual tiredness fully experienced in the present moment.

Sleeping is when you let go of everything and fully relax, which is what the Buddha always does even when he's fully awake.

Another time my teacher was talking to a different group and he said, "For half a year I just sat up in a monastery on a mountain eating cornflakes for breakfast. Doing zazen cut through the clouds of delusion. Then one day those clouds burst into thunder and I was invited to become the master of the temple. And don't those red apricot blossoms look great this time of year?"

The great ancient teachings of the Buddhist masters is always "sitting and eating cornflakes." If you want to become a Buddhist master, just master the art of eating cornflakes. Nobody knows how many clouds of delusion any one of us has to deal with. Even though my teacher metaphorically heard a thunderclap, those apricot blossoms were still just hanging out doing their thing. Apricot blossoms are red, which symbolizes a raw and sincere mind. When my teacher mentions them looking great this time of year, he's indicating that sincerity is available right here and now. The indescribable state is what happens when you eat a nice bowl of cornflakes.

Another time my teacher made up a poem that went like this:

The wondrous form of Buddha
Is my clothes and the cornflakes I ate
Therefore I bow down to you — duh
I sleep in and I get up late
Talking of the formless can really inspire
Unless the old stories set you on fire

This is something you can understand right away. The wondrous form of Buddha is the same as wearing a T-shirt and eating cornflakes. You don't need to ask what kind of person gets dressed and eats cornflakes, because everybody does that. You don't have to think that someone else has the wondrous form of Buddha and you don't. If you can just avoid that kind of stuff, then whatever you say will be the truth. That's why he says he bows down to you. This is why we have to be careful about getting too excited — or "set on fire," as he says in the poem — by old Zen stories of great awakenings and stuff like that.

One time another old Zen master named Enchi Daian (Ch. Changqing Daan, 793-883 CE) said, "For thirty years I lived on Isan Mountain, eating Isan cornflakes and shitting Isan shit. I didn't learn a damned thing about Zen. I just kept an eye on myself. When I got distracted, I got back to my practice. When I worried that others were better than me or that I was inadequate, I reminded myself that I am just what I am. I was a pitiful person. I suffered when others made fun of me. But now I'm a contented old man. I live in a constant state of bright clarity. Even if I try to get rid of that clarity, it never goes away."

We should pay attention to this teaching. Enchi Daian made thirty years of effort without ever worrying about it. If you do that, you'll end up contented and happy, too.

Once master Joshu Jushin (Ch. Zhaozhou Congshen, 778-897 CE) asked a newly arrived monk, "You ever been here before?"

The monk said, "Yes, I have."

The master said, "Have some tea."

Then the master asked another monk, "Have you ever been here before?"

The other monk said, "Nope. Never."

The master said to the second monk, "Have some tea."

Then the temple director asked the master, "How come you said 'have some tea' to the guy who'd been here before and to the guy who hadn't?"

The master said, "Hey, director!"

The director said, "Yeah?"

The master said, "Have some tea!"

The key to this story is the word *here*. The master is asking the two monks about what here and now really is. It's beyond anything you can think of, beyond any answer you can give. This place — here — is indescribable reality. But the monks just think he's asking if they've come to the temple before. They don't know that *here* is always new at every instant and that none of us has ever been *here* before, even if the here we're referring to happens to be a place we've been to a million times before.

My teacher used to say, "Which of the people in this wonderful world we live in has ever really drunk Master Joshu's tea?"

The everyday life of a real Buddhist practitioner is just eating cornflakes and having some tea.

— Preached to the assembly at Yamashi Peak in the Etsu District on December 12, 1243

I already talked about the cornflakes thing. And, as you surely knew, there's nothing in the original dialogue about the current president and George Washington and Abraham Lincoln. Tosu Gisei says something more like, "When the [current] emperor issues a decree in his territory, does he depend on [ancient emperors] Yu, Tang, Yao, or Shun?" That's the Kaz Tanahashi translation. Since you folks are probably like me and know Washington and Lincoln better than those ancient Chinese emperors, I made a substitution. You're welcome.

Where I have Tosu Gisei ask Dokai, "Are you sure about that?" the original is more like, "Has the disciple arrived at the state without doubt?" That's the Nishijima/Cross translation. That's pretty much what the original says. I like making it a more colloquial question.

After this I have Dogen say, "Do you think you'd be able to get into the mind of this question and jump out? Maybe you should try." Tanahashi's translation is, "Leap over the summit of the question *Besides this, are there any words and phrases for teaching?* Try to see whether leaping is possible." The italics are in the original and represent Dokai's question. In the Nishijima/Cross translation it's, "We should spring out in experience from the brains of this question." The word they're alternately translating as "summit" or "brains" is *chonin* (頂顑). The first character is a normal one, while the second is no longer used in Japanese. As a compound they mean "the top of the head." The Nishiyama/Stevens version doesn't even bother with translating this weird word and just says "the question...must be transcended." Smart move on their part.

And, of course (again), Master Sekito Kisen probably didn't have a wallet or eat mac and cheese. The original is more like, "I live in a hermitage that contains nothing of value; after taking my meal if I feel sleepy I nap." That's the Nishiyama/Stevens translation. I just wanted to remove some of the exoticness.

There is some difference among the translations as to how to deal with the phrase Dogen uses right after he quotes the story about Sekito Kisen taking a nap. I've paraphrased it as, "Sekito Kisen ate mac and cheese all the time. Every time he ate a bowl, he entered fully into the experience. Not eating mac and cheese means not being satisfied with an experience."

Nishijima and Cross see Dogen as simply saying that Sekito Kisen ate food every day and that this is the essence of the Buddhist teaching. Their version goes, "'[I] have finished a meal' — [an experience] that he repeats, repeats again, and repeats over again — is the idea and words of a Buddhist patriarch who experiences meals. One who has not yet finished a meal is not yet satisfied with experience."

Tanahashi has Dogen saying, "Words come, words go, words come and go, filled with Buddha ancestors' thoughts and phrases. Not yet having rice means not yet being satisfied."

This is another spot where Tanahashi and Nishijima/Cross reverse their usual way of translating Dogen. Nishijima/Cross, who generally stick strictly to Dogen's actual words, are interpretive here, while Tanahashi, who is usually interpretive, sticks to the actual words Dogen uses. I also chose to be a bit interpretive here.

In my paraphrase I then have Dogen say, "Even so, the truth of just having eaten some mac and cheese is there before he eats, it's there while he's eating, and it's there after he finishes. If you think satisfaction comes only after having an experience, you don't really understand satisfaction."

Dogen's idea about how you can be satisfied before, during, and after an experience is interesting. On this point the translators agree, and their translations read pretty much like my paraphrase

— although I'm the only one who makes Sekito Kisen eat mac and cheese.

I can't find any commentaries on this line, so I guess it's up to me. I feel like Dogen is indicating something that I have found tremendously important in his writings. He's saying that we can be completely satisfied with any part of any experience.

Instead of talking about mac and cheese, maybe let's make the story be about a hot date. In this case, Sekito Kisen is satisfied before the hot date, during the hot date, and after the hot date. Does that help make it clearer? If you're like me, you've probably missed out on a huge portion of your life by fixating on exciting things that are going to happen later or ruminating about exciting things that happened a long time ago — hot dates being a good example. This also goes for terrible or sad experiences. Or, also like me, you've probably divided your experiences into stuff you do in order to get satisfaction and then...ah yes, right there, baby...satisfaction! We all do the same thing.

In doing so, we're really missing most of our lives. Maybe if we were more fully present in the hours leading up to a hot date, we'd end up being more fully present when we actually got together with the object of our desire.

Moving right along, in the story about Dogen's teacher talking about miracles, I've followed the Nishijima/Cross translation. The word they translate as "miracles" is *tokuji* (特事). This just means "special thing." Tanahashi translates this as "extraordinary thing." Nishiyama and Stevens translate it as "the most important thing in the world." Shasta Abbey's translation has "Miraculous Matter," with the *M*s capitalized like that.

In the context of the story it feels like he's talking about something more extraordinary than your average "special thing." So I went with "miracle."

And, of course, there's no mention of cornflakes in the original here, either. But Dogen's teacher refers back to the story that I translated using cornflakes in my version. So that's why I put it in this story, too.

This story has the same message as the earlier story. The most extraordinary miracle is your everyday life.

As I said in the intro, I know a lot of people run around saying shit like this in cheery little voices: "Everyday life is a miracle!" I just want to slap those people sometimes.

I used to want to slap them because I thought they were wrong. I was a really depressed character, and I thought everyday life was shit. For most of the first half of my adult life I pretty much never had any money or prospects. The world felt like it could end any day. It still feels like the world could end, but now we're imagining a slow death from global climate change rather than being fried to death by nuclear bombs.

I feel a lot better about life these days. But not because I'm no longer worried that we might fuck everything up. I do worry about that still. And not just because my financial situation has gotten marginally better than it was back in those days — though not all that much better, actually. No. I feel better about life because I've come to understand how amazing it is, no matter what's happening.

I mean, what are the odds against me being alive at all? It must be in the trillions. Or maybe the odds against my existence are infinite. Yet here I am. How extraordinary is it that there's even a planet here for me to complain about? That's bloody amazing.

And yet I still want to slap people who run around cheerily declaring that it's a miracle to be alive. I want to slap them because I don't think most of them really mean it. They're just optimistic because they're so totally focused on some kind of shiny tomorrow while completely ignoring today. Of course I could be wrong. Maybe they're really connected to the present moment. Maybe I just hate cheery people.

Yet I have also learned to accept the fact that I hate cheery people. I've learned that it's more useful and less unpleasant to be amused at my own curmudgeonly tendencies than to be annoyed at the things that set them off. Knowing how to do that has changed my life for the better in so many ways it's hard to count.

Moving right along again, a bit after this I have Dogen call his cereal bowl a "bottomless bowlful of crunchy satisfaction." You probably think I'm really stretching things there. But in the original, Dogen calls his begging bowl "bottomless" and says that it "swallows the open sky." So there! Again, a begging bowl would be as common a thing to Dogen and his original readership as a cereal bowl is to us — or to me, at least.

After this I have Dogen quote his teacher as saying, "When I'm hungry I eat. When I'm tired I sleep. Whatever you really need to bring you to the truth, it's always there." The first two sentences are pretty much the same in every translation. The last one is a puzzler, and I have completely changed it.

Nishijima/Cross translate what Dogen actually wrote in the third sentence as, "Forges span the universe." Tanahashi's version has "furnaces and bellows" instead of just forges and has them spanning the sky rather than the universe. The original is four Chinese characters, 炉鞴亙天 (rohai wataru ten). The translations are both correct; they're just different ways of dealing with the words.

But what in the holy heck does that even mean? According to a footnote in the Shasta Abbey translation, "Forges and bellows is a traditional Zen Buddhist metaphor for the conditions and expedient means that intensify the heat of training, whereby a trainee is forged into a True Monk. As Tendo Nyojo [Ch. Tiantong Rujing, 1163–1228 CE, Dogen's teacher in China] points out, these conditions and expedient means are available everywhere. In other words, all things have the capability of teaching us the Dharma." The folks at Shasta Abbey capitalized "True Monk," by the way, not me. Even so, I'll accept their answer because it makes sense and nobody else seems interested enough in this weird phrase to explain it. My paraphrase is based on their explanation.

A little further down, I took some liberties with the line I para-phrased as, "Sleeping is when you let go of everything and fully relax, which is what the Buddha always does even when he's fully awake." In the Nishijima/Cross translation it's, "'Sleeping' is sleep-ing that borrows the eyes of Buddha, the eyes of Dharma, the eyes of wisdom, the eyes of patriarchs, and the eyes of outdoor pillars and stone lanterns." Which is pretty much how everybody else translates it.

I pondered this for a while and decided that Dogen's comparing the fully relaxed and realistic state that the Buddha experienced all the time to what we encounter only when we're asleep. That's also why he mentions pillars and lanterns. These are Dogen's favorite examples of inanimate objects.

In Buddhist philosophy, even inanimate objects are believed to partake of the same five aggregates that make up everything else in the universe: form, feelings, perceptions, impulses to action and action itself, and consciousness. The consciousness of a pillar or a lamp isn't the same as that of a human, though. They are free from worry because there's nothing they could do if they worried about whatever a pillar or lamp might worry about anyway.

Dogen then tells us another story about something his teacher, Tendo Nyojo, said about sitting in a monastery on a mountain. I didn't alter the first part much except to change "rice" to "corn-flakes." Once again I did this to eliminate the distraction of having him say something quaint and Oriental. I realize this sets up another distraction since you obviously know the original word was not cornflakes. Hopefully that's offset by using an example as ordinary and unexotic to us as the example of rice would have been to the audience for whom this was intended. I could have also had him sit in a Zen center in, like, Pittsburgh or someplace, but I figured that was too much.

I did alter a couple of other parts of the story. In the original Dogen just says "one sudden clap of thunder," without getting into what that symbolizes. In the footnotes of the Nishijima/Cross translation it says, "The thunderclap symbolizes the invitation to become master of Jōji Temple." I thought it was important to add that since I wouldn't have known it without checking the footnotes, so I wouldn't expect you to know it, either. But Dogen's audience would have known what he was referring to.

The other change I made is that the final line is, "The color of spring in the capital is apricot-blossom crimson" (Nishijima/Cross translation, which is very similar to Nishiyama/Stevens). Tanahashi changes "capital" to "mystic village" but his version is otherwise pretty much the same. Tendo Nyojo was referring to what was going on at the time he was speaking. He could probably see the apricot blossoms through the doors as he spoke — they usually keep the temple doors open during a Zen teacher's talk. I wanted to make sure that sense was properly conveyed.

I didn't change much about the explanation Dogen gives after he quotes his teacher.

Next up we get another poem, which I have butchered. Here is the Nishijima/Cross translation: "The golden and fine form / Is to get dressed and to eat meals / That is why I bow to you / I sleep early and get up late / Aye. Talk of the profound and preaching of the fine are enormously free / Sternly be on guard lest a twirling flower inflames you."

The twirling flower he's talking about is the one that the stories say Buddha twirled as a way of symbolizing that he was making his student Mahakashyapa the new leader of his order. So I just changed that to "old stories." He means that we can learn from those old stories, but if we get too excited about them, we totally miss the point — the same as what happens when we, today, get too excited about the exotic aspects of old stories about Dogen and his teacher.

Dogen then quotes a teacher who lived on Isan Mountain, eating Isan cornflakes and shitting Isan shit. I took some liberties once again with the original text. But not, you may be surprised to note, the reference to shit. Here is the Nishijima/Cross translation: "Daian [referring to himself in the third person, as Zen teachers often do] lived on Isan Mountain for thirty years, eating Isan meals, shitting Isan shit, not learning Isan Zen, just watching over a castrated water buffalo. When it strayed into the grass, I dragged it out. When it invaded another's seed patch, I whipped it. Though disciplined for a long time already, as a pitiful creature, it suffered people's remarks. Now it has turned into a white ox on open ground. It is always before me. All day long it is in a state of conspicuous brightness. Even if driven away, it does not leave."

That's a pretty standard translation, and there aren't many big variations. My paraphrase is my own understanding of the story. That term *castrated water buffalo* shows up a lot in old Zen stories. For some folks the term has an appealing exoticism. To me it just sounds horrifying. The last thing I want to be is a castrated water buffalo!

The image is about something that starts off wild and uncontrollable but ends up tame and friendly. It's a reference to the effects of the discipline of Zen temple life. So the water buffalo in the story is Daian himself.

The "open ground" in the story is a reference to a story in the Lotus Sutra in which the open ground represented enlightenment. As for the bit in the end where he says "it doesn't leave," it's usually thought that *it* means the water buffalo and that the water buffalo doesn't leave the open ground of enlightenment even when driven away. I took a slightly different approach and made it the enlightened state that doesn't leave. I think that's also what Dogen was saying here.

Last, we get that story about Zen Master Joshu Jushin offering the monks tea, no matter how they answer his question. People love to quote this story. But I think most of them just imagine it's a bit of Zen nonsense.

To me, the master is offering his hospitality and his Zen practice to anyone who comes seeking it, whether or not they understand the philosophical stuff. When he offers them tea, he's offering to allow them to join his practice.

There are two lessons in this story. One is the overall lesson of the whole essay, which is that everyday life is enlightenment itself. The other is that this is still true whether or not you understand it intellectually. Let me try to explain that a little.

I remember once someone at a lecture asked Nishijima Roshi, "Can you notice your own enlightenment?"

Nishijima Roshi said, "No."

At the time I hated this response. Why should I keep working for enlightenment if I'll never even notice when (or if) it happens? But I think Nishijima was right. Noticing enlightenment implies that enlightenment is an object that can be noticed by you as a subject. But enlightenment is when there is no subject and no object, where you and the thing you notice merge into one. This is already the case, though. We don't need to be like the Zen master who tells the hot dog vendor, "Make me one with everything." We are already one with everything. Our everyday life — right this very moment — is already the state of unsurpassed, complete, perfect enlightenment.

So don't avoid the mundaneness of your ordinary life. That's your enlightenment staring you in the face!

One part of our everyday lives that many of us would like to be able to avoid is cause and effect. Sometimes we've done something that we wish we hadn't. Or sometimes the state of the world, which is the present effect of innumerable past causes, is not to our liking. The next two essays talk about whether we can ever be free from cause and effect.

7. GARBAGE IN, GARBAGE OUT
Jinshin Inga
Deep Belief in Cause and Effect

DOGEN WAS A contradictory fellow. One of the most famous of all Dogen's many contradictions in *Shobogenzo* involves his treatment of an old Zen story called Hyakujo's Fox. We met Mr. Hyakujo in the previous chapter. Same guy. In two chapters of *Shobogenzo* Dogen recounts the story of Hyakujo and a fox. But in each one he gives it a completely different interpretation. Or does he?

In working on these two chapters it has been my mission to discover the answer to that question, which is, Are these interpretations really all that contradictory? I invite you to join me on my quest. I will try to present you with a clear reading of both chapters and then explain what I think they mean.

In ancient India one of the big controversies was over whether an enlightened person was subject to the law of cause and effect. This is because some folks ascribe a great deal of importance to whether enlightened people develop magic powers.

Here's why I say "magic powers." To me the definition of magic is "activity that violates the law of cause and effect." Remember the old TV show *Bewitched*, or its botched movie version starring Will Ferrell? If you don't, it was about Samantha, a witch, who marries Darrin, a regular person. Samantha has magical powers. With just the twitch of her nose, anything can happen. She'll turn Darrin into a crocodile, or make a five-course dinner appear on the table, or transport the family two hundred years back in time, all with a cute little wiggle of her nose.

This violates the law of cause and effect for a lot of reasons. But the main one is that there is not enough power in the twitch of a nose to cause the kinds of effects we see on-screen. So that's magic, in a nutshell. The cause and the effect do not match up.

Most Buddhists in the olden times didn't necessarily want to imagine that after becoming enlightened, a Buddhist master could twitch her nose and turn Uncle Arthur into a poodle. Yet they still wanted to believe that the enlightened state somehow exempted them from the effects of past karma. This controversy has persisted throughout the history of Buddhism and still comes up today.

In researching this chapter, I learned a new word that relates to all this stuff: *antinomian*. I came across it in a scholarly article about this essay of Dogen's. It's one of those words certain writers in my field use to prove they're smart. It derives from a Greek word meaning "lawless" and usually refers to the Christian idea that faith in Jesus releases you from the obligation to be an ethical person because your sins are already all forgiven. This, I think, is close to what those early Buddhists were interested in.

The theory of sin and forgiveness, if I can call it a theory for a second, holds that if you masturbated every day throughout junior high, then when you die Jesus will hold you accountable. However, if you become born again in Christ when you're old, Jesus will forgive you of your past sins, and you can still go to heaven in spite of all your teenage wanking. I think when we hear these Buddhist stories we imagine it's something like asking, "Will Buddha forgive my sins if I get enlightened?" I don't think it's too much of a stretch to say that this is sort of like what the early Buddhists fretted about, too. They were used to religions in which supernatural gods had the ability to transcend cause and effect — like most of our religions today.

But the Buddhist theory of karma is different. Sin is arbitrarily decided by God. There's nothing inherently bad about masturbation or about many of the things that are considered sinful. Karma, on the other hand, is simple cause and effect that we see at work in everything we do. If you drop a wineglass, it breaks. If you pull a puppy's tail, the puppy bites you. Or to put it in computer programmer lingo: garbage in, garbage out. Or vice versa: good stuff in, good stuff out. What goes around comes around. That sort of thing.

Buddhist philosophers extended that idea to areas of ethical action and believed that, with some causes, it could take a long time before the effects were felt. Even so, supernatural forces did not need to be invoked to make this happen any more than supernatural forces needed to be invoked to explain why stepping on someone's toe might get you punched in the face. Except that, to those Buddhists, there could be cases in which the punching of the face happens twenty years after the stepping on of the toe, during which time the person whose face gets punched has forgotten he ever stepped on anyone's toe. And maybe someone totally different from the person whose toe he stepped on punches him in the face.

The story we're about to look at, then, asks if enlightenment magically absolves you of every stupid thing you've ever done, or if you're still gonna get punched in the face because of that toe you stepped on twenty years earlier, even though now you're enlightened.

Dogen wrote two essays on the story of Hyakujo's Fox. I'm going to tackle them in reverse order from the way they're usually presented.

What we'll be looking at in this chapter is the second essay Dogen wrote about the fox story. In this essay, the answer to the question of whether an enlightened person is exempt from the law of cause and effect is fairly straightforward. I won't keep you in suspense. In this version, the enlightened person is not exempt. No one is. As for the other essay, which we'll look at after this one, the CliffsNotes version of Dogen's answer might be, "It's complicated."

This essay was probably written in the early 1250s and was part of the twelve-chapter version of *Shobogenzo*. There were a bunch of different versions of *Shobogenzo*, often identified by the number of chapters they contained. The only two that may date back to Dogen's time are the twelve-chapter edition and the seventy-five-chapter edition.

There is some debate as to whether this twelve-chapter version of *Shobogenzo* was put together by Dogen. But many scholars these days assume it was. Yet Ejo, Dogen's student, mentions in his postscript note to the essay we're about to read that the essay was unfinished. So maybe the whole twelve-chapter version wasn't Dogen's idea. We simply do not know, and we probably never will.

In any case, lots of scholars say that the twelve-chapter version was intended for newbies, while the seventy-five-chapter version was intended for more advanced students. They say Dogen may have worried that his deeper, more convoluted philosophical stuff might be misunderstood and therefore decided to make a more straightforward primer for novice monks, a work he never properly finished. We'll talk about that theory some more later. The other essay on the fox story, the one we'll look at in the next chapter, is from the seventy-five-chapter version of *Shobogenzo*.

One interesting fact I learned while doing research, which makes this story more interesting, is that Obaku, who appears near the end of the fox story, was reported to be nearly seven feet tall and to have a weird egg-shaped lump on his forehead. He's a young monk in this story but went on to be an important Zen master who was very stern and known to smack his students around sometimes as a way of teaching them. Which also accounts for what he does in the fox story.

In any case, this commentary on Hyakujo's Fox is easier to understand than Dogen's other commentary. So that's why I'll address it first and then deal with the more mystical one after. Here goes!

Whenever the Zen master of Hyakujo Mountain (we'll just call him Hyakujo to keep things simple; he's called Hyakujo Ekai in Japanese and Baizhang Huaihai in Chinese, and he lived 720–814 CE) gave a talk, this old guy showed up and stood at the back, just listening. Whenever the talks were over, the old guy just sort of wandered away. But one day he stayed behind after all the monks had left. So the master said, "Who is this person standing in front of me?"

The old man said, "I'm not actually a person. Millions of years ago, in the age of Kashyapa Buddha, I used to live on this mountain, where I was the Zen master. One day a student asked me if a person of great practice was subject to the law of cause and effect. I said that such a person does not fall into cause and effect. Since then I have been reborn as a wild fox for five hundred lifetimes. Now I'd like to ask you, master, to help me out and give me a word of transformation to free me from the body of a wild fox. Does a person of great practice fall into cause and effect, or what?"

The master said, "The law of cause and effect is as clear as noonday."

Upon hearing these words, the old man finally got it. He bowed to the master and said, "I'm free from the body of a wild fox. But can you do me a big favor and perform the funeral rites for a dead monk?"

The master then called the monks together and said, "After lunch we're gonna perform a funeral for a deceased monk!"

The monks were pretty shocked because nobody among them was even sick.

After lunch the master went behind a rock and with his stick pulled out the body of a dead wild fox. They cremated the body and performed the ceremony just as if they were cremating a monk.

Later that evening, the master told the monks what had happened. His student Obaku (Obaku Kiun; Ch. Huangbo Xiyun, d. 850 CE) said, "The old guy was asked for a word of transformation and gave the wrong answer, then he fell into the body of a wild fox for five hundred lifetimes. What would he have become if he hadn't made any mistakes?"

The master said, "Come up here, kid, and I'll tell you."

Obaku stepped forward and smacked the master in the face.

The master clapped his hands and laughed, saying, "I thought Bodhidharma had a red beard. But you just said that the guy with the red beard is Bodhidharma!"

That's the way the old story goes. Even so, people who should know better are still unclear about cause and effect. Buddhism has declined so badly these days. Sad.

Saying "they don't fall into cause and effect" is a negation of cause and effect. Anyone who says so suffers the consequences. Saying "cause and effect are as clear as noonday" shows deep belief in cause and effect. Anyone who says that gets free of bad effects.

Lots of folks these days who claim to be Zen students deny cause and effect. We can be sure they deny cause and effect because they think that the statements "they don't fall into cause and effect" and "cause and effect are as clear as noonday" are the same.

The ancient Indian master Kumaralabdha (the nineteenth successor of Shakyamuni Buddha, dates unknown; I would guess somewhere around 300 BCE) said, "Sometimes the effects of an action are not felt until a very long time after the action itself. But sometimes folks see, like, a really bad person making tons of money and getting elected president or, like, a really good person dying young, and they think there's no point in leading an ethical life. They don't know that the effects of whatever you do never go away even after a million, billion, quintillion years."

Obviously Kumaralabdha believed in cause and effect. Students these days are just plain ignorant. Listen up, you wanna-be so-called Buddhist masters! Don't ever tell your students cause and effect isn't a real thing. That is not the teaching of Buddhism. It's just a load of random bullshit.

These days in China you'll even hear certain dummies who dress up like monks saying stupid crap about this. They'll say stuff like, "We don't remember even one or two past lives. But the old man / wild fox in the story knew five hundred! So he must have been super-enlightened. Maybe he was reborn as a fox in order to enter the animal realm as an enlightened being so he could teach animals the truth."

This is not the teachings of Buddhism. There may be people or even animals who have the power to recall their former lives. This does not mean they understand anything about the truth. In fact, the ability to know former lives can be the result of poor conduct in the past.

Buddha spoke the truth. But even being able to recall ten

thousand lives does not produce anything like Buddha's teachings. There are people who claim to know millions of past lives, but they still have nothing useful to say. Knowing just five hundred past lives is kids' stuff.

It's a real shame that students in China these days don't realize that saying "they don't fall into cause and effect" is wrong. It's even more of a shame that there are whole schools of so-called Buddhism that believe that garbage.

Real practitioners of Zen need to remember the principle that "cause and effect are as clear as noonday." Don't be ignorant about this stuff. We know that if we do something we get the effect of the causes we create. This is what we should teach others.

The ancient Buddhist master Nagarjuna (ca. 150–250 CE) said, "If you deny cause and effect, then there is no present or future. If you deny that cause and effect are part of the Buddha's truth, then nothing else about Buddhism makes any sense."

The idea that some kind of immortal spirit or soul inhabits our physical bodies but is eternally enlightened is what I would call a "denial of the present." Some dweebs say that when people die they return to the spiritual world and that even if a person never practiced Zen they'll be enlightened after they die. For this reason, they say, there is no future.

That's just nihilism, not Buddhism. Even if those who say such things wear Buddhist robes, they're not Buddhists at all. Don't listen to that kind of garbage. Nagarjuna had it right.

A long time ago there was a Zen master named Yoka Genkaku (Ch. Yongjia Xuanjue, 665–713 CE). Once, while Genkaku was reading the Nirvana Sutra, a golden light filled the room and he had a huge awakening in which he realized there is no birth or death. His teacher, the sixth patriarch of Zen, Daikan Eno (Ch. Dajian Huineng, 638–713 CE), gave Genkaku his seal of approval. Later on Genkaku said, "Thoughtless ideas about emptiness negate the belief in cause and effect. People who believe such ideas get loose with their ethics and make a lot of mistakes, and then they end up in a bad way."

Was he ever right about that! But even though we are coming along very late in the process, we too can learn the truth of the law of cause and effect.

Zen Master Wanshi Shogaku (Ch. Hongzhi Zhengjue, 1091–1157 CE) made up a poem about this:

One foot of water in a ten-foot wave
Wandering through five hundred lifetimes in all
The wild fox struggles like a senseless knave
With "clear as noonday" and "does not fall."

People make everything way too complicated
And in the end they get all stuck
They never reach the understanding they awaited
I look at them and laugh, "Yuckety-yuck!"

If you don't get it, I'll keep saying gobbledygook
I'll dance and clap any time that I please
Maybe I'll look just like a crazy old kook
But I'll be exactly as free as the breeze!

In the poem Wanshi says, "The wild fox struggles like a senseless knave / With 'clear as noonday' and 'does not fall.' / People make everything way too complicated." He's saying that "clear as noonday" and "does not fall into cause and effect" mean the same thing. That's because the story of Hyakujo's Fox is not complete, so people wonder about it.

We don't know if the old man / wild fox goes on to be reborn as a human being or if he goes on to be reborn in heaven. In fact, the story doesn't tell us what state the old man / wild fox ends up in.

If the old man / wild fox deserves to be born in a better state, he'll be reborn as a human or reborn in heaven. If he doesn't, he'll get reborn in a worse place. After he dies he's gotta go somewhere. There are endless places he might be reborn. But people who don't believe in the Buddha's teaching think that once someone dies they return to the ocean of enlightenment or that maybe they just vanish forever.

Zen Master Engo Kokugon (Ch. Yuanwu Keqin, 1063–1135 CE) wrote a poem that goes like this:

A swimming fish makes the water murky
Birds fly and feathers fall, unless it's a turkey
The ultimate mirror you cannot avoid
And boundless is the great, great void
Once something's gone, it's gone forever, I suspect
Five hundred lives of great practice due to cause and effect
Lightning strikes the mountain and the seas they do shake
Pure gold doesn't change color, for goodness's sake!

This poem seems to me to deny cause and effect, which is an idealistic way of looking at things. And it also seems to uphold the false idea that there is a permanent self.

Master Daie Soko (Ch. Dahui Zonggao, 1089-1163 CE) praised the story of Hyakujo's Fox in a poem that goes like this:

"Not falling" and "clear as noonday"
These are stones and are clods, so dirty
When you meet them on a pathway
The Silver Mountain is crushed, ain't it purty?
Seeing it, the foolish priest from Ming
Can't stop himself from laughing

Back in China people think Soko was some kind of a genius. But Soko didn't get it at all, if you ask me. He seems more like a naturalist who believes in spontaneous enlightenment than a real Buddhist master.

There are more than thirty poems and commentaries on the story of Hyakujo's Fox, but not one of them understands that the phrase "such a person doesn't fall into cause and effect" is a negation of cause and effect. It's a shame they're so confused on such a simple point.

When you study the Buddhist Way, your first priority is to be clear about the principle of cause and effect. Those who deny cause and effect usually end up craving fame and money and negate whatever good they did in their lives.

Cause and effect has got to be the single most obvious thing in the world. Those who do bad end up in bad places, and those who do good end up in good places. There are no exceptions.

It is only because of cause and effect that Buddhas appear in the world. It is only because of cause and effect that Bodhidharma brought the true teachings to China and they reached us here. Without cause and effect we would never encounter the dharma.

Confucius, the famous philosopher, and Lao-tzu, the founder of Taoism, didn't understand cause and effect. Only Buddha and those who followed him understood and taught it. If students in this degenerate age don't hear the right teachings, they end up not understanding the principle of cause and effect. If we deny cause and effect, we end up suffering all sorts of bad stuff. The view that denies cause and effect is a kind of poison.

So if you want to get any kind of real enlightenment, you need to be very clear about the truth of the principle of cause and effect.

— During the summer retreat of 1255, I, Ejo, copied this from the rough draft Master Dogen left behind. It was never really finished, and I'm sure he would have revised it, had he lived longer

The question the old man / wild fox asks is, "Does a person of great practice (大修行, *daishugyo*) fall into cause and effect?" I almost changed "person of great practice" to "enlightened person" to try to make the story a little easier to follow. But since the next chapter delves into the question of what "great practice" means, I decided to leave it as it was. However, it's worth noting that the notion of a person of great practice implies that the person in question has practiced for a very long time and achieved some sort of realization.

I left the weird grammar of "fall into cause and effect" because that's there in the original. The words Dogen actually used are *raku inga* (落因果). They literally mean "fall (into) cause (and) effect." Some translators preserve this oddball grammar, whereas others change it into more standard English phrases like "subject to the law of cause and effect." Normally I would side with the latter and just make it sound like normal spoken English, because that's what it means. It's just a linguistic idiom that the verb happens to mean "fall (into)." Still, I like the imagery so I kept it.

In my version I have the master answer, "The law of cause and effect is as clear as noonday." I stole this translation from Joshu Sasaki's book *Buddha Is the Center of Gravity*. The original is in Chinese, not Japanese, and it says *fu-mai inga* (不昧因果). Let's break that down. *Inga* (因果) means "cause and effect," or "karma." *Fu* (不) is a character that negates whatever comes after it. *Mai* (昧) means "dark, foolish, or unclear." So probably the best translation would be, "The law of cause and effect is not unclear."

This phrase contrasts with what the student asks the master, which is whether or not a person of great practice is *fu-raku inga* (不落因果). This phrase could be translated as "not subject to (or literally doesn't fall into) cause and effect." The master in the story changes one character in the phrase and says *fu-mai inga* (不昧因果). Throughout the essay, Dogen contrasts these two four-character Chinese statements. I've tried to preserve that by putting my versions of these statements in quotes whenever I used them in the paraphrase.

The difference between the two statements is that *mai* (昧, unclear or dark) is substituted for *raku* (落, "fall" or "be subject to") in Hyakujo's "word of transformation" to the old man / wild fox. As I said, *mai* (昧) means "dark" or "unclear." For *fu-mai inga* (不昧因果), the Nishijima/Cross translation has, "Do not be unclear about cause and effect." This could also be a way of interpreting the original Chinese, since it could be a command. Tanahashi has, "Do not ignore cause and effect," which, if you ask me, is a little bit of a stretch, but okay. Nishiyama/Stevens have, "No one is beyond the effect of causality," which again is not quite what the original says, but okay. The Shasta Abbey translation has, "Such a one is not blind to causality." I actually think this is a little wrong, but it's still not so bad. These translations are all close enough for rock and roll, as we used to say when we couldn't get the guitars quite in tune. They're adequate and they don't really change anything that much, but they do change it.

The reason I used the Sasaki version, even though it also doesn't say quite what the original does, is (1) that that's the way I first heard it and it stuck in my mind and (2) that it's a compelling image. I think this is as close as you can get in English to the intention of the original. It's not just that the law of cause and effect is not unclear. It's super-clear, like noonday.

What the master is saying to the old man / wild fox is that *obviously* the law of cause and effect works on a person of great practice because — duh! — you were reborn as a wild fox for five hundred lifetimes. But notice that the master is also inferring that the old man / wild fox is a person of great practice. This is something I hadn't thought of the past few times I went over this story. I think it's interesting. So just because you're an enlightened person doesn't mean everything you say is necessarily correct. You still make mistakes. Or do you?

We'll get more into the idea of what is a mistake and what is not in the next chapter. But rather than saying it's correct or it isn't, maybe the question is whether or not the statement was the right one to say to that person at that time in that place. You can be correct and still say the wrong thing. More on that in the next chapter. Stay tuned.

At the end of the story there's a line about Bodhidharma and his red beard. In the original, Bodhidharma is not mentioned by name. It says *ko* (胡), which means "barbarian." But it's understood that the barbarian in question is the famous master Bodhidharma, who brought Zen Buddhism to China from India (or maybe Afghanistan) and was considered by the Chinese to be a barbarian. He is usually depicted in artworks as having a red beard.

In my paraphrase I have the ancient Indian Buddhist master Kumaralabdha say, "Sometimes the effects of an action are not felt until a very long time after the action itself." He actually says something about karma in the "three times" (三時, pronounced *sanji*).

Dogen wrote an essay about this concept called "Karma in the Three Times" (三時業, *sanji go*). I wrote about that essay in my book *Sit Down and Shut Up*.

In that essay Dogen talks about how the effects of our actions are sometimes felt immediately, sometimes felt after a little while, and sometimes felt a long, long time later. This is one of the essays that some people take as evidence that Dogen taught reincarnation or rebirth because he says that sometimes the effects of an action taken in one life are not felt until several lifetimes later. As I mentioned earlier, I devoted a whole chapter of my book *Don't Be a Jerk* to whether or not Dogen believed in rebirth/reincarnation, so I won't get into that here. I just wanted to let you know that a possible interpretation of the idea that causes and effects can be widely separated includes this idea of rebirth. So you might not notice the effects of something you've done in this lifetime until seven hundred years from now when you've been reborn as a colonist on one of the planets circling the star Epsilon Eridani. Be careful!

Still, it's not necessary to invoke reincarnation. The basic idea is that effects always follow causes, just sometimes not immediately.

There's a paragraph in my paraphrase where I have Dogen calling out Buddhist teachers who deny cause and effect. I changed his wording somewhat, but Dogen doesn't pull any punches in the original. The Nishijima/Cross translation has him saying, "Those who are negligent in emulating the ancients and yet randomly call themselves good counselors to human beings and gods, are great nuisances to human beings and gods and are the enemies of practitioners." So my paraphrasing isn't that far off.

Also in my paraphrase I have Dogen lament that Chinese Buddhists in his time said stuff like, "We don't remember even one or two past lives. But the old man / wild fox in the story knew five hundred! So he must have been super-enlightened. Maybe he was reborn as a fox in order to enter the animal realm as an enlightened being so he could teach animals the truth."

I just want to note that the direct translation of the last sentence in that quotation had me stumped. The Nishijima/Cross version is, "He goes forward among alien beings and, for the present, lets the wheel turn." Other translations are similarly baffling. But the translation by Nishiyama and Stevens makes better sense. It says, "As an enlightened being he entered the animal world to fulfill a vow to save all creatures." That is far easier to understand than any direct translation!

The reason other translators' versions get so confusing is that this line is actually a quotation from an old poem whose point, according to a footnote in the Nishijima/Cross translation, is "our efforts to order our lives are always in vain, so we should live freely and independently without worrying about cause and effect." Dogen is refuting that attitude, by the way. But if you don't know that this is a quotation from some old poem, the line is just confusing. The Shasta Abbey translation makes it explicit that Dogen is referring to this poem. Points go to them!

Right after this, Dogen says that just having the power to recall past lives doesn't mean you understand anything about the truth. I really appreciate his saying that. I've often wondered why people are so impressed by so-called paranormal abilities like recalling past lives and suchlike.

I remember, when I was in college, watching some people who were supposedly able to channel disembodied spirits. It was entertaining, but those disembodied spirits didn't seem to be particularly wise. In fact, every time I've seen anyone who claimed to channel the dead or recall past lives or bring forth messages from aliens or anything else along those lines, they never seem to say anything very interesting. Even if their claims are real, so what? Thank you, Dogen, for calling bullshit on that.

After this, Dogen quotes Nagarjuna as saying, "If you deny cause and effect, then there is no present or future." My paraphrase is close to Nishijima and Cross here. Tanahashi has Nagarjuna saying,

"If you deny cause and effect...you negate this present life as well as any future lives." There is no explicit reference to rebirth in the original. It just says *konsei* (今世), which means "now world," and *gosei* (後世), which means "future world." No other translations I've consulted see this as a reference to rebirth.

Anyway, I find this line interesting. The very existence of anything we can call "the present" or "the future," as well as anything we can call "the past," is a confirmation that the law of cause and effect is real. *Time* and *cause and effect* are actually two names for the very same thing. Trippy, huh?

In the story about Genkaku, I have Genkaku say, "Thoughtless ideas about emptiness negate the belief in cause and effect. People who believe such ideas get loose with their ethics and make a lot of mistakes, and then they end up in a bad way."

Tanahashi's version of this line is, "Carefree views of emptiness ignore cause and effect, and invite endless calamity." That's pretty much what other translations say. I added some words to clarify what I think it means.

The idea of emptiness is one of those really tough parts of Buddhism. It's an important teaching, but it's hard to present it so that it doesn't end up being misunderstood. Lately I've been trying out using the word *silence* instead of *emptiness*. Kobun Chino Roshi preferred the word *nothing*. But any way you phrase it, people will still misconstrue it.

The basic idea is that no explanation of the way things work is ever truly adequate. Therefore, one way to think of it is to consider everything as a manifestation of emptiness, or silence, or nothing. But it's easy to misinterpret that as meaning that everything is meaningless and therefore we can do whatever the hell we want. That's clearly not the teaching of Buddhism, which, as we've seen, has a very strong ethical basis. But still, lots of people have misinterpreted Buddhism that way for just about as long as there has been Buddhism. It continues to be an issue even now.

Moving along. As I usually do with poems, I have completely destroyed the poem by Wanshi that Dogen quotes after this part. Here's the Nishijima/Cross translation of the poem:

"One foot of water and a one-fathom wave. / [What happened] five hundred lives ago is of no consequence. / Even as [people] discuss 'not falling' and 'not being unclear,' / Still they are forcing themselves into nests of entanglement. / Ha! Ha! Ha! Do you understand, or not? / If you are free and easy / There is nothing to prevent me going 'Ta! Ta! Wa! Wa!' / Gods sing, spirits dance, and music naturally plays. / In between hand claps, a chorus of hoorays." Other translations are similar.

After Wanshi's poem, we get some lines that explicitly refer to the concept of rebirth / reincarnation. That's in the original, too, and appears in all the translations. I take these references with a grain of salt, especially given that Dogen seems to refute the idea of rebirth/ reincarnation in other writings, such as "Bendowa" and "Genjo Koan." You're free to interpret it any way you choose. As I mentioned earlier, you can read my opinions on this stuff in my book *Don't Be a Jerk*. Basically I'm agnostic on the subject, but I see some evidence that Dogen may have believed in some version of rebirth.

Back to Dogen's essay. The next thing we get is that poem by Kokugon, which I mutilated, of course. The Tanahashi translation goes:

"A fish swims making the water murky / A bird flies, shedding its feathers / The ultimate mirror is difficult to escape / The great void is boundless / Once you go, you go endlessly / By virtue of causation, the one who practices completely / lives five hundred lifetimes / Thunder cracks the mountains and storms shake the ocean / The color of purified gold does not change."

About the ultimate mirror, a footnote in the Nishijima/Cross translation says, "A mirror symbolizes a standard, a criterion, or a law — in this case, used as a concrete simile for the law of cause and effect." And about gold not changing color, Nishijima and Cross explain the meaning in a footnote that says, "This world is very changeable, but at the same time, it has an immutable essence."

They translate Dogen's comment at the end of the poem as, "Even this poem of praise has a tendency toward negation of cause and effect. At the same time, it has a tendency toward the eternity view." The Nishiyama/Stevens translation of the same line is a bit easier to follow: "Even this verse contains contradictions: it denies the principle of causality at one point, while it affirms eternity in another." In a footnote to this line, Nishijima and Cross say, "In general, *joken*, 'eternity view,' and *danken*, 'cutting-off view,' may be interpreted as traditional expressions of the two extreme views that modern philosophy calls idealism (championed by Hegel) and materialism (championed by Marx)."

I have to admit I find that poem and Dogen's comment hard to follow. I don't get why he even put that poem in the piece. This and the poem that follows must be two of the thirty-odd commentaries on the story that Dogen mentions. But even so, why reproduce the poem in its entirety, only to dismiss it in a single sentence? I'm afraid Dogen just loses me here, and all I can do is report to you what Nishijima and Cross have to say about it.

Let's keep going. My version of the next poem has even more forced rhymes than the others. Sorry! Here is the Nishijima/Cross translation: "*Not falling* and *not being unclear*/Are stones and clods/Met along the path by any rice paddy/Having crushed the silver mountain/I clap my hands and laugh, ha! ha!, in every situation/In Minshū [a.k.a Ming] there lived that foolish Happy Buddha."

Again, Dogen reproduces the poem, only to refute it. In their footnotes Nishijima and Cross give us a clue as to why this poem was included. They say, "Master Daie Sōkō (1089–1163 CE), [was the] successor of Master Engo Kokugon. Master Sōkō was a leading proponent of so-called kōan Zen, as opposed to mokushō [silent illumination] Zen of Sōkō's contemporary, Master Wanshi Shōgaku. Master Dōgen often praised Master Wanshi as an eternal buddha (see, for example, [Dogen's essay] *Zazenshin*), but strongly criticized Master Daie Sōkō (see, for example, [Dogen's essays] *Sesshin-sesshō* or *Jishō-zanmai*)."

There is a lot of cross talk in Zen circles about whether Dogen practiced and taught what folks these days call "koan Zen." This is the kind of Zen in which your teacher gives you a tricky question like, "What is the sound of one hand clapping?" or "If a tree falls on a mime does he make a sound?" and you meditate on it. Then you're supposed to go to your master and present your answer.

Dogen did not teach this sort of "koan Zen." Period. End of debate. Forever.

I have no idea why this is even a question. Dogen wrote very extensively about what kind of Zen he *did* practice and teach. He is abundantly clear about it, especially in his essay "Fukanzazengi," which is easy to find online and which I paraphrased in my book *Don't Be a Jerk*. There is nothing in that or, indeed, in any of Dogen's writing in which he recommends that anyone sit and contemplate a koan and then try to answer it for their teacher. Those who claim that he did have to twist obscure things Dogen said into bizarre shapes to try to make their case and, even worse, they also have to completely ignore the things he very clearly said when he wrote pieces specifically about how to do zazen practice. If he practiced that way, why didn't he write about it? In all his thousands of pages of writings he just somehow forgot to mention it? I don't think I'll ever understand why this is up for debate.

It is true that Dogen used koans extensively in his teachings. This essay that we've been looking at is one example of how he used them. He talked them through and then gave explanations of what he thought they meant. It's safe to assume he also had discussions with individual students about their meaning. So yes, Dogen did use koans in his teachings. But the idea that he assigned them to students for them to answer is absurd, and it's annoying that I even have to waste time refuting it.

End of rant.

So anyway, that was the first of Dogen's commentaries on the koan of Hyakujo's Fox that I want to look at in this book. As you've seen, the conclusion is as straightforward as can be. Denying cause and effect is wrong. Affirming it is right. No ambiguity. In fact, this might be one of the few places where Dogen comes off as almost completely unambiguous.

The other version is not quite as clear-cut. Join me in looking at it next, won't you?

8. WAIT! WHAT WAS THE DEAL WITH CAUSE AND EFFECT AGAIN?
Dai Shugyo
Great Practice

THE FOLLOWING ESSAY, "Great Practice," was written in 1244. We don't know the date of "Deep Belief in Cause and Effect," the essay I wrote about in the previous chapter. Ejo, Dogen's foremost student, copied it in 1255, two years after Dogen died. Scholars speculate that "Deep Belief in Cause and Effect" was written about six or so years after the essay we're about to look at, so maybe 1250, or possibly 1251. They are both commentaries on the same old Buddhist story "Hyakujo's Fox." Yet in them Dogen seems to draw opposing conclusions about the meaning of the story.

Since "Deep Belief in Cause and Effect" was never finished, we don't really know why Dogen wrote it. The easiest answer would be that he changed his mind about the meaning of the story of Hyakujo's Fox and wrote "Deep Belief" as a replacement for "Great Practice" but then died before he could make the substitution. This would make things neat and tidy. Problem is, there is no evidence to support such a conclusion.

As I mentioned in the previous chapter, as far as we know two versions of *Shobogenzo* may have existed while Dogen was alive, one consisting of seventy-five chapters and another consisting of

twelve.* It appears that Ejo compiled the seventy-five-chapter version and that this version was approved by Dogen. The essay we'll
be looking at in this chapter is number sixty-eight in the seventy-
five-chapter version.

The essay we looked at in the previous chapter, "Deep Belief
in Cause and Effect," though it was never finished, is in the twelve-
chapter version. The fact that it contains unfinished pieces is one of
the things that cast doubt on the idea that the twelve-chapter version
was compiled during Dogen's lifetime. It's possible it was but that it
was a work in progress. Again, nobody really knows.

So there is some evidence that both the seventy-five-chapter
version *and* the twelve-chapter version — many of whose chapters appear to directly contradict things he wrote in the seventy-
five-chapter version — had Dogen's approval. What on God's
green Earth was he thinking?

Steven Heine wrote a whole book about Hyakujo's Fox called
*Shifting Shape, Shaping Text: Philosophy and Folklore in the Fox
Kōan*. How nerdy can you get? Anyway, here's how Heine explains
the matter of the differences between the seventy-five and twelve-
chapter editions of *Shobogenzo*: "The conventional interpretation,
which relies on the theory of two levels of truth, is that the message
reflecting a nondual religious vision is the same [in both of Dogen's
essays about Hyakujo's Fox] but the earlier [seventy-five-chapter]
version is appropriate for a philosophically advanced monk who
could appreciate the subtleties of nonduality whereas the former

---

* By the way, there were also versions of *Shobogenzo* with sixty and twenty-eight
chapters, and those are very old, too. Plus other versions with other numbers
of chapters. I'm leaving out a lot of historical details here. You're welcome!
If you're a masochist and need to know all the gory and complicated minu-
tiae, check out an essay called "Textual Genealogies of Dōgen" by William
Bodiford in a book called *Dōgen: Textual and Historical Studies*, edited by
Steven Heine. It's listed in the bibliography at the back of this book.

[twelve-chapter version] is appropriate for a novice only able to grasp the literal meaning of karma."

This theory has it that, late in his career, Dogen found himself teaching a lot of young monks with very little background in the subtler aspects of Zen philosophy, as well as laypeople who would have known even less. He was worried that stuff like the chapter you're about to read would be misunderstood by these youngsters and laypeople. So he wrote more straightforward versions of some of his earlier teachings, like the one in the previous chapter of this book, for them. Those straightforward versions were gathered as the twelve-chapter edition of *Shobogenzo*, either by Ejo, after Dogen died, or perhaps by Dogen himself, though he never quite finished the job.

Anyhow, scholars will probably debate this stuff until forever. It's one of those unresolvable questions that certain types of people love to argue about. If you want my guess, I'd say that Dogen was not attempting to rewrite his earlier stuff, nor did he have any kind of major change of mind regarding his philosophical outlook. It is true that lots of his later pieces seem to take positions that are almost polar opposites of his earlier views. Yet if you read his earlier pieces you see that they even contradict themselves. My personal guess, for whatever it's worth, is that he intended for both his contradictory commentaries on Hyakujo's Fox to be published as part of his complete *Shobogenzo*. Let me explain why I think so.

Dogen, I think, would agree with Walt Whitman, who famously said in his poem "Song of Myself," "Do I contradict myself? Very well, then I contradict myself. I am large, I contain multitudes." Contradiction is actually part of Dogen's philosophical outlook.

Gudo Nishijima summed it up like this:

After I had read the *Shōbōgenzō* many, many times, I began to see that with his use of contradictions, Master Dōgen was pointing to an area which was outside the area of intellectual debate; he was pointing to existence outside the rational and intellectual area. When I was young it was difficult for me to believe in a world that was different both from the world of my thoughts and also from the world of my perceptions. Master Dōgen talks about the ideal world of theory and the world of matter as we perceive it. But he uses these two viewpoints to point to or describe the real world, the reality in which we exist. And after reading the *Shōbōgenzō* I too began to see that the world in which I existed was neither the world of ideas nor the world of objects and perceptions, but something different from both.

The first commentary on Hyakujo's Fox we looked at is pretty straightforward and reasonably easy to follow. The one we're about to look at is very different. The original version of this essay begins with the story of Hyakujo's Fox, told in the same words as it is in "Deep Belief in Cause and Effect." The version of the fox story that I'm including below is exactly the same as the one I included in the last chapter, just as it is in Dogen's original. You can skip over it if you want.

Another interesting fact I learned while researching this chapter is that Hyakujo was the author of some of the earliest codes of monastic conduct, as well as rules about how and when Buddhist ceremonies should be performed. Dogen alludes to this in his commentary. He doesn't state it outright, but his original audience would have been aware of this aspect of Hyakujo's history and it would be a factor in how they understood some of what Dogen says.

Also, one of the most famous stories about Hyakujo is that when he was very old he still insisted on working, just like any other monk. When his young monks hid his tools, he refused to eat, saying, "One day no work, one day no food." That doesn't have much to do with this essay, but it's a neat story and says a lot about the Zen attitude.

Anyhow, here's Dogen's crazy commentary on Hyakujo's Fox.

Whenever the Zen master of Hyakujo Mountain gave a talk, this old guy showed up and stood at the back, just listening. Whenever the talks were over, the old guy just sort of wandered away. But one day he stayed behind after all the monks had left. So the master said, "Who is this person standing in front of me?"

The old man said, "I'm not actually a person. Millions of years ago, in the age of Kashyapa Buddha, I used to live on this mountain, where I was the Zen master. One day a student asked me if a person of great practice was subject to the law of cause and effect. I said that such a person does not fall into cause and effect. Since then I have been reborn as a wild fox for five hundred lifetimes. Now I'd like to ask you, master, to help me out and give me a word of transformation to free me from the body of a wild fox. Does a person of great practice fall into cause and effect, or what?"

The master said, "The law of cause and effect is as clear as noonday."

Upon hearing these words, the old man finally got it. He bowed to the master and said, "I'm free from the body of a wild fox. But can you do me a big favor and perform the funeral rites for a dead monk?"

The master then called the monks together and said, "After lunch we're gonna perform a funeral for a deceased monk!"

The monks were pretty shocked because nobody among them was even sick.

After lunch the master went behind a rock and with his stick pulled out the body of a dead wild fox. They cremated the body and performed the ceremony just as if they were cremating a monk.

Later that evening, the master told the monks what had happened. His student Obaku said, "The old guy was asked for a word of transformation and gave the wrong answer, then he fell into the body of a wild fox for five hundred lifetimes. What would he have become if he hadn't made any mistakes?"

The master said, "Come up here, kid, and I'll tell you."

Obaku stepped forward and smacked the master in the face.

The master clapped his hands and laughed, saying, "I thought Bodhidharma had a red beard. But you just said that the guy with the red beard is Bodhidharma!"

The old man / wild fox asks the current Zen master of Hyakujo Mountain, "Does a person of great practice fall into cause and effect, or what?" So the main point of the story of Hyakujo's Fox is "Great Practice."

The old man / wild fox says that Hyakujo's mountain existed in the age of Kashyapa Buddha, the Buddha who lived millions of years before Shakyamuni. That, in itself, is a clue to understanding the story.

Even though that's so, it's not the same mountain, nor is it a different mountain. The mountain is not the accumulation of what it was in the past. The mountain that existed in the past has not become the mountain that exists now. The present mountain didn't used to be the mountain in Kashyapa Buddha's time.

Yet the old man / wild fox begins by saying, "I used to live on this mountain." That itself is a fundamental question.

The relationship between the old man / wild fox and Hyakujo applies to all of us today. You should ask the same question the old man / wild fox asks. What you do right now is not what you did in the past, yet it is related to what you did in the past. If you do two things at the same time, you are still doing just one thing, even if it's a combination of two or more things. You only live in this very moment, and you can only ever do just one thing.

The old man / wild fox asks, "Does a person of great practice fall into cause and effect, or what?" Don't be in a rush to give your answer! For the first time in hundreds or even thousands of years the question comes from this wild fox — namely me — to you wild foxes listening to me. This is a very rare thing, for sure.

Great practice and *cause and effect* are really the same thing. Asking about one is the same as asking about the other. Real causes always have real effects. The effect is always exactly equal to the cause. So it makes no real sense to talk about falling into cause and effect, or about being unclear about cause and effect. If the answer, "They don't fall into cause and effect" is a mistake, then the answer, "The law of cause and effect is as clear as noonday" might also be a mistake.

When we admit that mistakes are mistakes and move on, there is still being reborn as (literally, "falling into") the body of a wild fox, and there is getting free of the body of a wild fox. It's entirely possible that the answer, "They don't fall into cause and effect" was a mistake back in Kashyapa Buddha's day but isn't a mistake here in the age of Shakyamuni Buddha. And it's also possible that the answer, "The law of cause and effect is as clear as noonday" frees someone from the body of a wild fox nowadays but that things were different in Kashyapa Buddha's time.

The old man / wild fox says he was reborn as (literally, fell into the body of) a wild fox for five hundred lifetimes. So what the holy heck does that mean? It's not as if there was an empty wild fox body that lured the old man into falling into it. And the old man was not originally a wild fox. The idea that the old man's soul left his body and was reborn in the body of a wild fox is not Buddhism. And a wild fox didn't just jump out of the bushes and swallow the old man.

If you say the old man changed into a wild fox, then he must have gotten rid of his former body so that he could fall into the fox body. But a Zen master can't be replaced by a wild fox!

How could cause and effect work like that? Cause and effect doesn't sit around waiting for people to make it happen. Effects follow causes naturally. Even if the answer, "They don't fall into cause and effect" is wrong, the person who says it doesn't always get reborn as a wild fox. Hell, if being reborn in the body of a wild fox was the inevitable consequence of giving a wrong answer the world would be full of nothing but wild foxes! But that's not the case. There have been a lot more far worse answers than, "They don't fall into cause and effect." Plenty of people don't even believe in cause and effect in the first place. So you can't say that answering questions wrongly causes somebody to be reborn as a wild fox.

The story doesn't say what happened after the old man got rid of his wild fox body. But I think it's safe to assume there was a pearl of wisdom within him.

There are folks who don't understand Buddhism who say that once a person gets rid of the body of a wild fox he returns to the great ocean of original enlightenment. That's just poppycock! If you say that a wild fox is something other than enlightened, then there is no such thing as original enlightenment. If you say you become enlightened upon getting rid of the body of a wild fox, then you're saying that it wasn't the wild fox who got enlightened. That doesn't make sense, either.

The story says that Hyakujo said something and the old man who'd been a wild fox for five hundred lifetimes got free. There is an important principle in that. If you say there are some kinds of words of truth that can free people, then all of nature must be repeating those words over and over, 24/7 all around the world, since nature always demonstrates, and therefore speaks of, the truth. But in the past, the old man / wild fox didn't get free. He got free when Hyakujo spoke to him.

However, if you say Hyakujo's words had some kind of magical power, that is not the philosophy of Buddhism. If you say that nature doesn't speak words of transformation, that would be the same as saying Hyakujo couldn't even open his mouth to say a single thing.

Plus, lots of masters of the past have said that "not falling into" and "clear as noonday" are the same thing. But they haven't clearly understood falling into the body of a wild fox and getting free of the body of a wild fox right down to the center of their bones. When the head ain't right, the tail ain't right, either!

The old man / wild fox says he fell into the body of a wild fox for five hundred lifetimes. But what fell and what did it fall into? What is the subject and what is the object? At the very moment this falling happens, what form and what color does the eternal universe have? Why should a simple string of words like "doesn't fall into cause and effect" cause five hundred repetitions? What actual place did the body of a wild fox that Hyakujo pulled out from behind a rock with his stick come from?

To say "doesn't fall into cause and effect" is to fall into the body of a wild fox, and to hear "cause and effect is as clear as noonday" is to get free from that wild fox body. These instances are exactly the causes and effects of the wild fox, the reality of being a wild fox.

Even so, lots of people since long, long ago have said that "they don't fall into cause and effect" is a saying that refutes cause and effect and that's why the guy who said it fell into the body of a wild fox. There's no reason to believe that's true. People who say it don't know what they're talking about. Even if the old man said, "They don't fall into cause and effect," his great practice could not delude anyone and he couldn't refute cause and effect.

Some other folks say that the meaning of "cause and effect is as clear as noonday" is to not ignore cause and effect. They say great practice transcends cause and effect and gets rid of the body of a wild fox. I give that answer a B-plus.

So in the time of Kashyapa Buddha the old man lived on the mountain. In the time of Shakyamuni Buddha the old man lives on the mountain. The former body and the present body are like the faces of the sun and moon. He covered up the ghost of a wild fox and he manifested the ghost of a wild fox.

How could a wild fox know five hundred of its past lives, anyway? Foxes don't even remember a single lifetime, let alone five hundred of them. When a fox knows its own falling down for five hundred lives, that's the real point. There's stuff that a wild fox knows and stuff that a wild fox doesn't know. Body and knowing do not appear and disappear together, so how can you count five hundred lifetimes? Maybe the whole "five hundred lifetimes" deal is just made up.

If you say that the wild fox knows by using something other than its own intelligence, then you can't really say the wild fox knows anything. And anyhow, who else could possibly know these five hundred lifetimes on behalf of the wild fox?

If you don't understand knowing or not knowing, we can't really talk about falling into the body of a wild fox. And if there's no falling into the body of a wild fox, well, then how can there be any getting free of the body of a wild fox, either?

And if it's neither falling nor getting free, then how can there be any old man who did those things? And if there's no old man who did those things, how could there be any Hyakujo to meet him? You can't just accept this stuff. You have to look at it in detail for yourself. Use your reasoning, and you won't be fooled by the bad explanations of this story that have been around for hundreds of years.

Then the old man / wild fox asks Hyakujo to perform the ceremony for a deceased monk.

What the *what*?

How come nobody is ever surprised about that part? How can a dead fox be regarded as a monk? He never took the Buddhist precepts, he never attended a single meditation retreat. How could he possibly be a monk? Come on! If you do a monk's funeral for a dead fox, why not just give everybody a monk's funeral? That's not the Buddhist Way.

Then we are told that Hyakujo does the formal cremation ceremony. Is that even true? Personally, I doubt it. I mean, there is a whole big ceremony for a monk's funeral; there are all sorts of rites and rituals. It's not just some random kind of thing.

Even if there really was a dead fox under a rock, as the story says, how could such a creature be a full monk? Who would know that the fox really was the past master of the mountain?

Don't mock the ancient principles of Buddhist practice by just accepting this story as accurate. We monks are trying to uphold the high standards and values of our ancestors. If someone makes the kind of inappropriate request of you that the old man / wild fox makes of Hyakujo in this story, don't do it.

Don't be led by sentiment or follow vulgar secular customs. It's hard to even hear about the Buddhist Way in any form, let alone get a chance to be a monk. This is especially true for us in Japan, where true Buddhism is super-rare. We need to revere Buddhist customs as if they were valuable jewels.

Those who don't understand the relative importance of things are unhappy. They lack the wisdom of five hundred years and lack the wisdom of a thousand years.

Even so, we need to be able to encourage ourselves and encourage others. Maybe all you've been able to get from the Buddhist tradition is to learn how to bow, or maybe you've just done meditation a single time. Even if that's all it ever adds up to, you should still celebrate your good fortune. Do you know how few people even get that far? It's not easy and it's not common.

Those who don't have the right mind-set won't get any virtue or benefit, even if they should happen to encounter a thousand Buddhas. They might act like they're all "into Buddhism" or whatever, but you'll get no evidence of that if you listen to the crap they say.

To sum it all up, if somebody who isn't a monk — even if it's someone real important like a king or whatever — asks for the funeral rites of a dead monk, don't do it. Tell them to come back after they've done all the necessary work to become a fully ordained monk. It doesn't do any good to offer that kind of honor to someone who is still stuck in the world of trying to acquire fame and money. It defiles everything that being a monk is about.

The story then says, "Later that evening, the master told the monks what had happened." That's pretty ambiguous! What sort of discussion did they have? It sounds like he must have told the monks that the old man got rid of his wild fox body after five hundred lifetimes. Should we count those as five hundred human lifetimes? Or should they be counted as five hundred fox lifetimes? Should we count these as lifetimes spent pursuing the truth?

And anyway, how could a wild fox even see Hyakujo? Wild foxes only see the ghosts of wild foxes. Hyakujo sees the Buddhist ancestors. That's why Zen Master Hojo wrote:

> Hyakujo met with a wild fox
> When it asked him a question he was deeply distressed
> Now I ask you, my monks in your socks
> Have you spat out the wild fox's silly mess?

So a "wild fox" is like the eye of Hyakujo's intimate experience. Being able to spit out the wild fox's silly mess is how you speak a word of transformation like a Buddha. The very moment we do so, we get free of the wild fox, get free of Hyakujo, get free of the old man, and get free of the entire body of the universe.

Then Obaku asks, "The old guy was asked for a word of transformation and gave the wrong answer, then he fell into the body of a wild fox for five hundred lifetimes. What would he have become if he hadn't made any mistakes?"

This question is the actualization of the words of the Buddhist ancestors. And Obaku went on to become one of the greatest Zen masters of all time. Even so, the old man / wild fox never actually said he gave a mistaken answer. So why does Obaku just casually ask the question as if he did?

If Obaku means that the old man's answer caused him to be reborn as a wild fox five hundred times, then Obaku didn't really understand Hyakujo. It's almost like Obaku never researched the Buddhist ancestors' mistaken answers or studied their answers that are beyond mistakes. Keep in mind here that the old man / wild fox never says anything about giving a mistaken answer, nor does Hyakujo say anything about the old man / wild fox's answer being a mistake.

However, using five hundred bodies of a wild fox, the old man lived on the mountain and expressed himself for the benefit of his students. The pointy hairs of the wild fox's skin are liberated. Because of this, Hyakujo exists as a regular old stinky person. When you think about him, he's sort of like someone in the actual process of getting free of the body of a wild fox.

Falling into the body of a wild fox and getting free of it are what Obaku is referring to when he asks, "What would he have become if he hadn't made any mistakes?" Cause and effect speaks words for others. That in itself is great practice.

If Obaku were to ask me, "What would he have become if he hadn't made any mistakes?" I'd say he still would have fallen into the body of a wild fox.

If Obaku asked me why, I'd say, "You ghost of a wild fox!"

But it still wouldn't be a matter of mistakes or nonmistakes. Don't just assume that Obaku asked the right question.

If Obaku asked me again, "What would he have become if he hadn't made any mistakes?" I'd ask him if he could even touch his own face. Then I'd ask him if he had gotten free of the body of a wild fox. Then I'd ask him if he'd have told the student that people of great practice don't fall into cause and effect.

But Hyakujo said, "Come up here, kid, and I'll tell you." This is his way of saying that what the old man would have become is just *this*.

Obaku steps up. He's totally forgotten the past and he's oblivious to the future. When he slaps Hyakujo, that slap is endless transformations of a wild fox.

Hyakujo clapped his hands and laughed and said, "I thought Bodhidharma had a red beard. But you just said that the guy with the red beard is Bodhidharma!" There's no such thing as complete perfection. What Hyakujo said is just 80 or 90 percent of realization. Whenever you say there's 80 or 90 percent of realization, there isn't really 80 or 90 percent of realization yet. And whenever you say there's complete perfection, there's not really 80 or 90 percent realization. No matter how good your description of reality is, it's still just a description. And there are always multiple ways to accurately describe the same reality.

Here's a little poem I wrote about this:

Hyakujo's expression goes out all around
But he's still inside the wild fox's grotto
Obaku's got his feet firmly planted on the ground
But like a mantis he hesitates a lot, oh
Slap and clap are one, get that through your head
they are one and they are never, ever two
Bodhidharma's beard indeed is very red
and the red beard's Bodhidharma, not a kangaroo
—Presented to the audience at Yoshimine Temple
in Echizen Province on March 9, 1244

The very first line in Dogen's commentary is *jikon genjo no koan, kore daishugyo nari* (而今現成の公案、これ大修行なり). Sharp-eyed readers will spot the words *genjo* and *koan*, which refer back to Dogen's most famous piece of writing, "Genjo Koan." Nishijima and Cross translate this opening line as, "The kōan realized just now is 'great practice' itself." Tanahashi's version goes, "The fundamental point actualized just now is great practice."

I went into the meaning of *genjo* at length in my book *Don't Be a Jerk*. The first character in *genjo, gen* (現), means "the present," "existence," "reality," or "consciousness," depending on context. The second character, *jo* (成), means "to turn into" or "become" or simply "is." Nishijima and Cross translate it as "realize." Others have translated it as "manifesting." Still others just leave it untranslated.

In *Don't Be a Jerk*, I said Dogen made up the word *genjo*. That was incorrect.* The word was in use before Dogen's time, but its use was, and still is, pretty much confined to a small group of Zen Buddhist writers and speakers. It's not a word you'll find in a standard Japanese-to-English dictionary. In Dogen's usage *genjo* means the

---

* How many times will I be reborn as a wild fox for that?

actual moment when one puts the deepest truths of Buddhism into concrete action.

The phrase *daishugyo* (大修行), which also appears in the opening line of Dogen's commentary, means "great practice." It is the title and subject of this essay and relates to the question the wild fox / Zen master asks the then-current master of Hyakujo Mountain, "Does a person of great practice fall into cause and effect?"

In my version of the essay Dogen says that the fact that the old man / wild fox says that Hyakujo Mountain existed in the age of Kashyapa Buddha and still exists now is in itself "a clue to understanding the story." What Dogen actually says instead of "clue" is *ichitengo* (一転語). This literally means "one turning word" or "one word of transformation."

There's an idea in Zen circles that certain words or phrases, when spoken by just the right person to just the right other person in just the right circumstances, have the power to change someone's entire outlook. These are called "turning words."

These are not magic words, though. It's not like you just say them and, presto!, enlightenment! But you can study them as clues to understanding why they might have worked for the people for whom they made a profound difference. In my paraphrase I have Dogen say, "So it makes no real sense to talk about falling into cause and effect, or about being unclear about cause and effect." This is because cause and effect doesn't care whether or not you believe in it. A lit match will burn your fingers, even if you believe it won't.

In the original text, Dogen does not specifically point out that Kashyapa Buddha lived millions of years before Shakyamuni. But since his audience would have known that and my audience probably doesn't, I added it in there. I didn't mention that in the previous chapter because it wasn't as relevant as it is in this one, in which that part of the story falls under Dogen's careful scrutiny.

In Dogen's time, most people didn't have any concept of how

long mountains existed. As far as they knew, mountains lasted forever. Nishijima Roshi sometimes speculated that Dogen intuitively understood that the Earth does not remain eternally the same, as most people in his time thought. He cited lines like Dogen's statement about mountains walking in the Mountains and Waters Sutra as examples. Japan being an earthquake- and typhoon-prone country, it is quite possible Dogen realized that, over long stretches of time, entire mountains might move or even disappear and that islands like Japan could sink into the sea.

But Dogen is also indicating a more philosophical position. It is a cornerstone of Buddhism that nothing ever remains the same. From moment to moment we newly appear in the universe, and, in fact, the entire universe bursts into existence and disappears thousands of times each second. In that sense, even without speculating about Dogen's possible nascent understanding of plate tectonics, it's still absurd from a Buddhist standpoint to say the mountain on which the old man / wild fox met Hyakujo is the same one that existed millions of years ago.

Yet there is still some kind of continuity from the past to the present, and we all know that. This is another one of those paradoxes Buddhism likes to play with. You are not the same person you were two years ago — or even two seconds ago. But if you killed someone two years ago, you should still go to jail for it. That paradox is the law of cause and effect. And that's what this whole essay is about.

In my paraphrase I have Dogen say, "The mountain is not the accumulation of what it was in the past." What Dogen actually said is more directly translated as "the mountain is not three and three before, and not three and three after." In a footnote, Nishijima and Cross explain this by saying, "Three and three before, three and three after, suggests for example the differences in the mountain in different seasons: white in winter, green in spring, blue in summer, yellow and red in autumn, etc. The real Hyakujo Mountain here and now is beyond any accumulation of past impressions."

Buddhist ideas about causality are difficult because they don't take for granted a lot of things most of us assume are true. And there is also that matter of the inherent contradictions of reality. As I said a few seconds ago, we are not the same people we were even a few seconds ago. And yet I have the same haircut I had ten seconds ago. My first teacher used to use an old Buddhist metaphor to explain this. He'd ask, "If you use one candle to light another candle and then immediately blow out the first candle, is it the same flame?" You can't really answer yes or no. It's both and it's neither. It's a contradiction, but it's also a fact.

I changed a lot of stuff in the paragraph that begins, "The relationship between the old man / wild fox and Hyakujo applies to all of us today." The translations all differ here, and the original Japanese is also confusing. My version of the paragraph is a mash-up of the Nishijima/Cross, Tanahashi, and Nishiyama/Stevens translations, with a bit of my own interpretation thrown in. I suggest you consult those or the original Japanese if you feel you need a second opinion.

The line "For the first time in hundreds or even thousands of years the question comes from this wild fox — namely me — to you wild foxes listening to me" is also my interpretation of Dogen's very convoluted Japanese, mixed in with what various translations say. I believe I'm giving you a true sense of what Dogen means. But, as always, I don't insist you take my word for it if you have any doubts. Specifically, in the original, Dogen doesn't directly say he's referring to himself and his audience. It just seems that he's strongly implying that he is, so I put that in there.

What I've paraphrased as "when we admit mistakes are mistakes and move on" is actually *shosaku shusaku* (将錯就錯), which is a Chinese expression meaning something like "to muddle through after making a mistake." Tanahashi translates this phrase as "when mistakes surpass mistakes," which sorta says the same thing but in a confusing way. Nishijima and Cross say "when mistakes are put in their place as mistakes," which is also a little awkward.*

Later in my paraphrase Dogen says, "Hell, if being reborn in the body of a wild fox was the inevitable consequence of giving a wrong answer the world would be full of nothing but wild foxes!" In the real essay, Dogen doesn't say "hell." But he does use the opportunity to take a shot at certain Zen masters who he thinks sometimes made big mistakes in their teachings, specifically Rinzai and Tokuzan and their followers. Then he goes on to say there would be tons of wild foxes since everybody gives wrong answers at some point in their lives. I decided the criticism of Rinzai and Tokuzan wasn't very relevant to an audience who, like me, barely knows anything about them or their teachings. But I make note of it here so I won't be accused of smoothing over some of Dogen's prickly nature concerning certain teachers.

In my paraphrase, Dogen says, "If you say that a wild fox is something other than enlightened, then there is no such thing as original enlightenment. If you say you become enlightened upon getting rid of the body of a wild fox, then you're saying that it wasn't the wild fox who got enlightened." Here is the Nishijima/Cross translation of that section: "If we say that a wild fox is not the original essence and that there is no original enlightenment in a wild fox, that is not the Buddha-Dharma. If we say that when we realize the great enlightenment we have departed from and discarded the body of a wild fox, then it would not be the wild fox's great enlightenment, and we would make the wild fox serve no purpose. We should never say so."

Nishijima and Cross add a footnote:

[As for] *Hongaku* [the word they translate as "original enlightenment"], *hon* means "original" or "inherent." *Kaku* is the

---

* For those of you who've read my earlier books, this Chinese phrase is probably what Shunryu Suzuki, author of *Zen Mind, Beginner's Mind*, was thinking of when he famously misquoted Dogen as saying, "Our life is one continuous mistake."

Chinese character used to represent the Sanskrit *bodhi*, which means a buddha's state of intuitive wisdom, or enlightenment. In the Tendai sect the concepts *hongaku*, "inherent [or original] enlightenment," and *shikaku*, "initiated enlightenment," represent opposing views of the buddha nature. It is said that this opposition set up a conflict in Master Dōgen's mind during his teenage years as a monk in the Tendai sect. The conflict was finally resolved when Master Tendō Nyojō recommended Master Dōgen to "just sit."

The idea of original enlightenment (*hongaku*) has become quite controversial in Japan lately. According to Noriaki Hakamaya (as translated by Steven Heine in his book about Hyakujo's Fox), "Although some interpret the doctrine of original enlightenment as a theory of equality because it claims to recognize the fundamental universal enlightenment of all people, in reality, this is a gross misunderstanding. In fact, the doctrine of original enlightenment, which in a facile way requires seeking out the fundamental unified ground of enlightenment, must be considered the primary source of (social) discrimination [in contemporary Japan]." Heine explains this position saying, "By denying causality…[the concept of original enlightenment] promotes a false sense of equality that mitigates the need for moral responsibility."

Certain Japanese Buddhists have used the doctrine of original enlightenment to promote Japanese nationalism and ethnic injustice against minorities in Japan. It is difficult for me to understand how you could use the doctrine this way. It seems that some interpret original enlightenment to mean that everyone is equal, so there's no reason to discriminate among people. Which sounds good so far. But certain misguided folks apparently see the idea of nondiscrimination as an excuse not to help those members of society who clearly fare worse than those in the majority and to take no responsibility for the way the majority sometimes steps all over the rights of minorities.

That just seems like a stupid way to interpret the idea of original

enlightenment, if you ask me. It only proves that, if you're an asshole, you can bend pretty much anything into a justification for being
an asshole. I don't think it's a problem inherent in the doctrine itself,
which just says that all people are originally enlightened, are originally Buddhas. To me that means you have to treat everyone with
dignity and respect, even if they're a member of a minority, and also
even if they have stupid ideas about original enlightenment.

Moving right along, in my paraphrase Dogen says, "If you say
that nature doesn't speak words of transformation, that would be
the same as saying Hyakujo couldn't even open his mouth to say
a single thing." Nishijima and Cross add a footnote that says, "In
other words, if the state of natural balance did not have in itself the
power to effect change, then Master Hyakujō would be powerless.
Hyakujō's action was conscious human intervention, and at the same
time it was natural."

The part after this where I have Dogen say, "I give that answer a
B-plus" in the Nishijima/Cross translation is, "Truly, this is eighty-
or ninety-percent realization of the eyes of learning in practice." In
other words, he gives that answer a B-plus.

That thing where I have Dogen say foxes don't even know one
lifetime, let alone five hundred, is me trying to make sense of a line
that Tanahashi translates as, "If you say that it knows five hundred
lifetimes with the intelligence of a wild fox, the wild fox's intelligence does not even know the matter of a single lifetime, much less
a life rammed into a wild fox's skin bag." Other translations are
equally confounding. I did what I could. I guess it means something
like what I wrote. Your guesses may vary.

A bit further down the page I have Dogen say, "Body and knowing do not appear and disappear together, so how can you count five
hundred lifetimes? Maybe the whole 'five hundred lifetimes' deal is
just made up." Here again the Japanese is hard to follow, and the
translations all say somewhat different things. What I'm giving you

is what I think it means. As always, there is a list of translations in the back of this book if you want to consult other versions.

If you ask me, though, in this section Dogen appears to be cautioning his readers not to take the story literally. This struck me as funny because it never would have occurred to me to take a story like this as an account of something that actually happened. Not even when I first read it and I was dumb as a box of rocks.

Still, even today, even in the West, some people actually do take the story of Hyakujo's Fox literally. I've met some of them and even argued with them. The mind boggles! Please don't you take this story literally, dear reader. That'd be like thinking Noah's flood really happened or that there was a real Adam and Eve. Of course, some people take those stories as fact, too. Stories like these are metaphors intended to emphasize a principle through fiction.

That being said, even though the Zen tradition often mercilessly mocks anyone who believes in the supernatural, it is common for Zen teachers to use stories that involve the supernatural to make philosophical points. They also use stories that they know are not factual. Hyakujo's Fox is just one example.

If you're talking about a true story, then you can talk about there being a single explanation for it. For example, most of the evidence involved with the assassination of John F. Kennedy indicates that Lee Harvey Oswald did it and that he acted alone. His motivations may never be clear, but the evidence all indicates that his motivations were personal and psychological, and that he wasn't an agent of the CIA or the KGB or anyone else. Some of you probably disagree, but perhaps you can put your disagreements aside to look at the point I'm trying to make with this admittedly controversial example.

The point is, when we sift through and examine the evidence of something that actually happened, like the assassination of JFK, we can draw some definite conclusions about it. However, if we are looking at a myth or a work of fiction, like Hyakujo's Fox, it becomes a little bit murky. When we talk about a novel, for example, we might ask what the story means to the person who wrote it. But lots of novelists insist that their interpretation of a novel that they themselves wrote is not necessarily the single, correct one.

That's also how it is with myths like Hyakujo's Fox. Someone must have made up the story, and whoever it was probably had a specific meaning in mind. Tradition has it that Hyakujo himself made it up. Whatever the case, the story then entered the collective human consciousness and got modified. So it doesn't really matter anymore what the original author of the story meant. Plus, there are a number of different versions of Hyakujo's Fox, and sometimes important details vary from version to version. We will never know exactly what the original said.

So Dogen isn't really presenting a conclusion based on evidence like he would if he were examining the assassination of JFK. He's presenting a philosophical interpretation of a myth. And he's using that myth to put forth his philosophy.

Anyway, let's keep going.

In my paraphrase I have Dogen say, "Those who don't understand the relative importance of things are unhappy. They lack the wisdom of five hundred years and lack the wisdom of a thousand years." My paraphrase doesn't deviate too much from the standard translation here. I'm unaware of anyone commenting on this line, but I think it's an important one.

When Dogen says that people "lack the wisdom of a thousand years," I believe he is talking about our ability to receive and benefit from the wisdom of those who came before us. There is no sense in revering old ideas just because they're old. However, there are ideas that have lasted for centuries because they have proven their usefulness to generation after generation. Buddhism represents one stream of such time-proven wisdom. Even though you still have to check it out for yourself, it is useful to allow the best wisdom of the past to inform you.

A little ways after that I have Dogen say, "Those who don't

have the right mind-set won't get any virtue or benefit even if they should happen to encounter a thousand Buddhas. They might act like they're all 'into Buddhism' or whatever, but you'll get no evidence of that if you listen to the crap they say." The Kaz Tanahashi version of this line is, "Those who lack this heart will not possess a single virtue or acquire any benefit even if they were to encounter the emanation of a thousand Buddhas. There are people outside the way who have been mistakenly entrusted with the buddha dharma. Though they may sound like they are learned in the buddha dharma, the buddha dharma they expound lacks the fruits of realization."

Dogen is probably talking about people in his time who became monks without really understanding the deeper philosophy of Buddhism. In our day, though, I think it can also refer to that huge mass of people you often encounter, particularly online, that pretend they know loads about Buddhism but don't really know a damn thing. They've read a *Wikipedia* entry or two, but they've never actually practiced. You have my permission to ignore that stuff.

Then we have Dogen asking about what Hyakujo told his monks concerning his encounter with the old man / wild fox. In my version he says, "It sounds like he must have told the monks that the old man got rid of his wild fox body after five hundred lifetimes. Should we count those as five hundred human lifetimes? Or should they be counted as five hundred fox lifetimes?"

That's based on the Nishijima/Cross translation, which is pretty close to what the others say here. I was curious what Nishijima and Cross were translating as "count," so I checked the original. The word Dogen used is *sansu* (算数). In contemporary Japanese this means "arithmetic." In Dogen's usage here it means "to calculate." Dogen then asks how they should be counted with the question, *butsudo no gotoku sansu suru ka* (仏道のごとく算数するか). *Butsudo* is "Buddhist Way." *Gotoku* means "the same as." *Suru* is what you add to the word for arithmetic to turn it into a verb meaning "to calculate." And *ka* turns the whole thing into a question. It's sort of like a question mark.

Nishijima and Cross translate this as, "Should they be counted as in the Buddha's truth?" Tanahashi's translation says, "Are they counted in the manner of the Buddha Way?" Tanahashi gets my vote here for the closest to literal translation. But it's a funny question. Is Dogen asking if we should regard the old man / wild fox as having been practicing the Buddha Way all those five hundred lifetimes? Honestly, I don't know. But that's what I think he must be asking, so that's what I put in my paraphrase.

Right afterward I have Dogen say, "And anyway, how could a wild fox even see Hyakujo? Wild foxes only see the ghosts of wild foxes. Hyakujo sees the Buddhist ancestors." That's a pretty standard translation. Nishijima and Cross add a footnote saying it "suggests affirmation of Master Hyakujō; in [Dogen's essay] *Kenbutsu* [Seeing Buddha], Master Dogen says that only a buddha can see a buddha."

We get another poem after this, which I have, of course, butchered. The Nishijima/Cross translation is, "Hyakujō has intimately experienced meetings with a wild fox / Questioned by it, he is greatly ruffled / Now I dare ask all you practitioners / Have you completely spat out a fox's drivel or not?" I added the stuff about socks just to make it rhyme.

Dogen's commentary on the poem deserves some commentary. My paraphrase goes, "So a 'wild fox' is like the eye of Hyakujo's intimate experience. Being able to spit out the wild fox's silly mess is how you speak a word of transformation like a Buddha. The very moment we do so, we get free of the wild fox, get free of Hyakujo, get free of the old man, and get free of the entire body of the universe." If you look up other translations, you'll see I'm staying pretty close to everybody else. The only thing I changed is that Dogen makes reference to "the wide, long tongue sticking out." The "wide, long tongue" is one of the supposed physical features of the Buddha. So sticking it out means to speak like a Buddha.

The "eye of Hyakujo's intimate experience" is a puzzling phrase. It's a perfectly good translation, and one that both Nishijima /Cross and Tanahashi agree on. Nishiyama and Stevens just say that Hyakujo and the fox had "a meeting of minds." I think it means something like that. When Dogen refers to something as "an eye (of whatever)" he usually means a real, concrete experience of that thing.

In the Japanese phrase that I paraphrased as "the very moment we do so" Dogen uses his old standby word *inmo*. You'll recall that *inmo* literally means "what" and is usually translated as something like "the ineffable" or "suchness." It's Dogen's way of referring to something real that cannot be adequately named. Both the Tanahashi and Nishijima/Cross translations just have this as "the very moment." But it sort of means something like "in that real but unnameable momentary experience."

My takeaway from this section is that Dogen is saying that when we speak the truth we achieve complete liberation from the bondage of concepts and ideas. Speaking a word of transformation means saying what's true. Of course, truth is a hard thing to define precisely. Still, we know when we are lying and we know when we are saying something true.

After Dogen restates Obaku's question I have him say, "This question is the actualization of the words of the Buddhist ancestors." That's another pretty standard translation. The word I've given as *actualization* is that old fave of Dogen's that I mentioned earlier, *genjo* (現成).

Then we get a really confusing little section. This is one of those fascinating junctures at which you can clearly see that nobody quite knows what the heck Dogen is trying to say. So we've all just done our best to put together a string of words that represents some close equivalent to what he wrote. Check it out.

I've paraphrased the lines in question as, "The pointy hairs of the wild fox's skin are liberated. Because of this, Hyakujo exists as a regular old stinky person. When you think about him, he's sort of like someone in the actual process of getting free of the body of a wild fox." The Nishijima/Cross translation goes, "Because the skin of a wild fox has pointed hairs in the liberated state, the present Hyakujo exists as one stinking skin bag, which, when we fathom it, is half a wild fox skin in the process of getting free." Tanahashi's version goes, "Because the pointed strands of hair on the wild fox skin dropped off, the current Baizhang [a.k.a. Hyakujo] is one stinky skin bag. I presume this is dropping off half a wild fox's skin." Shasta Abbey's translation says, "In that the stubble of a wild fox's coat had fallen away, the later Hyakujo had the stinking skin bag of a human being, which, when we take the measure of it, is half a wild fox's skin striving to get free." Nishiyama and Stevens give us, "If just one hair is liberated then we will have the present Hyakujo's stinking bag of bones. On thorough examination we will find that this is only half of the meaning of liberation." The "later/current/present Hyakujo" means the master of Hyakujo Mountain who encounters the wild fox / Zen master, and who I just call Hyakujo.

Yep. It's crazy-pants any way you translate it. I went through the Japanese original myself, and what I came up with in my paraphrase is not much better than anyone else's guess. I have no idea what Dogen means when he says the wild fox's pointy hairs are liberated (literally, "have fallen away"). But the word he uses here for "liberated / fallen away" is *datsuraku* (脱落). This word also appears in one of Dogen's pet phrases, *shin jin datusraku* (身心脱落), which is usually translated as "body and mind have fallen (or dropped) away."

Dogen attributes this phrase to his teacher in China, Tendo Nyojo, who said that the practice of zazen was the dropping away of body and mind. My own teacher liked to say that "dropping away of body and mind" was what happened when mind and body came into perfect balance. When that happens, one loses any sense of either body or mind as separate entities. As for what this has to do with fox hair, I really don't get it. And, frankly, it doesn't look to me like any of the other translators do, either. Sorry guys. I calls 'em as I sees 'em!

You may have noticed that the word *half* appears in everyone's translation except mine. When Dogen says that something is "half-*whatever*," he generally means it is that actual, concrete thing. I've never read anyone's guess as to why he uses the word *half* this way, but many Dogen scholars agree he uses the word to refer to actual, real-world stuff as opposed to concepts or ideas. So I just paraphrased it that way.

Moving right along, just after this my paraphrase says, "Falling into the body of a wild fox and getting free of it are what Obaku is referring to when he asks, 'What would he have become if he hadn't made any mistakes?' Cause and effect speaks words for others. That in itself is great practice." Here I think my paraphrase stays close to most translations, so I'll let you look those up yourself if you want.

What Dogen's saying here is that we are all manifestations of cause and effect. We imagine that we are independent beings moving around and doing stuff. And maybe to some extent that's true. But we are also causes and effects. When you think of it that way, cause and effect writes this book, and cause and effect reads it. We call part of that chain of causes and effects "you" and we call part of it "me." To take this idea further, you can call various things that take place within cause and effect "mistakes," and conventionally that's true. But in the greater scheme of things, maybe the concept of a mistake is in itself a mistake. It's just a concept we humans have invented. Trippy, huh? Even so, this is no excuse for being careless.

After this I have Dogen say, "There's no such thing as complete perfection. What Hyakujo said is just 80 or 90 percent of realization. Whenever you say there's 80 or 90 percent of realization, there isn't really 80 or 90 percent of realization yet. And whenever you say there's complete perfection, there's not really 80 or 90 percent realization." The Nishijima/Cross translation of this section is, "This expression is not the boldness of spirit that belongs to one hundred percent perfection; it is barely eighty or ninety percent of realization. As a rule, even when we acknowledge eighty- or ninety-percent realization there is not yet eighty- or ninety-percent realization, and when we acknowledge one hundred percent perfection there is nothing left of eighty- or ninety-percent realization." Other translations are similar.

Nishijima and Cross add a footnote here saying that the reference to 100 percent realization is "an ironic expression; perfection does not exist in reality." Shasta Abbey adds a footnote that says, "That is, even if a way of putting the Matter is right on target one hundred percent, it is not the only way of putting the Matter, and hence is less than one hundred percent, or even eighty or ninety percent." By "putting the Matter" (they're the ones who capitalized the word *Matter*, not me), I believe they mean describing reality. That's why I added the lines, "No matter how good your description of reality is, it's still just a description. And there are always multiple ways to accurately describe the same reality." Those lines aren't in the original.

And last, of course Dogen's final poem in this essay did not originally mention a kangaroo. Here's the Nishijima/Cross translation of the poem at the end: "Hyakujō's expression pervades all directions / Yet he still has not left the wild fox's den / Obaku's heels are touching the ground / Yet he seems to be stuck on the path of a praying mantis / In a slap and a clap there is one, not two / Red-beards are foreigners and foreigners' beards are red."

◆

So there you have it. To answer the question I posed to myself at the beginning of the previous chapter, I don't think these two essays are completely contradictory. They're just taking different points of view on the same subject. In a way, it's sort of like one of the lessons of the story of Hyakujo's Fox. Sometimes speaking the truth means saying things one way to one person at one time and saying them a different way to somebody else at another time.

In their introduction to this essay, Nishijima and Cross put it like this:

> There is a famous Chinese story about Master Hyakujō Ekai and a wild fox; the story concerns the relation between Buddhist practice and the law of cause and effect. This relation is explained in two ways, each totally at odds with the other. The first explanation says that someone of great practice "does not fall into cause and effect"; in other words, it denies the influence of cause and effect upon someone of great practice. The other explanation says "do not be unclear about cause and effect"; in other words, it affirms the influence of cause and effect upon someone of great practice. But Master Dōgen considered the difference between these two explanations to be only a matter of intellectual thought, and that the situation in reality had no such dichotomy. He explained that someone of great practice transcends both the negation and the affirmation of the law of cause and effect, by acting here and now in the real world.

I'll leave you with one more thing before we move along. The footnotes in Shasta Abbey's translation contain an intriguing speculation. They say, "Something that is not explicitly stated but is implied by Dogen's commentary is that the old man in the story may be one of Hyakujo's past lives, the karma from which Hyakujo cleanses by helping the old man turn his thinking around."

After working with the chapter I can see why they say this. But I still don't know if that's necessarily what Dogen's commentary implies. I just think it's an interesting speculation, so I offer it for your consideration as well.

9. BUDDHIST SUPERPOWERS
Jinzu
Mystical Power

WHEN I FIRST started going to Kent State University, I was very interested in religions. I wasn't raised with a religion, and I wanted to know if I could believe in God. I was open to the possibility that all that stuff about Jesus dying for my sins was true, but I was also highly skeptical. I remember talking to a guy from some campus ministry organization who basically told me that Jesus Christ did miracles, therefore he was God, therefore I should worship him.

I'd heard that line before, but it never made any sense. Still doesn't. Jesus lived and died — and rose from the dead, if you believe that — two thousand years ago. All we have left now is a book. But there are lots and lots of books in which people say they saw someone perform miracles. So I asked the guy why I should believe the book about Jesus rather than any of the other books about miracle workers. Like that fat Chinese dude, Buddha.

The campus ministry guy said that several of Jesus's disciples had died horribly rather than recant their stories about him and his extraordinary powers. I remember thinking that maybe there was something a little more to it. But then I went to the library. After a few minutes of research, I discovered that the stories of the apostles dying for their belief in Jesus's miracles were even less well documented than the stories of Jesus's miracles themselves. So much for that.

Which is all well and good. But I bet you've heard that argument a thousand times. And either you already believed it or you just rejected it out of hand. The upshot is that not a single person in all of history, anywhere on Earth, has ever been persuaded by logic to believe in miracles and God(s), or persuaded by logic not to believe in them. Okay. Maybe one guy has, but belief in the supernatural is remarkably resistant to logic.

So you can go get yourself a nice Sam Harris or Richard Dawkins book if you want to read someone using logic to counter the belief in the supernatural. But Harris, Dawkins, and the rest might as well give it up, if you ask me. Because you can mock the logic of believing in miracles all you want. It won't stop people believing in them.

Eight hundred years ago Dogen was already aware that such tactics were never going to work. So he doesn't use them in this essay. In fact, I can't think of a single place where he mocks anyone's belief in the supernatural, as a lot of Zen teachers did and still do. And yet his attitude is highly realistic and very much grounded in this world.

When Buddhism first appeared in the West, lots of people were super-excited to find a religion that seemed completely free from superstition and belief in the supernatural. But recently, as more Westerners are taking vacations in parts of Asia they once were unable to travel to or just reading about them on the Internet, Western folks are getting different ideas about what Buddhism "really is."

These folks saw the rituals and heard about some of the supernatural beliefs of certain sects of Buddhism in Southeast Asia and boldly declared that we in the West had gotten Buddhism all wrong. This whole "rational Buddhism" thing, they said, was a Western invention of recent origin. Buddhism is actually just as superstitious as any other religion, and they worship Buddha as a god!

But as I've already pointed out, just as with Christianity, Buddhism includes a wide variety of practices and belief systems, many of which are completely incompatible with each other.

So, yes, it's true, you can find Buddhists who do believe Buddha was a supernatural being with awesome miraculous powers who demands our worship. But this does not mean the rational forms of Buddhism that reject such ideas are a new development or are some kind of perversion of the religion created to attract Westerners. The more rational, less superstitious versions of Buddhism are actually older and better established than the versions of Buddhism that focus on stories of the supernatural.

Even so, Buddhists who believe in the supernatural have been around for a very long time. But rather than mocking such beliefs or using logical arguments to disprove them, Dogen goes for something very different.

Submitted for your approval, here is Dogen, eight hundred years ago, telling his listeners that if they want to know about real miracles they shouldn't look for the weird or the paranormal, because the real miracle is just being alive. He doesn't deny those other kinds of miracles. He just says those are "small-stuff" miracles and that we really ought to focus on the much more astounding miracle that we are even here to talk about those other miracles at all.

Oh, and, by the way, when that word we saw earlier that means "tea and rice" appears in this chapter, this time I went with "burgers and fries" instead of "cornflakes and washing dishes." I know I said I thought that was too specifically American before. But it just sounded better that way in this essay. So sue me!

As for the word I'm paraphrasing as "superpowers," it's *jinzu* (神通), the original title of this essay. This word is often combined with the suffix *riki* (力), which means "power," and defined as "supernatural power." Tanahashi translates the word as "miracles," the Nishiyama/Stevens version says "miraculous powers," Zen scholar Carl Bielefeldt calls them "spiritual powers," and Nishijima/Cross have "mystical powers." I'm just saying "superpowers" because it's funnier and more cartoonish. The original word refers to the kinds of superpowers spiritual-type people often claim to possess, like mind reading or levitation or whatever. They did that bullshit back then, and they still do it now.

Anyway, let's watch Dogen do his thang!

Superpowers are the burgers and fries of Buddhism. Nobody can ever get enough of 'em. Sometimes they say there are six kinds, and sometimes they say there's one. There's also a state without superpowers, and there's a state that goes beyond having superpowers.

There are three thousand superpowers every morning, and eight hundred superpowers every evening. Superpowers appear simultaneously with Buddha, but Buddha doesn't pay any attention to them. They disappear along with Buddha, but that doesn't demolish Buddha.

Whether way up in heaven or coming down from heaven, superpowers are always the same. When doing training and experiencing enlightenment, they're still the same. They're one with the Himalayas. They're trees and rocks, too.

Way back in the day, some of Buddha's followers brought him a robe and a little statue called a stupa. Buddha said, "What an amazing superpower!" Any other Buddha, of the past, present, or future, would have said the same thing.

Once upon a time a really super-cool Zen master named Isan Reiyu (Ch. Guishan Ling-yu, 771–853 CE) was lying down in his room when a student named Shemp* came to see him. Isan turned so he was facing the wall.

Shemp said, "Hey, man! I'm your student! Don't show me your butt!"

Isan started to get up. But then Shemp just left.

Isan called him back, "Hey, Shemp!"

When Shemp returned, Isan said, "Let me tell you about this weird dream I just had."

Shemp leaned in so he could listen. Isan said, "See if you can tell me what the dream means."

---

* His name was actually Kyozan, but there's another character in this story named Kyogen. The names are so similar it's easy to get them confused. So I've changed their names to Shemp and Larry. You're welcome.

Shemp then left and got Isan a basin of water and a towel. Isan washed his face to wake himself up. Then he sat there for a couple of minutes.

Right then this other guy named Larry* showed up. Isan said to him, "Me and Shemp have been practicing our superpowers together! We got us some mad super-skills! It's not just small stuff."

Larry said, "I was standing outside and heard the whole thing."

Isan said, "Why don't you try some of your own superpowers?"

Larry went out, made some tea, and brought it back into the room. Tea has caffeine in it. It's another symbol of waking up.

Isan said, "You two are even better at this than Buddha's most super-powered disciples!"

If you want to know the real Buddhist superpowers, pay attention to this story. These aren't just small powers they're exhibiting in the story. These are the real superpowers that have been transmitted from master to disciple in the Buddhist order. Don't listen to anyone who talks about other sorts of superpowers.

Everything in the story is an example of a Buddhist superpower; the master lying down, him turning his butt to his student, him getting up, him shouting his disciple's name, the whole thing about the dream, the water and towel, him telling his student he's using superpowers. It's all superpowers. Without superpowers none of this stuff would have happened. Don't miss any of it.

Notice that after he told Larry that he and Shemp were using superpowers, Isan said, "It's not just small stuff." That's important.

There are sects of Buddhism in which they believe in small-stuff-type superpowers. But those aren't the real Buddhist superpowers. What we're talking about in this story are the super-est of all superpowers, the ones that all the Buddhas use and maintain. People who believe in small-stuff superpowers have never even heard of them.

Without Buddhist superpowers, Shemp couldn't have gotten his teacher a bowl of water and a towel. His teacher couldn't have shown him his butt. There would have been no washing of the face.

---

* Kyogen, actually. See previous footnote.

These big-time superpowers contain within them the small-stuff superpowers. But small-stuff superpowers don't know anything about the big-time superpowers.

Small-stuff superpowers are things you sometimes read about in the old sutras. You know, like the one in the Vimalakirti Sutra where a tuft of hair swallows an ocean. That one was weird. Or the one in the same sutra about a poppy seed that contains a mountain inside it. Or that stuff in the Lotus Sutra about Buddha shooting water out of his lower body and fire out of his head. That sort of thing is what I mean by "small-stuff" superpowers.

The so-called Six Mystical Powers that I alluded to in the beginning of this essay are also just small stuff.* People who are impressed by that kind of small stuff haven't even dreamed of the real Buddhist superpowers. Small-stuff superpowers depend on developing special skills just to do some kind of impressive stunt. Such small-stuff superpowers might happen once, but they never happen again. They're selfish superpowers.

Big-time superpowers aren't like the small stuff. Big-time superpowers are not used only by Buddhas but occur everywhere. It's totally beyond anything you could possibly imagine. Big-time superpowers appear even before your own body appears. They're not connected with past, present, and future. None of the Buddhas could ever have become Buddhas without big-time superpowers.

The reason we live in a stable universe is because of big-time superpowers. All those small-stuff superpowers from the old sutras that I mentioned before are manifestations of the big-time superpowers. Buddhas hang out in this land of big-time superpowers.

There was a Buddhist layperson named Houn (Ch. Pang Jushi, a.k.a Layman Pang, 740–808 CE). He was one of the greats. One time he said, "The greatest superpower is the ability to go get water and carry firewood."

Pay close attention to that statement. Because you need to do things for yourself and for others. You carry water. That's some kinda superpower right there, let me tell ya!

---

* I list what these are at the beginning of the commentary below, in case you just have to know.

Sometimes you notice superpowers and sometimes you don't. But even not noticing superpowers is still a kind of a superpower at work. Just because you don't know that carrying water is a superpower, that doesn't mean it's not a superpower. It's just as super whether you know it's super or you don't.

Carrying firewood is one of these three thousand superpowers in the morning and eight hundred superpowers in the evening that I talked about right at the beginning. The way people attain enlightenment is by practicing superpowers like this one. From ancient times up till today people have carried firewood. That kind of big-time superpower is totally unlike any of the small-stuff superpowers.

Once upon a time Master Tozan Ryokai (Ch. Dongshan Liang-jie, 807–869 CE, one of the founders of the Soto school of Zen) was attending to his teacher, Master Ungan Donjo (Ch. Yunyan Tan-sheng, 780–841 CE). Ungan asked Tozan, "What's your superpower, Tozan?"

Tozan folded his hands like in prayer and took a step forward.

Ungan then asked Tozan, "How can I describe that superpower?"

Tozan said, "Smell ya later!" and left.

The superpower on display here is the ability to understand the real meaning of someone's words. It's like when a lid perfectly fits on top of a box. The meaning and the words merge completely.

Superpowers like this have children and grandchildren. They are discovered by our predecessors and are passed down to us, unchanged from the distant past.

Don't sit there thinking these big-time superpowers are anything like the small-stuff superpowers some people get all excited about. Everything everywhere is making use of big-time superpowers. It's beyond anyone's ability to speculate about.

A long time ago in a land far away there lived a wizard who had the so-called Five Superpowers. He served under the Buddha. The wizard asked the Buddha, "You got six superpowers. I only got five. Which one am I missing?"

The Buddha said, "What up, wizard!"

The wizard looked his way.

The Buddha said, "That's the power you should be asking about!"

We should look into this carefully. Why did the wizard think the Buddha had six superpowers? The Buddha had all kinds of superpowers! If the wizard noticed only six of them, then he doesn't even know anything about those six superpowers. He couldn't even have dreamed of the Buddha's other superpowers.

Ask yourself, even though the wizard is looking right at the Buddha, does he see the Buddha or not? Like, does he actually *see* the Buddha? Has the wizard ever even seen himself? The wizard needs to study entanglements and study what happens when you cut away entanglements. His whole idea about Buddha having six superpowers is sorta like counting up how much stuff your neighbor has. But it doesn't even make as much sense as doing that.

So what does the Buddha mean when he says, "That's the power you should be asking about?"

He's not saying the wizard has that power or that the wizard lacks it. Even though the wizard talks about getting that power, how could he ever get it or even understand what it was? Even if the wizard really does have five superpowers, they aren't five of the six superpowers that the Buddha has.

The Buddha can see what superpowers the wizard has, but the wizard can't see what superpowers the Buddha has. Even if the wizard had superpowers that *looked* kinda like the Buddha's superpowers, the wizard didn't have superpowers like the Buddha's. Even if the wizard acts like the Buddha, he doesn't have the superpowers of a Buddha. The wizard is just a big ol' phony.

The Buddha tells the wizard he should ask about that one power. But there's no way a wizard could ever understand that kind of superpower. You might call the things a wizard can do "superpowers," but those kinds of superpowers are totally different from the superpowers of a Buddha.

Here's a poem that Master Rinzai Gigen (Ch. Linji Yixuan, d. 866 CE) made up:

The Buddha had special marks on his body
It wasn't because he wanted to be gaudy
They were there just to help him to teach…
…folks to drop nihilistic views he couldn't reach

Sometimes we say there were thirty-two
Sometimes we say eighty if that seems too few
But his body wasn't his enlightenment substance
Having no form is how the Buddha could dance

Master Rinzai said further, "Look. Maybe you think Buddha has six superpowers or whatever. But then you think that all sorts of wizards, demons, evil spirits, demigods, and suchlike also have superpowers. Are they Buddhas, too? If not, then what's so special about having superpowers?

"If these thingies have superpowers, whatever powers they have are due to cause and effect. Maybe they worked on attaining those powers. So what? Buddha's superpowers aren't like that.

"When Buddha enters the world of forms, and sounds, and smells, and tastes, and sense objects, he isn't distracted by them. He's not even distracted by the dharma. So, when a person realizes that all the sense objects are essentially empty, then nothing can bother that person, either.

"Listen up, people! Although the old scriptures say that everything is made up of the five aggregates, everything is ultimately a mystery. Nothing has any fixed form.

"Even when you find what you think you've been searching for, what you find is ultimately no more real than a ghost or a hallucination. That's not what Buddhist practice is all about."

So what Master Rinzai was saying was that the six superpowers of a Buddha can't be attained by gods or demons or anybody else. These six superpowers are only transmitted directly from Buddhas to those who sincerely practice with them. Anybody who hasn't practiced directly with a Buddha can't get 'em.

Zen Master Hyakujo Ekai (Ch. Baizhang Huaihai, 720–814 CE, the wild fox guy) had this to say: "Eyes, ears, nose, and tongue are not greedy for material things or even spiritual things. This state is what happens when someone first perceives the truth. When none of the six senses leave any trace, that's what's called the six superpowers.

"Like, for example, when you don't rely on knowing and understanding stuff, that's a superpower. Or when you don't get all excited about superpowers, that's a superpower. Any person who manages to go beyond superpowers like this is so awesome they're kind of like a god."

Hyakujo knows what he's talking about. Being free from the senses and free from superpowers is the real superpower. The real superpowers make all the senses clear, by leaving no trace of them. Every Buddha there ever was knows this.

A long time ago a guy said, "The six superpowers aren't emptiness and they aren't *not* emptiness. They're like a big ball of light with no inside or outside."

Having no inside or outside means the same thing as leaving no traces. When we do zazen we enter this state without traces by not disturbing the six senses. So try to get working on that.

The only people who know about this are those who've studied the Buddhist masters. Others try to get it by wasting their efforts doing totally the wrong thing.

To sum it all up, the only way to understand the truth of Buddhism is through the use of real superpowers. Understanding the truth is itself the most super of all superpowers. How can you possibly doubt that?

— Preached to the audience at
Kannon-dori-kosho-horin-ji Temple on November 16, 1241

According to a footnote in the Nishijima/Cross translation, the six superpowers Dogen refers to are "1) the power of mystical transmutation, 2) the power to know others' minds, 3) the power of supernatural vision, 4) the power of supernatural hearing, 5) the power to know past lives, 6) the power to end excess." Dogen addresses some of these in his essay. Carl Bielefeldt gives the same list in his footnotes. On the other hand, Kaz Tanahashi's translation adds a parenthetical statement that the "six miracles" are "freedom from the six-sense desires." Nishijima/Cross's and Bielefeldt's versions make better sense in the context of the essay, if you ask me.

The story about the Zen master and his dream is especially interesting to me. So let's look at it a little closer. First off, Dogen doesn't just call Zen Master Isan "super-cool." He actually drools about how great he is for about half a page. I spared you that. You're welcome.

In the original story, Isan doesn't just compare Shemp and Larry to "Buddha's most super-powered disciples." He names Shariputra and Maudgalyayana, who were reputed to have supernatural abilities.

If you've never studied with a Zen teacher, you might not really get this story completely. When I heard it, I put myself in the position of Larry and imagined what it would be like if one of my teachers ever said something like, "Hey, Brad, let me tell you about this weird dream I just had." If Tim or Nishijima Roshi had ever said anything like that to me, you'd best believe I would totally have wanted to hear their dreams. Are you kidding? An enlightened master offering to tell me their dreams? I'm all ears!

So I am really impressed with Shemp and Larry and their ability to resist that kind of temptation. They're truly grounded. You can tell their teacher was impressed as well.

Lots of people, when they hear this story, tend to assume the teacher, Isan, didn't really want to tell Shemp and Larry his dream. It was all just some kind of Zen test.

I don't see why it has to be that way. I'm not saying it couldn't have been some kind of a test on the teacher's part. But maybe Isan really did want to talk about his weird dream. In fact, if he did, that would make the story even more compelling. So that's how I picture it. I also like to imagine that later that day Isan finally found someone else to talk about his dream with.

As a teacher myself, I think that's a much more realistic version of the story. There's an idea that Zen teachers are some kind of omnipotent entities who would never be so human as to want to tell someone their dreams. To me that's just another way of believing in the supernatural.

And just by the way, I once heard what might be a modern-day version of this same type of story. Apparently early one morning a student knocked on the door of Mel Weitsman, the head of the Berkeley Zen Center. When Mel opened the door, the student said, "You have to hear this dream I just had!"

Mel said, "No I don't" and shut the door in his face.

Back to Dogen. After the story of Shemp and Larry and their teacher we get to the discussion of big-time superpowers and small-stuff superpowers. I actually copped the phrase *small-stuff* from Bielefeldt's translation of the word *shosho* (小\小\) that appears in his translation of this essay. So "small-stuff" and variations thereof are a fairly standard way of translating the word Dogen uses. Tanahashi calls them "great miracles" and "minor miracles." That's also pretty standard.

A little further along in my paraphrase I have Dogen say, "Small-stuff superpowers depend on developing special skills just to do some kind of impressive stunt. Such small-stuff superpowers might happen once, but they never happen again. They're selfish superpowers."

Bielefeldt's translation of this is, "To say that the five powers or six powers are small spiritual powers is [to say that] the five powers and six powers are defiled by practice and verification; they are cut off in time and place. While we have them in life, they do not appear after the body. They belong to the self and not to others. Though they may appear in this land, they do not appear in other lands. Though they may appear when we do not show them, they fail to appear when it is time to show them." That's a fairly standard translation. Mine is a little interpretive, but I think it's essentially correct. Let me explain why.

It seems that Dogen didn't take the view of a contemporary atheist who would say that so-called supernatural or paranormal powers are completely impossible. He seemed to believe they could happen, or at least he doesn't mock those who think so. But he also very firmly believed that such acts, if they happened, were not truly supernatural.

He says they take skills to develop (they're "defiled by practice and verification"). He's willing to concede that things that seem paranormal might occur, but only under very special circumstances (they are "cut off in time and place" and "Though they may appear in this land, they do not appear in other lands"). He says they're used selfishly ("They belong to the self and not to others").

He also believes these small-stuff superpowers never occur through the intervention of anything outside the laws of cause and effect. This last assumption comes from my reading of some of Dogen's other essays in which he strongly criticizes the idea that anything can occur outside the laws of cause and effect. We just looked at one of those essays a couple of chapters ago.

There's an old Buddhist story that goes like this. The Buddha runs into a yogi who claims he can walk on water. The Buddha asks for a demonstration, and the yogi happily obliges, walking across a river.

The Buddha asks the yogi how long it took him to attain that skill. The yogi says that he worked at it for thirty years. The Buddha says, "Huh. So much trouble when you could have just paid a ferryman fifty cents for a ride!"

If that sounds like a joke, just stop and consider it for a minute. In this vast universe full of mostly empty space and gamma ray bursts that can wipe out all the life-forms on entire planets before they even get a chance to develop into anything more complex than worms, how amazing is it that there are humans who can make little boats to ferry other humans across rivers? And how amazing is it that you just happen to live on one of those planets? Assuming there even is more than one planet with intelligent life like this one, which, for now, we can't even be certain of.

Sorry for yet another digression. Let's return to Dogen. My paraphrase, "Big-time superpowers appear even before your own body appears" is my interpretation of a sentence that goes *yuishin yori saki arawasu* (有身よりさきに現す). A literal translation would be "(They) appear before the body has appeared." This idea follows from the Buddhist formula about how the universe comes into being.

In Buddhist cosmology it's not that the universe appeared billions of years ago and that much, much later here we are in it. Buddhists believe the universe appears instantaneously, perhaps we could even say miraculously, at every moment. Even though this appearance seems to us to happen all at once, there's a belief that Buddha was so enlightened he could break it down into individual steps. The appearance of the body, and thus of the material universe as a whole, is one of the last things that occurs in this process.

So the word *body* here means the entire material universe. And the superpowers he's talking about appear before the entire universe comes into being.

What I've paraphrased as, "The reason we live in a stable universe is because of big-time superpowers" is, in the Nishijima/Cross translation, "That the present limitless ocean of Dharma worlds is constant and unchanging is entirely the mystical power of Buddha." This is pretty much the way everyone translates that line.

Of course we now know that the universe we live in is far from constant and unchanging. Although people of Dogen's time generally assumed the heavens and earth were permanent, there's evidence in Dogen's writings to suggest he did not see it that way. So I'm going to go ahead and assume he is using the phrase *constant and unchanging* (常不変, *jofuhen*) metaphorically rather than literally.

Here's how I take this line. The fact that we live on a planet that can support life is kind of amazing. The more we learn about the universe, the more incredible it seems that we are even here at all. Dogen sees this as evidence of a kind of superpower at work. And, although the universe is not literally constant and unchanging, it is stable enough to have allowed us to evolve and develop. Another superpower!

This isn't quite the same as the so-called strong anthropic principle, which says that the universe can support human life because it is made to support human life. Yet it isn't miles away from that idea, either. It doesn't postulate that there has to be some sort of intelligent design at work. But it does see the human mind as a manifestation of something much bigger that plays a part in the creation and establishment of the universe. Trippy.

The line right after that one in my paraphrase is, "All those small-stuff superpowers from the old sutras that I mentioned before are manifestations of the big-time superpowers." This is my distillation of a much longer section. In the actual text Dogen goes into each of the mystical powers that he talked about earlier, such as the tuft of hair swallowing an ocean (whatever the hell that even means), and he dissects them into little pieces. It's all very hard to follow. I suggest looking it up in one of the standard translations if you feel like you need to know. You'll probably just end up thanking me for cutting that stuff out. (And you already know what I'll say to that.)

I then have Dogen say, "Sometimes you notice superpowers and sometimes you don't. But even not noticing superpowers is still a kind of a superpower at work. Just because you don't know that carrying water is a superpower, that doesn't mean it's not a superpower. It's just as super whether you know it's super or you don't."

Bielefeldt translates this section in part as, "Even though people do not know it, the dharma is the dharma as it is. Even if we do not know that bearing water is the spiritual powers, [the fact] that the spiritual powers are bearing water is irreversible." I just thought I'd let you know in case you thought I was making stuff up.

Then we get that little story about Tozan and Ungan. Of course the phrase "smell ya later" is not a direct translation. The Nishijima/ Cross version is, "Tozan then conveys best wishes and leaves." Same thing, if you ask me.

After this I have Dogen say, "Superpowers like this have children and grandchildren. They are discovered by our predecessors and are passed down to us, unchanged from the distant past."

The Nishijima/Cross rendering of this section is, "Remember, the mystical power and the wondrous function will surely have children and grandchildren; they are not subject to regression. And they must properly have their founding patriarchs; they are not subject to evolution." My version takes some liberties, but not that many.

Bielefeldt's footnote here says, "The powers and functions have a family lineage, a posterity with its founding figure." My paraphrase is an attempt to put what I think Dogen means and what Bielefeldt has to say about it in easier language.

After this I make Dogen say, "Everything everywhere is making use of big-time superpowers. It's beyond anyone's ability to speculate about." I crunched a big, huge paragraph into these two sentences. Again, Dogen takes apart a bunch of the miracle stories he talked about earlier in the essay and breaks them down piece by piece. And again it's really convoluted and confusing. I'll let you check out the standard translations for yourself. As always, there's a bibliography in the back of this book that will direct you to them.

In the story that comes up after this about the wizard and the Buddha, I have Dogen say, "The wizard needs to study entanglements and study what happens when you cut away entanglements."

The word I'm giving as "entanglements" is actually *katto* (葛藤). Here's what Bielefeldt has to say about that part: "The term kattō, translated 'entanglements,' literally means 'arrowroot and wisteria'; from the image of the intertwined tangle of these vines, comes the sense 'complications,' 'entanglements.' The term is regularly used in Zen to indicate the entanglements of language, including sometimes the language of the Zen masters; the Zen masters' language is also sometimes described as 'tangle cutting phrases' (*katto dan ku*, 葛藤斷句) for its power to overcome such entanglements. Dogen's own language here is rather tangled and subject to somewhat varied interpretation."

My own interpretation of this bit is that the wizard has become entangled in his own concepts concerning superpowers. Dogen is advising him to see that entanglement for what it is and thereby learn how to free himself of it.

Later on, when I have Dogen call the wizard a big ol' phony, that's based on a footnote to this section in the Nishijima/Cross translation that says, "A phony can imitate a buddha's forms but cannot imitate the state of buddha." We see a whole lot of phony Buddhas these days. They're all over the Internet and everywhere else. Lots of people put on an act based on what they think a Buddha must be like. But it doesn't take much to see that it's all for show.

Then we get to Master Rinzai's poem. My version sucks. Bielefeldt's version goes, "The Tathagata's presentation of the bodily marks is done to accord with the sentiments of the worldly. / Lest people produce nihilistic views, we expediently set up vacuous names. / We provisionally speak of the thirty-two and the eighty, just empty sounds. / Having a body is not the substance of his enlightenment; / Having no marks is his true form."

All the other translations are similar. Basically it's saying that the Buddha appeared to people in ways they could understand. His body was supposedly covered with certain marks that showed he was special. Some of these were things like having webbed fingers and having a big "wisdom bump" on the top of his head. Sometimes you see these in statues. Whether or not this is factually true is anybody's guess. But that's the legend.

Dogen seems to accept these legends. Or at least he knows his listeners accept the legends. But he cites Master Rinzai, who makes the case that these special marks — if they existed at all — weren't what was really important about the Buddha. What was really important about him was formless, in the sense that it wasn't something anyone could see.

After the poem, Dogen continues quoting from Master Rinzai. Rinzai talks about how legendary demons and whatnot have superpowers and asks if that makes them Buddhas. Once again, this is a truncation of a longer segment. In it Dogen cites a legend about the god Indra battling eighty-four thousand demons.

In the original, the stuff I have in there about these demon thingies working on their powers refers to the demon thingies having their powers due to karma. I didn't want to get real mystical there so I avoided using the word *karma*. Karma is just action; it's just cause and effect. So he's basically saying that they have their powers because they worked on them. Like that story about the Buddha and the yogi who spent thirty years learning to walk on water.

Master Rinzai mentions the theory of the five aggregates (called *skandhas* in Sanskrit). That's Buddhism 101. In his first sermon, the Buddha said that human beings did not have souls. Rather, he said, all things are made of five aggregates. The usual translation of the five are (1) form, (2) feelings, (3) perceptions, (4) impulses to action and actions themselves, and (5) consciousness.

The theory of aggregates was Buddha's counterpunch to the theory of atman, which is basically analogous to the Christian idea of the soul. Notice that consciousness is just one of the aggregates. So Buddhism isn't one of those philosophies that says we are beings of pure consciousness inhabiting inert material bodies. Form, the first of the aggregates, is our body as well as the material universe.

But even though this idea of aggregates is an important doctrine in Buddhism, Rinzai says everything is ultimately a mystery. Bielefeldt's translation of this part is, "Therefore, when he realizes that the six types — form, sound, smell, taste, touch, and dharma — are all empty marks, they cannot bind this person of the way who depends on nothing. Though his is the defiled quality of the five aggregates, it is yet the spiritual power of walking the earth."

The Nishijima/Cross translation finishes this thought: "True Buddha has no set shape and true Dharma has no fixed form. You are only fashioning images and inventing situations on the basis of fantastic transformation."

What I think is even more interesting is the part that comes next.

I paraphrased it as, "Even when you find what you think you've been searching for, what you find is no more ultimately real than a ghost or a hallucination. That's not what Buddhist practice is all about."

Bielefeldt translates this part as, "Even supposing you get something through your seeking, it will all be fox spirits." As we saw in the previous two chapters, "ghost/spirit of a wild fox" is a standard Buddhist phrase that means something deceptive. Foxes were thought of as being crafty and devious animals, so ghosts of foxes must therefore be even more deceiving. Dogen is probably referring to the story of Hyakujo's Fox.

This is great stuff. Even if you find what you're seeking for, that's still another illusion. I've found this idea incredibly useful to keep in mind.

In my paraphrase, Dogen quotes Hyakujo as saying, "Eyes, ears, nose, and tongue are not greedy for material things or even spiritual things." What he actually says is more like, "The eyes, ears, nose, and tongue are each without the stain of craving for all the dharmas, whether being or non-being" (Bielefeldt). That's how it's usually put. Although Tanahashi's translation says, "The eyes, ears, nose, and tongue are not defiled by form and formlessness." He eliminates the word *greed* or *craving* that appears in the other translations. So I looked it up, and the word *ton* (貪) appears in the original sentence. This word is the standard Chinese translation (the quote from Hyakujo is in Chinese) for the Sanskrit word *raga*, a Buddhist term meaning "desire" or "craving."

The part of my paraphrase of this line that might strike you as being a bit of a stretch is where I have Hyakujo say "material things or even spiritual things." In the original the words are *issai umu shoho* (一切有無諸法). This basically means "all existent or nonexistent things/dharmas."

In their footnotes Nishijima and Cross say that this phrase "means all material and immaterial things — for example, material possessions and Buddhist teaching." Dogen often writes about "existent and nonexistent things." It sounds real trippy, I know. But Nishijima Roshi always explained phrases like that as meaning material or nonmaterial things. "Nonmaterial things" means stuff like ideas, or philosophy, or unquantifiable but nonetheless real things like love or happiness or freedom. In my paraphrase I'm designating this non-material stuff as "spiritual."

It's an absurd statement on the surface. I know for darn sure that *my* eyes, ears, nose, and tongue are very greedy for material and spiritual things. Hyakujo knew this, too, of course. So he's being deliberately provocative here.

That's why he follows up by saying, "This state is what happens when someone first perceives the truth." In the original version, he cites two specific examples of this. Tanahashi's translation refers to "receiving the four-line verse of vows" and "receiving the four fruits of the arhats." Arhats are Buddhas. (That is not a misprint of *asshats*.) These are both just fancy ways of saying that someone had a profound Buddhist awakening.

After this, Hyakujo talks about how, when none of the six senses leave a trace, that's a superpower. In Buddhism they count six senses instead of five. The sixth sense isn't like what's depicted in that old Bruce Willis movie. It doesn't refer to psychic powers or anything like that. It refers to the mind as a sense organ that senses thoughts and feelings. When he says that stuff about the senses not leaving a trace, he means when you sense things but don't get hung up on them.

After this he says, in my paraphrase, that "when you don't rely on knowing and understanding stuff, that's a superpower." In the Tanahashi translation what I've paraphrased as "when you don't rely on knowing and understanding stuff" is "not depend[ing] on intellectual understanding." That's a pretty standard translation.

Hyakujo is not advocating the kind of anti-intellectualism that's been eroding the political system in the United States for the past few decades. Sometimes people mistakenly imagine that Zen is super anti-intellectual. Which is funny because other people imagine it's totally all about being intellectual. It's neither.

But there is a tendency among all us human beings to get too wrapped up in our own heads. This is not limited to so-called intellectuals, either. You don't have to ever read a book to get too wrapped up in your own head. In fact, if you do nothing but sit on your couch drinking beers and watching Honey Boo-Boo, you're just as likely to end up "relying on knowing and understanding" as any brainiac with a PhD in phlebotomy.

It doesn't mean being too smart. It means getting overinvolved in fixed and inflexible ideas and then depending too much on those ideas to guide your behavior. We all do this, to some extent. Buddhist practice is intended to help us put a stop to that kind of thing.

In my paraphrase I have Dogen say, "The real superpowers make all the senses clear, by leaving no trace of them." The Nishijima /Cross translation of this line is, "Those six mystical powers make the six senses clear, in the state of being without any trace."

Dogen's not saying we have to block off the senses in order to attain freedom. A lot of silly people try to do this. They build these complicated isolation tanks that are supposed to deaden all the senses, leading to a grand spiritual awakening. But remember that Buddhism also looks at the brain as a sense organ. Your isolation tank can't block that one. So, in Buddhist terms, you're not blocking off all the senses in your isolation tank; you're just completely focusing on a single sense. You might as well, for example, shut your eyes and turn your headphones up real loud to focus on hearing alone. It would be pretty much the same thing.

Since you can't shut down all your senses — without being dead, of course — the trick is to learn to allow them to be as they are without leaving traces. This is easier said than done. But meditation practice can help.

A bit further along I have Dogen say, "When we do zazen we

enter this state without traces by not disturbing the six senses." A more standard translation of the same line is, "When you practice, study, and realize no-trace, you are not disturbed by the six sense organs" (Tanahashi). Tanahashi has Dogen saying we aren't disturbed *by* the senses, while Bielefeldt and Nishijima/Cross have Dogen saying *we don't disturb* the senses. When I looked at the original, it looked to me like Tanahashi had it right. It says *roku-nyu wo docho sezaru nari* (六入を動著せざるなり). Nishiyama/Stevens split the difference and say, "There is no functioning of the six sense organs."

Be that as it may, the quibble you probably have is with my changing "practice, study, and realize no-trace" into "do zazen." I know that might seem like a stretch. But honestly, I can't think of anything else Dogen could be referring to here. Let me try to explain.

When you do zazen, you don't attempt to stop the functioning of the senses. You don't even try to stop your brain from doing its thing, which tends to be the main focus of lots of meditation techniques. Rather, you sit and let the brain and senses continue to function. You even leave your eyes open instead of closing them. In doing so, you gradually learn how to let the senses function without leaving too many traces. I don't think many people get to the point of having them leave no traces at all. But you can significantly reduce the traces the senses leave, and that's really useful.

Right after this part I cut out about a paragraph or so in which Dogen cites a number of old Zen stories and then rephrases them and connects them to each other. It's good stuff, but you have to know all the old stories in order to have any hope of following what he's saying about them. Most of what it amounts to is covered in the earlier parts of the essay, so I made an executive decision and dropped it. Apologies to Dogen.

I changed the ending somewhat, too. In the Nishijima/Cross version it ends, "In sum, the Buddha's truth is mastered, in every case, through mystical power. In such mastery, a bead of water swallows and spews the vast ocean, and a particle of dust holds up and lets go of the highest mountain — who could doubt it? This is just the mystical power itself." There aren't too many big variations in the other translations.

I sat and pondered that for a while before I typed out my ending. I decided that what Nishijima/Cross translate as "in such mastery" (その達する, *sono tatsu suru*) refers back to mastering what I'm calling the "real superpowers." To master these real superpowers is to live a life unencumbered by trying to master any superpowers.

All that stuff about beads of water swallowing the ocean and specs of dust holding up mountains refers to the balance of our small subjective selves and the incredibly huge outside world. This is our natural state of balance that we aim at returning to. In a larger sense, we can't ever really leave that state of balance. Yet we live inside our unbalanced minds so much that we fail to see what we really are.

◆

I think this essay is really interesting and that contemporary people can learn a lot from Dogen's attitude here.

What usually happens when folks like Richard Dawkins, Sam Harris, or the late Christopher Hitchens and their followers try to convince people that religions are wrong is that they mock the old miracle stories and point out how flimsy the evidence for them is. Then they belittle those who believe in such ridiculous stuff as being stupid and naive.

This never works. In fact, in spite of what I told you in the introduction to this piece, it didn't even work on me. I could see for myself that the evidence for Jesus's miracles was inadequate. Yet when I heard smarty-pants guys sneer at that stuff, that actually made me *want* to believe in it. The problem for me was that I just couldn't. I tried to believe. I really did. But I could not be convinced.

Still, it's amazing how many people do believe this kind of stuff. In cultures all over the world we find exactly the same thing, going back thousands of years. Some guy is reported to have done miraculous stuff a long time ago and millions of others believe these stories and worship that guy. This approach worked in Japan in Dogen's time, too.

I cut out a lot of Dogen's specific references to stories of Buddha's miracles because I didn't think most of you nice folks would have heard of them. But I think it's good to keep in mind that many in Dogen's original audiences did know of those stories and believed in them. Not only that, but probably many in his audience thought that the very reason to have faith in Buddhist philosophy was that Buddha and his followers were able to work miracles.

This didn't go for everyone. Since there was already a long Buddhist tradition of skepticism about the supernatural, many in Dogen's audiences wouldn't have been bothered by this sermon. But it's wrong to assume that none of them would have been bothered by it. In fact, I'd imagine it would have been shocking to quite a few of the folks who originally heard it. Let me see if I can make that aspect of it come to life a little.

Dogen never heard of Jesus. But I'll assume most of you know more about the miracles of Jesus than about the crazy supernatural stuff the Buddha supposedly did. So I'm gonna try using Dogen's approach, as applied to Christian miracle stories. Here goes.

Jesus fed a multitude with two fishes and five loaves of bread (Matt. 14:13–21), and he raised Lazarus from the dead (John 11:1–44) and was himself raised from the dead three days after his crucifixion (Mark 16:1–13, Luke 24:1–53, Matt. 28:1–10, John 20:11–18). These are indeed great accomplishments. But they are examples of small-stuff miracles, not the big-time miracle.

It is only because of the big-time miracle that such small-stuff miracles as the ones Jesus performed exist. Without the big-time miracle, even the most spectacular of small-stuff miracles could not occur. Jesus worked great wonders. But the greater wonder is that there is a world in which Jesus could have been born, that there is a universe in which that world exists, that you and I are alive to hear about his miracles. It is only the big-time miracle of existence itself that allows smaller miracles to occur.

Does that make it a bit more real?

Anyhow, this is why Buddhists say things like, "The mystical power and wondrous function is carrying water and lugging firewood." Your own real, three-dimensional existence with all its joys and sorrows, its pleasures and pains, its spectacular times and its mundane times, that's the most impressive miracle of all.

Whether or not you believe in small-stuff miracles doesn't really matter. But the big-time miracle cannot be doubted by anyone. It exists everywhere and at all times and all places. It's called the universe. Another name for it is *you*.

You can't investigate small-stuff miracles that happened long ago and far away. But you can examine the one big-time miracle for yourself using your own body and your own mind just as they are right here and right now.

I think if Dogen had ever been asked about Christianity, he might have responded something like that.

10. HE NOT BUSY BEING BORN IS BUSY DYING
Shoji
Living and Dying

THE JAPANESE TITLE of this chapter is 生死, which is pronounced *shoji*. The second character means "death." The first can mean either "birth" or "life," depending on the context. Translators are about evenly divided on whether to call this chapter "Birth and Death" or "Life and Death" in English. Kaz Tanahashi, Yuho Yokoi, Thomas Cleary, and the Stanford *Shobogenzo* translation project go with "Birth and Death." Nishijima/Cross, Nishiyama/Stevens, and Shasta Abbey go with "Life and Death."

I've gone with "Living and Dying" mostly just to add a bit of nuance to the standard "Life and Death" version. But "Birth and Death" is fine, too. Dogen was writing in Japanese for a Japanese audience, so he could play with the ambiguity of the term in ways you really can't in English.

My friend Greg Fain told me that his teacher Mel Weitsman, founder of the Berkeley Zen Center, the guy who didn't want to hear his student's dream, told him he prefers the title "Birth and Death" because birth and death are both parts of life. And life is what Mel believes Dogen is addressing in this chapter. That sounds reasonable to me. Choosing one interpretation doesn't necessarily mean that all the others are wrong.

The character combination 生死 (*shoji*) is also the Chinese

character combination used to represent the Sanskrit word *samsara*. When I first learned the term *samsara*, it was being contrasted to the word *nirvana*. My initial understanding was that nirvana was Buddhist heaven and samsara was Buddhist hell. This is pretty simplistic, but it's not completely wrong. For many Buddhists, samsara is what they're trying to avoid, and nirvana is where they want to get to. In common parlance, samsara is the name the ancient Indians (not just the Buddhists) gave this world of life, and death, and misery, and dental bills, and reality TV, whereas nirvana was the bliss and peace of the Buddhist enlightened state.

Literally, the Sanskrit word *nirvana* means "extinction" and the Sanskrit word *samsara* means "flowing together" or "journeying," as in the journey of life. The fact that *nirvana* means "extinction" sometimes leads people to conclude that Buddhism is nihilistic. But it's more about the extinction of craving. In any case, for those who crave nirvana and hate samsara, things get even trickier. Nagarjuna, in his famous *Root Stanzas of the Middle Way* (*Mulamadhyamaka-karika*), says that samsara and nirvana are one and the same. He wasn't the first person to say this, but he was among the first and remains one of the most famous. According to the *Shambhala Dictionary of Buddhism and Zen*, "The essential unity of *samsara* and *nirvana* is based on the view that everything is a mental representation, and thus *samsara* and *nirvana* are nothing other than labels without real substance."

Which is all well and good. But if you want to buy a Fender Jazz bass you gotta ask for a Fender Jazz bass or you're gonna get a Squier Bronco bass. And nobody wants one of those! We have to name things. So we use words like *samsara* and *nirvana*, even as we acknowledge that they're ultimately the same thing.

No translation I've ever come across calls this chapter "Samsara," although they could. Even my own teacher, Gudo Nishijima, doesn't comment on this meaning of *shoji* in his introduction or footnotes — and he footnotes everything! Among all the translations I consulted, only the Norman Waddell / Masao Abe version mentions this alternate meaning of the title.

I didn't even notice this was the character combination used for samsara until I started doing research for this chapter. I think it would be good if more translators made note of this, because Dogen's intended audience would have understood it right away. In this chapter Dogen sometimes contrasts *shoji* (生死) with *nehan* (涅槃), meaning nirvana, so we can be certain his intention was to get into these traditional pairs of opposites.

Anyhow, in my paraphrase I will indicate where I think the meaning of the key word *shoji* (life and death) is more like "birth and death" and when it's more like "samsara."

Much of this chapter is Dogen riffing on what Nagarjuna said about samsara and nirvana ultimately being the same thing.

We don't know when Dogen wrote this piece. He didn't put a date on it, nor did whoever copied it later. It was not included in either the seventy-five- or the twelve-chapter editions of *Shobogenzo* we talked about earlier. It's the shortest of all Dogen's pieces in the complete version of *Shobogenzo*. Kokyo Henkel of the Santa Cruz Zen Center notices similarities between this essay and one called "Zenki" (All Functions), which was written in 1242, and he believes this essay may have been written around that time. But that's just a guess. Nobody really knows.

Anyhow, let's see what Dogen has to say about birth/life and death, shall we?

Because there's Buddha in life and death, there isn't any life and death. Because in life and death there isn't Buddha, you don't need to get confused about life and death.

Master Kasan Zen-e (Ch. Jiashan Shanhui, 805-881 CE) and Master Jozan Shinei (Ch. Dingshan Shenying, 771-853 CE) said these things, and they were pretty smart cookies who didn't just go around saying goofy stuff.

If you want to get free from life and death (samsara) you gotta dig into what they said. If you're looking for Buddha outside life and death, that's like going to McDonald's and expecting a nutritious meal or putting on a Metallica album when you want to hear something soothing.

All you're doing is just collecting more of the causes of life and death (samsara) and losing any hope of getting free.

When we understand that life and death (samsara) is itself nirvana, there's no such thing as life and death to be a hater of, and no such thing as nirvana to get all hot and bothered for. That's when you can start getting free of life and death (samsara).

You're mistaken if you think we move from birth to death. Birth is a single moment that happens at the time of birth. It has its own past and its own future. That's why we Buddhists say birth isn't really birth, or appearance isn't really appearance. Death, too, is a single moment that happens at the time of death. It also has its own past and its own future. That's why we Buddhists say disappearance isn't really disappearance, or death isn't really death.

When you're alive there's nothing but life. When you die there's nothing but death. So when life comes, be alive. When death comes, die. You don't need to dodge either one, and you don't need to long for either one.

Your own life and death are exactly the sacred life of Buddha. If you despise your real life and want to toss it aside, you're throwing away the sacred life of Buddha. On the other hand, if you grab on to your life like there's no tomorrow, that's another way to throw away the sacred life of Buddha. That's just you pretending to be Buddha.

You only really get inside the mind of Buddha when you can stop wanting life and stop fearing death.

But don't think about it, and don't talk about it. Just let go of your body and forget your mind. Throw them into the house of Buddha. Then Buddha does it all. Follow this way, and you become a Buddha without making any effort or coming up with any plan. Who would want to get stuck in their own mind?

It's easy to become a Buddha. Don't be a jerk. Don't get hung up on life and death. Have compassion for everybody and everything. Show some respect to people who deserve it and kindness

to people who need it. Don't get all caught up in hating stuff or in
wanting stuff. Don't think too much. Don't worry.

That's what we call being a Buddha.

You don't need anything else.

— Date and place of composition not recorded

Dogen starts right off with a confusing statement: "Because there's
Buddha in life and death, there isn't any life and death. Because in
life and death there isn't Buddha, you don't need to get confused
about life and death." My paraphrase is pretty close to the standard
translations. It's tricky, so let's look at it in detail.

This section sounds a little like the opening lines of his famous
essay "Genjo Koan":

> When all dharmas are [seen as] the Buddha-Dharma, then
> there is delusion and realization, there is practice, there is
> life and there is death, there are buddhas and there are ordi-
> nary beings. When the myriad dharmas are each not of the
> self, there is no delusion and no realization, no buddhas and
> no ordinary beings, no life and no death. The Buddha's truth
> is originally transcendent over abundance and scarcity, and so
> there is life and death, there is delusion and realization, there
> are beings and buddhas. And though it is like this, it is only
> that flowers, while loved, fall; and weeds while hated, flourish.
> (Nishijima/Cross)

When Dogen says "Buddha" in these essays, he's not referring
to the guy who lived in India 2,500 years ago. What he's talking
about here is the more transcendent meaning of Buddha, which
scholars trace back to the Lotus Sutra. That sutra, written a few
hundred years after the historical Buddha died, is where the word
Buddha started to refer to something bigger than just Mr. Siddhartha Gautama. It's sort of like the way the word *Christ* came to mean
something much greater than the historical person Jesus of Nazareth.

First Dogen says, "Because there's Buddha in life and death, there isn't any life and death." Here we can take *Buddha* to refer to the viewpoint that takes the entire universe as a single unified thing. In terms of the universe as a whole, the words *life/birth* and *death* don't have any meaning. We don't yet have a scientific consensus about how the universe was born or how the universe will die, or even if it can be said to be born and die in any way that we can comprehend. What we can say for now is that even though individual aspects of the universe like stars, planets, and ourselves come into being, last a while, and then die, nothing ever really goes away. Matter and energy change form, but they don't disappear.

Then Dogen says, "Because in life and death there isn't Buddha, you don't need to get confused about life and death." My take on this part is that there is a sense in which we can say that in life and death there *is* Buddha, and a sense in which we can say that in life and death there *isn't* Buddha. One the one hand, objectively, from an impartial, universal sense there is Buddha. But on the other, subjectively, on a day-to-day basis, it can feel like there isn't Buddha. It's just me going through the shit I gotta go through. Whereas most religions would insist that the "there is Buddha" sense is real while the "there isn't Buddha" sense is false, Buddhism takes the view that both views are equally false. Yet it acknowledges that we feel both ways, sometimes simultaneously. So we gotta deal with both of them.

The word I paraphrased as "confused" as in "confused about life and death" is usually translated as "be deluded about." For once, the Waddell/Abe, Nishijima/Cross, and Tanahashi translations all use the same wording! Nishiyama/Stevens say, "There is no illusion in life and death," which is pretty much the same thing. The Shasta Abbey translation says, "Because the Buddha did not exist within life and death, He was not infatuated with living and dying." I'm going to leave their translation alone because I don't understand why they put it that way.

Where I've said "confused" and others have said "deluded," in the original, Dogen used an old Japanese word, *madohazu* (まどはず).

This is an older way of writing the negative of the word *madowasu* (惑わす), which means to be "bewildered," "perplexed," or, as per the usual translations, "deluded."

I take this as meaning that we don't need to try to figure out life and death, which is why I paraphrased it as "confused." Any which way we attempt to figure out something as mysterious as life and death is bound to be mistaken. So trying to figure it out amounts to a big waste of time. Whatever we say about it is going to be a kind of delusion. Especially since, in the sense Dogen points out in the previous sentence, life and death don't really exist anyway.

Moving along, obviously Dogen didn't say anything about McDonald's or Metallica, as I have him saying a few lines later. He actually said it's like pointing your cart north and heading for Etsu, which was a legendary place everybody knew about back then that was supposedly really far south. Or, Dogen said, it's like facing south and looking for the North Star (or the Big Dipper, depending on whose translation you look at). I could have used those metaphors, too, but it wouldn't have been funny.

The next line in my paraphrase is, "All you're doing is just collecting more of the causes of life and death (samsara) and losing any hope of getting free." That's pretty much the standard translation. By getting all worked up about life and death, you're reinforcing your confused delusion that what you think of as life and what you think of as death are real things. But maybe you're wrong.

My paraphrase says, "When you're alive there's nothing but life. When you die there's nothing but death." The best direct translation I can come up with would be, "In the time called life/birth, there is nothing other than life/birth. In the time called extinction, there is nothing other than extinction." Most translators translate the character 生 (*iki* or *sho*) in this sentence as "life" (Nishijima/Cross, Nishiyama/Stevens, Shasta Abbey, Waddell/Abe). Tanahashi goes with "birth." So his version says, "In birth there is nothing but birth, and in death there is nothing but death." The outlier is Yuho Yokoi, whose version goes, "In the time of rise, there is nothing but rise. In the time of decay, there is nothing but decay." It's an odd choice, but there is some precedent for the character *iki* (生, also pronounced *sho*) referring to things as arising or appearing.

In this line Dogen uses *metsu* (滅), meaning "destruction" or "extinction," rather than *shi* (死), meaning "death," which is the character he used in the title. He makes this substitution a few other times in the essay. Often *iki/sho* (生) and *metsu* (滅) are used as paired opposites, as in the line in the Heart Sutra *fusho fumetsu* (不生不滅), usually translated as "(they) neither arise nor cease." So you could make a case for translating the line as, "In the time of arising, there is nothing apart from arising. In the time of ceasing there is nothing apart from ceasing."

This line was one of Nishijima Roshi's favorites. It echoes another of his favorite lines of Dogen's, the line in "Genjo Koan" that goes, "Life is an instantaneous situation, and death is also an instantaneous situation." Nishijima Roshi often paraphrased these lines in his talks, saying things like, "When you are alive there is nothing but being alive, and when you die there is nothing but dying." He also said, "Our life always exists just at the present moment, and the length of the present moment is always the shortest time. Actually, the present moment is much shorter than a single breath. Therefore, we can say that the length of our life is much shorter than the length of one breath."

When Nishijima Roshi was dying in a Tokyo hospital, the attending physician wanted to put him on a respirator. But Nishijima refused, saying, "I will decide the time of my own death."

I don't know if I'll be that brave when I die, but I deeply admire his stance. He really lived up to what he taught. Death didn't scare him at all. Lots of people say that, but he actually meant it. He regarded death as a necessary part of living. He didn't speculate about what did or did not happen after a person dies. He just knew death was something none of us can avoid. When his time came, he chose to just do it.

In the essay "Zenki" (All Functions), which I mentioned in the introduction to this chapter, Dogen says something similar. He says, "Realization is life, and life is realization. At the moment of this realization, there is nothing that is not the total realization of life, and there is nothing that is not the total realization of death." He also quotes an old Zen master of the past who said, "Life is the manifestation of all functions. Death is the manifestation of all functions." Further along in that essay, Dogen says, "Life does not get in the way of death and death does not get in the way of life. The whole earth and the whole of space are both present in life and are both present in death." These lines are all from the Nishijima/Cross translation, by the way.

This relates to the next line I'd like to look at. In my paraphrase, I have Dogen saying, "You don't need to dodge either one (i.e., life or death), and you don't need to long for either one." I think this describes Nishijima's attitude toward death when it was actually happening to him.

The Nishijima/Cross translation of this line is, "Do not say, confronting them, that you will serve them, and do not wish for them." Their footnote describes "serving life" as things like being a hypochondriac or excessively health conscious and "serving death" as being a drug addict or someone who drives unreasonably fast. My guess is that this footnote was sparked by a conversation between Nishijima and his co-translator, Mike Cross. It sounds like the kinds of things I heard them discuss.

"Your own life and death are exactly the sacred life of Buddha," Dogen says a bit further along in my paraphrase. Again, I didn't deviate much from the way everybody else puts that line. This may be one of the key lines in this essay. Lots of us imagine our lives to be just...whatever. But we think that things like "the sacred life of Buddha" must be a whole lot more important and cool and special.

Dogen says here that it's not like that. This very life you're living right now, no matter how schlubby and ordinary you might think it is, is the sacred life of Buddha. How could it get any more uplifting?

The part a few lines later that I translated as "if you grab on to your life like there's no tomorrow...that's just you pretending to be Buddha" is a little bit different from what you'd get in most standard translations. The actual line is *hotoke no arisama wo todomuru nari* (仏のありさまをとどむるなり). Everybody I know, other than Nishijima/Cross, reads the last part of this line as something like "what remains will be the mere form of Buddha" (that's Tanahashi's translation, but others are very similar). Nishijima/Cross give us "we confine ourselves to the condition of Buddha." The key word is *todomuru*, which is a medieval Japanese word nobody uses anymore. It means something like "(you) stop (at)" or "(you're) limited/confined (to)."

I think my paraphrase is pretty true to Dogen's intentions as they might be expressed to contemporary Western people. He's saying that making a big show of holding on to the sacred life of Buddha is just pretending to be like what you imagine a Buddha must be like. Don't do that.

Right after this part I have Dogen say, "You only really get inside the mind of Buddha when you can stop wanting life and stop fearing death." The one major change I made is to add the words *life* and *death* as objects of the wanting and fearing that Dogen is talking about. In the original it's more like, "Without dislike and without longing, that's when the mind of Buddha begins to appear." It's implied that life and death are the objects of this longing and dislike, but it's not directly stated. It could also refer to longing and dislike in a more general sense.

This echoes the first line of a famous Buddhist poem called "Shin Jin Mei" (Faith Mind Inscription), which goes, "The Great Way is not difficult, just avoid like and dislike." Sometimes it's translated as "just avoid preferences" or "just avoid picking and choosing" or even "just avoid love and hate."

This idea of avoiding preferences can sound intimidating. It sounds sort of like Dogen is asking us to walk into an ice cream shop and say, "Give me whatever flavor you like, for I am without preferences." It sounds like he's demanding that we get rid of our ordinary tendency to like some things better than others. Or, worse yet, it sounds like a call for total complacency.

I don't think of it like that. Here's how I think of it. In any given moment, you may like what's happening, or you may not. But whether or not you like it, this moment is exactly what it is. That doesn't mean you shouldn't try to make things better. It doesn't mean you have to complacently accept whatever comes. But your like or dislike isn't going to change a bad situation. It's what you do that matters. So being able to put aside your preferences and act is much more useful than worrying about what you like or don't like.

Also, preferences aren't some fixed thing you have to eradicate once and for all so that you never prefer anything over anything else ever again. Preferences arise moment by moment. Sometimes they can be a guide to what you need to do in the next moment. Usually, though, preferences are not of much use. So while we don't try to eliminate them, it seems beneficial to set them aside and get down to business.

Let's keep moving along. The Waddell/Abe translation has a footnote about the stuff that shows up a bit later about throwing your mind into the house of Buddha and letting him do it all. They say that this might be a reference to the ideas of the Pure Land school of Buddhism.

Pure Land Buddhism is hugely popular in Japan and was just beginning to get off the ground in Dogen's day. There is a tradition in the Soto school of presenting this particular essay as something Dogen preached for people of the Pure Land school, although nobody knows for sure if it really was. One of the Pure Land school's main ideas is *tariki*, or "other power" as opposed to *jiriki*, or "self-power." In Pure Land Buddhism you're supposed to have faith that

Amida Buddha will use his "other power" to help you when you can't help yourself with your "self-power." It's a lot like the Christian idea of salvation through the power of Christ rather than by your own doing.

. I don't think Dogen would have put something he didn't believe into one of his essays just to appeal to a specific audience. So he must have really believed what he said about letting Buddha take care of things. It isn't quite the same as the Pure Land idea, but it is kind of close. To folks who are accustomed to Dogen's radical DIY ideals, hearing him talking about leaving it all in Buddha's hands must be kind of disconcerting.

I don't think he's saying that Buddha is some kind of God-like figure who can intercede on your behalf. To me he's saying that Buddha — the transcendent Buddha I spoke about earlier, not the guy who lived in India a long time ago — is bigger than our individual selves. Buddha is what Buddhists call the collective mind and body of the universe. Our own individual body/mind is a small part of that.

When we align ourselves with the larger universal body/mind, it's a little like accepting the grace of God, to put it in Christian terms. If you don't like the idea of God, you can think of it as the universal mind or something like that. Even though there's no Supreme Being in Buddhism, there is an idea that the universe as a whole can be said to have a mind and a will. I feel like that's what Dogen is talking about here.

Let's keep going. That little list at the end of the essay about what it takes to be a Buddha has a few variations. The part I've paraphrased as "don't be a jerk" is usually translated as "refrain from evil" or from "unwholesome action" or "committing wrongs." The word Dogen uses is *aku* (悪), which is probably best translated as "evil." But most translators into English don't like using the word *evil*, probably because of its Christian connotations. I used the phrase "don't be a jerk" as a reference to the Dogen essay I gave that title to in my previous book (the title of the whole book was also *Don't Be a Jerk*). He uses basically that same phrase here.

Where I have "don't get hung up on life and death," most translators go with something like "be without attachment to life and death." There's no big diff, as far as I'm concerned, but I just thought you might like to know.

"Show some respect to people who deserve it and kindness to people who need it" generally gets translated more like "venerate those above and pity those below." Sometimes *respect* is substituted for *venerate*. Sometimes *be kind* is substituted for *pity*. The Japanese people I've known who speak English tend to use the English word *pity* in a much broader way than we do. When they use it, it has a sense of being kind or compassionate to whomever you're pitying rather than being condescending to them.

"Don't get all caught up in hating stuff or in wanting stuff" usually gets translated more like "not excluding or desiring anything." Again, we're back to that idea expressed in "Shin Jin Mei" (Faith Mind Inscription) about being without preferences.

"Don't think too much. Don't worry" is a little more colloquial than most translators go for. But again, they all say something pretty similar. It's easier to say this than to do it, of course. That's why we practice zazen. A meditation practice can help you understand the true source of overthinking and worry. Once you see how it arises, it's much easier to avoid it.

Still, no matter how good you get, there will be some things you'll think too much about and some things you'll worry about. In and of itself, that's not really a problem. By saying "don't think too much" and "don't worry," Dogen is not asking us to start thinking about overthinking or to start worrying about worrying. That doesn't help anything.

For myself, when I'm sitting around and I notice that I'm overthinking or worrying, I try my best to let those thoughts go without judging or holding on to them, and without trying to make them go away. All those activities just make it worse.

When I can't let stuff go, I try my best not to try too hard to let it go. I try to see if I actually have to act on those thoughts and worries right now. If I don't have to act on them immediately or if I can't act on them even if I think I ought to, then I see if there's something else I can do instead. Like more zazen, or just going for a walk or something.

If it seems like I have to do something right now and I can actually do that thing, I'll do it. But when that happens, I also try to remember that my worried, overthinking state of mind is making it highly unlikely that I'll be able to act in the best possible way. So I try my best to do as little of whatever I feel like I need to do as necessary.

If I fail at all the above, well, life usually goes on anyway, and there's almost always another chance to get it right.

So that's Dogen's take on life and death. It's short and to the point. Next I'd like to talk a little about what modern science and contemporary Buddhists have to say about life.

11. DOES LIFE EXIST?

A LOT OF us who get into meditation and other similar types of deep inquiry get into it because we want to know the meaning of life. Often, though, we take it for granted that we know what life *is* even if we don't know what it *means*. At the very least, we generally believe that we know in broad terms the difference between people and things that are alive and people and things that are not alive. That much seems pretty obvious.

In Buddhist temples we often dedicate the merit of various ceremonies we do to "all sentient beings." I have always found this interesting. It immediately sets up a dualism between those beings that are sentient and those that are not, much like the dualism between what's alive and what's dead. The word that was translated as "sentient" that I recall hearing when I studied Zen in Japan was *seishinteki* (精神的), which literally means "possessing a spirit" or "possessing a mind."

The words for *spirit* and *mind* are interchangeable in Japanese. The word for *psychiatry*, for example, is *seishingaku* (精神学). *Gaku* means "the study of" and the same *seishin* that we just saw in the word for *sentient* could, in other contexts, refer to what we tend to define in the West as "spirit" as easily as to what we in the West call "mind." So the idea of designating some things as sentient and others as nonsentient is pretty much the same in Japan as it is in the West, except that Japanese philosophies never had a strong idea of the immaterial soul as something different from the material mind. And yet much of Buddhist philosophy admits of no distinction between that which is sentient and that which is not. I've often wondered why we make the distinction in our chants. I don't really know the answer to that. But here's a story that might help illustrate the problem.

> Once upon a time, Dogo, a Zen teacher, and Zengen, his student, were attending a funeral. As they stood by the coffin Zengen, the student, tapped the coffin and asked, "Is he alive or dead?"
>
> Dogo, his teacher, said, "I won't say alive and I won't say dead."
>
> Zengen said, "Why won't you tell me?"
>
> Dogo said, "I won't say! I won't say!"
>
> Later on, when they were walking home, Zengen said, "Please tell me the answer! I can't wait! If you don't tell me, I'll beat the tar out of you."
>
> Dogo said, "You can hit me if you want, but I won't say."
>
> Zengen smacked his teacher.
>
> Later on Zengen went to another teacher named Sekiso. Zengen asked Sekiso the same question. Sekiso said, "I won't say alive and I won't say dead."
>
> Zengen said, "Why won't you tell me?"
>
> Sekiso said, "I won't say! I won't say!"
>
> This time Dogo understood and had a great awakening.

Uh...what? Obviously there is some difference between alive and dead. But what that difference is may not be as obvious as we assume. The more you look at life, the less obvious it is what is and what is not alive. So let's see what science might have to tell us about Zengen's question.

In his article called "Why Life Does Not Really Exist," Ferris Jabr says, "For as long as people have studied life they have struggled to define it. Even today, scientists have no satisfactory or universally accepted definition of life."*

Every set of criteria developed by scientists to define what life is turns out to have so many holes and exceptions that a proper definition of life is still elusive. In the seventeenth century, a doctrine called vitalism was developed by a German chemist named Georg Ernst Stahl. This theory is very much like most religious theories of life that I am aware of.

According to the article, the vitalists said that "living organisms are fundamentally different from non-living entities because they contain some non-physical element or are governed by different principles than are inanimate things." In other words, living things possess what the Christians call a soul and the Hindus call atman. The Japanese would probably call it *seishin* and leave the argument about whether it is material or immaterial aside. But, alas, for those who believed in it, the theory of vitalism was largely abandoned by science, though it has never been abandoned by religion.

Science has progressed a lot in the past four hundred years. But even with today's sophisticated methods and theories, whenever science has attempted to find a clear dividing line between that which is alive and that which is not, that dividing line has proved to have too many exceptions.

To take just a few examples of how tricky this can be, Jabr says,

Most people do not consider crystals to be alive, for example, yet they are highly organized and they grow. Fire, too, consumes energy and gets bigger. In contrast, bacteria, tardigrades, and even some crustaceans can enter long periods of dormancy during which they are not growing, metabolizing or changing at all, yet are not technically dead. How do we

---

* *Scientific American* website, December 2, 2013.

categorize a single leaf that has fallen from a tree? Most people would agree that, when attached to a tree, a leaf is alive: its many cells work tirelessly to turn sunlight, carbon dioxide and water into food, among other duties. When a leaf detaches from a tree, its cells do not instantly cease their activities. Does it die on the way to the ground; or when it hits the ground; or when all its individual cells finally expire? If you pluck a leaf from a plant and keep its cells nourished and happy inside a lab, is that life?

Jabr says the reason we have failed to find the elusive something that differentiates life from nonlife is "because such a property does not exist. Life is a concept that we invented. On the most fundamental level, all matter that exists is an arrangement of atoms and their constituent particles. These arrangements fall onto an immense spectrum of complexity, from a single hydrogen atom to something as intricate as a brain. In trying to define life, we have drawn a line at an arbitrary level of complexity and declared that everything above that border is alive and everything below it is not. In truth, this division does not exist outside the mind."

This doesn't mean that there's no important difference between a living monkey and a sock monkey. Of course there is! But it does mean that even such an obvious distinction may break down at some level.

All our concepts are just maps to help us navigate our way through our day-to-day existence. But maps, by their very nature, must be incomplete. A map that has too many details is confusing and useless. The only way a map could be fully detailed would be for the map itself to actually be the territory it represents — in which case it's not a map anymore!

If life isn't what we think it is, maybe death isn't what we imagine it to be, either. Around the same time that I saw the *Scientific American* piece, a few people sent me links to an article called "Scientists Claim That Quantum Theory Proves Consciousness Moves to

Another Universe at Death" on a website called Spirit, Science and Metaphysics. The website was full of articles with similar titles, such as "Physicists Find Evidence That the Universe Is a Giant Brain" and "Science Proves That DNA Can Be Reprogrammed with Words and Frequencies." So I'm quite skeptical of the direction of the piece. However, the article did quote several working scientists on their opinion as to what happens after we die. I found that part interesting.

The article set out its premise in the first line, which said, "A book titled *Biocentrism: How Life and Consciousness Are the Keys to Understanding the Nature of the Universe* has stirred up the Internet, because it contained a notion that life does not end when the body dies, and it can last forever. The author of this publication, scientist Dr. Robert Lanza, who was voted the third most important scientist alive by the *NY Times*, has no doubts that this is possible." Already I was suspicious. But, okay, I read on.

The article summarized Lanza's theories by saying, "If the body generates consciousness, then consciousness dies when the body dies. But if the body receives consciousness in the same way that a cable box receives satellite signals, then of course consciousness does not end at the death of the physical vehicle." It went on to postulate that there is reason to believe that perhaps the brain is not so much the generator of consciousness as the receiver of it.

Now, I'm pretty cynical when it comes to supposed "scientific proof" of life after death, especially when it's promoted in breathless hyperbole like this website chose to employ. In the midnineties I read a book called *The Physics of Immortality: Modern Cosmology, God and the Resurrection of the Dead* by Frank J. Tipler. It had created a lot of hype and cross talk and seemed like the kind of weirdo stuff I often read, even though I don't put too much stock in most of it. *Library Journal* said of that book, "Tipler, a professor of mathematical physics at Tulane, presents a scientific argument for the existence of God." In the book Tipler offers what he insists is mathematical proof that everyone who ever lived will one day be resurrected and live forever.

Tipler's logic and mathematics have been disputed by many others in his field and would hardly be considered "scientific proof" of anything these days. Yet when it was new, lots of people who long for scientific validation of their pet theories were quick to tout the book as proof that science supported them. So I take all the "scientific proof" of immortality I often come across with several large grains of pink Himalayan rock salt.

And yet this idea that the brain receives rather than produces what we call consciousness is essentially the Buddhist idea of how things work. In traditional Buddhist thinking, the brain is considered one of the sense organs. It takes input from the other sense organs and organizes it into something that it can manipulate and deal with. It also senses consciousness, which is not assumed to reside within it or to be created by it. Though consciousness is not thought of as a signal the brain picks up like your cable box picks up episodes of *The Jersey Shore*, either. It's more the summation of sensory input.

The article from Spirit, Science and Metaphysics stated that,

> Consciousness resides, according to [Dr.] Stuart [Hameroff, physician and researcher at the University Medical Center in Tucson,] and British physicist Sir Roger Penrose, in the microtubules of the brain cells, which are the primary sites of quantum processing. Upon death, this information is released from your body, meaning that your consciousness goes with it. They have argued that our experience of consciousness is the result of quantum gravity effects in these microtubules, a theory which they dubbed orchestrated objective reduction (Orch-OR).
>
> Consciousness, or at least proto-consciousness, is theorized by them to be a fundamental property of the universe, present even at the first moment of the universe during the Big Bang.

All this stuff about consciousness residing in microtubules in the brain cells sounds pretty hokey to me. And if I've learned anything, it's that just being a scientist doesn't guarantee that you're any more immune to trying to find ways to make yourself believe you'll live forever than the average religious fundamentalist. See Frank Tipler, for just one example.

Still, science is based on experimentation and reason rather than on taking the word of ancient authorities. So it is interesting to hear scientists saying things that sound so much like Buddhism and yet so very unlike it as well.

Like science, Buddhism is also based on experimentation and reason. But our experiments are far more subjective. They probably wouldn't pass muster as truly "scientific." Yet they are not based on blind faith in received wisdom or ancient supposedly supernatural authorities. My friend Steve Stücky, former abbot of San Francisco Zen Center, died of cancer on December 31, 2013. Just a few days before he passed away he wrote a poem:

> This human body truly is the entire cosmos
> Each breath of mine, is equally one of yours, my darling
> This tender abiding in "my" life
> Is the fierce glowing fire of inner earth
> Linking with all pre-phenomena
> Flashing to the distant horizon
> From "right here now" to "just this"
> Now the horizon itself
> Drops away—
> Bodhi!
> Svaha.

Steve's poem expresses the basic Zen Buddhist view of what life and death are. The poem is not exactly scientific. But it does convey some of what he had come to understand, including the ambiguities of that understanding. This is not just received wisdom, memorized and then regurgitated on cue. It's what one discovers through meditation practice. It's been verified by many others who have followed the path.

Meditation is the direct observation of the workings of the human mind, not objectively, the way science might attempt to do such observation, but in a blatantly subjective manner. We observe the workings of the human mind by sitting quietly with our own brains and bodies and seeing what they do. This is what Dogen did, and it's why he says what he does about life and death.

The kind of introspective research I'm describing is a time-consuming process, because each and every one of us comes into the experiment with a lot of preconceived notions about ourselves. These notions have been built up throughout our entire lifetimes and draw on the entire lifetime of the human race for much of their source material. It's not easy to get through this, and it's never quick or completely painless. We need to give up all our most cherished notions of who and what we are in order to see clearly the truth of our own existence. But the rewards of doing this are unspeakably great.

We end up with a new map of our existence that's better than the one we used before. A map is just a guide, though. As I said, it has to be incomplete. We have to be careful never to mistake the map for the territory. And when we come across something in the territory that's not on our map, we need to revise the map, not try to change the territory.

Still, that doesn't mean that maps are useless just because they're incomplete or that all maps are equally good. Some maps are far better than others. A good map of what we ourselves are and what the world is can be very useful and guide us to a better life. A poor map, on the other hand, makes us miserable because we get lost.

The map that says we are immaterial souls trapped in material bodies is a poor one that doesn't adequately represent the territory of

reality. A map that says we are machines made out of meat that simply *think* we're sentient when we're actually not is also inadequate.

I am strongly biased toward zazen, particularly as Dogen describes it, over other forms of meditation. Sometimes the philosophy
surrounding these other practices is, I feel, an example of an inadequate map of the territory being explored. If, for example, a certain
meditative system is developed with the goal of helping to free the
immaterial soul from the confinement of the material body — and
many of them are — that appears to be a goal that can't possibly be
achieved because it is based on a misunderstanding of the situation.
As Dogen puts it, it's like trying to reach the south by pointing your
cart toward the north — or like going to McDonald's and expecting
a nutritious meal, as in my paraphrase.

Still, I do not believe this renders all such meditation systems
useless. I've found that people who get very deeply into just about
any kind of meditation practice come to more or less the same conclusions. Even though they will often talk about things like the soul
or the atman, or even God, when you look more closely at how they
define these things you very often see that they're using these words
in a different way from the way their less experienced colleagues use
them. Even Dogen, who very definitely did not believe in the existence of an immaterial soul residing inside the material body, sometimes described the practice of zazen as "playing with the soul." It
isn't that the thing we call soul does not exist. It's that the description
we have for what we call the soul is inadequate, like a poor map.

It's important to me that you, dear reader, know what my biases
are. I don't want to present myself as being wholly objective. But I'm
not closed-minded. I do not think Dogen's style of Zen is the best
or the only way for everyone. It happens to be the best and the only
way for me. If it weren't I wouldn't have devoted so much of my life
to it! But not everyone is like me. Zen may not be best for everyone.
So while I will always gravitate toward the Zen way, I think it's good

to point out the other available alternatives and let people decide for themselves what's right for them.

As for what life is and what death is, I have to agree with Dogen. When you get right down to it, all you can say with assurance is that life is what happens when you're alive and death is what happens when you die. The rest is just speculation.

12. A WILLINGNESS TO SEE THE TRUTH
Doshin
The Will to the Truth

THE TRADITIONAL TITLE of this essay is "Doshin" (道心). But Dogen never wrote an essay with that title. He did, however, write two very different essays both with the title "Butsudo" (仏道), which literally means "the Buddha Way." In the 1600s a guy named Kozen was putting together a version of *Shobogenzo*. He wasn't sure which of the two essays titled "Butsudo" was the right one, so he included both. But he changed the title of one of them to "Doshin" in order to avoid confusion — and because the word *doshin* comes up a bunch of times in that one.

In his article "Textual Genealogies of Dōgen,"* William Bodiford says Kozen "misled readers into assuming that Dōgen addresses the same themes in two separate books (rather than in a revised version of an earlier work)." The parenthetical statement is part of the original quotation, FYI.

Reading both essays, I can see no reason to describe "Doshin" as a "revised version" of "Butsudo." They're almost entirely different. Maybe Dogen just forgot he'd used the title already or something. We'll never know.

One of the main points Dogen makes in that other "Butsudo"

_____

* In Steven Heine's book *Dōgen: Textual and Historical Studies*.

is that we should never refer to what he teaches as "Zen." He says it's "Butsudo," the Way of Buddha, that he teaches and not some subsect called Zen. If you look up the word *butsudo* in a standard Japanese-English dictionary the word you get is *Buddhism*. So Dogen is basically saying there is no Zen, only Buddhism.

As you may have noticed, I often use the term *Zen Buddhism* to describe the stuff that Dogen and other like-minded Buddhists taught. I do so knowing full well that Dogen himself would bristle at being called a Zen Buddhist, as would my late teacher, Gudo Nishijima.

I use the term anyhow because I feel like we've come to a point where such a distinction has already been firmly established and because that distinction needs to be made, especially when speaking and writing for the kind of audiences I generally have.

I can't tell you how many times I've been interviewed by some podcaster, radio DJ, or journalist who sought me out because he or she liked my writings but didn't know anything else about Buddhism except what they'd gleaned from random references on TV, usually made by Lisa Simpson. These folks often assume that there is just one form of Buddhism and that all Buddhists believe and practice the same things.

So I use the term *Zen Buddhism* because I have to, not because I want to. Besides, if I followed Dogen's lead and insisted that what he taught was real Buddhism, as opposed to all the other Buddhisms out there, I'd never hear the end of certain types of people comparing me to the Nazis and the KKK. So apologies to Dogen and Nishijima Roshi for that. I'll also sometimes be using the word *Buddhism* to describe certain ideas that are very much specific to Dogen's form of Zen Buddhism, just like Dogen did. Apologies to anyone who gets offended.

But let's get back to the essay at hand.

The two Chinese characters used to write the word *doshin* mean "way" and "heart/mind." The Chinese characters for *heart* and *mind* are the same — though this is not the same character we looked at earlier that can be translated either as "spirit" or "mind." *Shin* (心, also pronounced *kokoro*) is more like the English word *mind* than the English word *spirit*. But *shin* can also mean "heart," both as in the organ in the center of the chest and as in phrases like "affairs of the heart."

Gudo Nishijima always translated the word *doshin* as "will to the truth." In the San Francisco Zen Center and its affiliate centers they tend to translate this phrase as "way-seeking mind." In Kaz Tanahashi's translation of this essay, which was created partially for use at the San Francisco Zen Center, this chapter is entitled "Heart of the Way." That surprised me. When I first looked it up I thought I must have the wrong chapter. I expected it to be titled "The Way-Seeking Mind."

There are numerous other ways to translate this phrase, which is one of the key phrases in Dogen's writing as a whole and indeed in much of Buddhism. Having *doshin* is seen by many teachers as the most important first step in establishing understanding of the truth that Buddhism seeks. The word itself is open to a lot of interpretations. I'll talk about these as we go along.

I'm using Nishijima's phrase "will to the truth" in my paraphrase. But you can also read it as "way-seeking mind" or "heart of the truth" or "the mind's search for the truth" or "mind of the way" or whatever other version you prefer. I like "will to the truth" because it makes me think not only of having a will — as in resolve, drive, or determination — to know the truth but also of the willingness to accept the truth once it becomes clear. Both are equally important.

This essay is about what *doshin* meant to Dogen. But it's interesting for another reason. It's the one essay that is most often referenced by people who are convinced that Dogen believed in, and taught his students to believe in, the idea of rebirth or reincarnation.

I wrote a chapter in my book *Don't Be a Jerk* entitled "Did

Dogen Teach Reincarnation, and Does It Matter If He Did?" In that chapter I included a passage from this essay in which Dogen appears to give a detailed explanation of what happens after we die. I pointed out that even though this stuff does appear in the essay, it is clearly not the point of the essay to say, "Hey, kids, listen up! Here's what happens after you die! You'd better believe it!" Rather, Dogen's point is that it is super-essential to revere Buddha, dharma, and sangha — I'll talk about what that means later. It's so important to revere these things that Dogen says you should chant praise to them even after you die.

I think it's interesting to discuss Dogen's outlook on the matter of life after death, which we already looked at a few chapters ago. So I'll talk about that after we get through with the essay. I'd also like to talk about the main point of the essay, that matter of what *doshin* means. So we'll do that as well at the end.

This is yet another undated essay that wasn't included in the earliest versions of *Shobogenzo*. We don't know when Dogen wrote it or why. We don't even know if he finished it to his satisfaction. Still, it is now included in the complete version of *Shobogenzo* and is generally considered part of Dogen's overall philosophical outlook. So let's see what it says.

The most important thing in Buddhism is to make the will to the truth your primary concern. Not too many people know what it means to have the will to the truth. It's useful to talk to people who clearly know what it means.

There are plenty of people who supposedly have the will to the truth, but they don't really have it. There are also people who actually have the will to the truth, but nobody else knows it. So the will to the truth is a tricky thing to find.

You shouldn't listen to dumb-asses. But you should also be careful about listening to yourself. The best thing is to pay attention to the dharma. Keep the dharma in mind all day and night. Hope and pray that the real truth can exist in this world.

These days, hardly anyone has a genuine will to the truth. Even so, if you keep in mind that everything is impermanent, you'll know how erratic the world is and how uncertain our lives can be. You don't need to constantly tell yourself, "I am now thinking about impermanence" or anything like that. Instead, we should consider the dharma as essential and consider our own lives and our own bodies as less important. You should be ready and willing to give up even your life and body for the sake of the truth.

Next up, we have to pay deep respect to the Three Treasures — Buddha, dharma, and sangha. We should dedicate everything we have to these three treasures, even our own bodies and lives. When we're awake and when we're asleep we should still keep chanting our dedication.

After we die and before we are reborn, there is said to be a state called Middle Existence, which lasts for seven days. Even during this period, we should keep on chanting our dedication to the Three Treasures without stopping.

They say that after seven days in Middle Existence you die there and receive another body in the Middle Existence. This other body lasts seven days, maximum. When you're in this body you can see everything and hear everything in the whole universe. Even at that time, we have to keep on chanting. The traditional way to do this in Japanese is by saying, "*Namu kie Butsu, Namu kie ho, Namu kie so.*" That just means "Praise to Buddha, praise to dharma, praise to sangha."

After this seven-day period you pass from Middle Existence and you start moving toward whomever will be your parents in your next life, who will be getting busy working on your conception — if you get my meaning. At this time, you gotta really keep up your resolve. Next you'll enter the Womb Storehouse World. This is where you go before you get sent to your next mom's womb. You have to keep on chanting in there, too.

Don't forget to chant even while you're being born. That should surprise your next mom's obstetrician!

You need to totally dedicate yourself to serving offerings to, chanting praises to, and taking refuge in the Three Treasures with all your sense organs.

When this life ends, both your eyes will go dark and you won't see anything. That's when you'll know your life is ending. At that moment you need to try with all your might to chant the praises of the Three Treasures, that chant I mentioned a few paragraphs ago.

If you do that, then Buddhas from every direction will dump tons of compassion on you. Even if you did awful things in this life such that you ought to be reborn in some horrible, hellish world, instead you'll get born into a heavenly realm. You'll end up right where Buddha is. If you manage that trick, you'd better worship Buddha and listen to what he has to say.

After your eyes go dark you gotta keep right on chanting to the Three Treasures. Don't stop in the Middle Existence. Don't even stop during your next birth.

Life after life, in age after age, in world after world, you need to keep right on chanting praise to the Three Treasures. Even after you get completely enlightened you can't stop chanting their praises. This is what all the Buddhas and bodhisattvas do. This is what we call "profoundly realizing the dharma." This is what happens when the great truth of Buddha is totally present and embodied by you. Don't ever pay attention to any other teachings than this.

In this lifetime, make a statue of the Buddha for yourself. Once you've made it, then serve it offerings of a place to sit, some soda pop, and some nice Christmas lights.

You should also make copies of the Lotus Sutra. Lots of them. Write 'em, print 'em out, keep 'em around for yourself, and preserve them for others. You should also prostrate to your copies of the Lotus Sutra and offer them some pretty flowers, stinky incense, more Christmas lights, some tasty food, more soda pop, and clothes. Keep your Lotus Sutras clean, and keep your head clean when you put them on top of your head to praise them.

You also need to wear your Buddhist monk's robe, which is called o-kesa in Japanese and kashaya in Sanskrit. Long ago a prostitute once put on a monk's robe as a joke and because of this she was later reborn as a Buddhist nun, whereupon she had a great awakening. It's the robe of all the Buddhas of the past, present, and future. You can't possibly overstate how valuable it is.

Zazen is not a practice of this world. It is the practice of the Buddhist ancestors.

— Date and place of composition not recorded

This is some wacky piece of work! I wanted to include it to give you a complete picture of the kind of stuff Dogen wrote. Lots of people cherry-pick the essays of his that are most palatable to contemporary Westerners. But this is an example of the types of Dogen writings that are not usually included in books like this. It seems to go against the idea that Dogen was a nice, modern, rational kind of guy. Parts of this essay seem pretty religious or even superstitious. Let's dissect it a little bit.

In the essay Dogen says we should "hope and pray" that the truth can exist in this world. It seemed weird for Dogen to use the word *pray*. But when I checked a few translations it seemed like everybody used the word *pray* in this sentence. So I looked it up in the original, and sure enough, the word Dogen used is *inoru* (いのる). It's one of those instances in which there is very little ambiguity for a translator. The Japanese word *inoru* has one meaning, and it is "pray."

Of course, Japan is not a Christian nation so the Japanese idea of prayer is a bit different. These days, the word *inoru* is used to describe what Christians do when they get on their knees by their beds at night. But it originally referred to what one did at a Shinto shrine when one asked one of the gods (*kami*) for some kind of help. In Shinto there's not a single God like Jehovah or Allah who runs the whole show. Instead there's a god of the sun, a god of the wind, a god of war, a god of rice, and so on. So there's a difference, but it's still what we would call "prayer."

This is not the only place where Dogen talks about praying. Dogen was a realist. He didn't believe in "petitioning the lord with prayer," as Jim Morrison of the Doors said. He didn't generally recommend asking supernatural forces to provide things. Yet he did see the value in prayer as a way to direct people into taking important matters seriously. We saw this in "Instructions for the Cook" when Dogen said the temple cook should chant a sutra to the kitchen god.

The way I look at it is that if you pray to God for help, you are also taking responsibility for doing whatever it takes to make that help happen.

After this stuff about praying, Dogen gets to the part about the Three Treasures: Buddha, dharma, and sangha. Basically *Buddha* means the guy Shakyamuni Buddha who started it all. *Dharma* means that guy's teachings. And *sangha* means the group of people who come together to practice what he taught. That's the most literal translation.

In a wider sense, Buddha is less a reference to the guy who died five hundred years before Jesus was born and more to Buddha in the cosmic sense that we looked at earlier. This gets a little tricky, though. Dogen wasn't from one of those sects of Buddhism in which Buddha is regarded as a god. The more cosmic sense of the term *Buddha* means Buddha as the living, intelligent aspect of the universe, that aspect that holds all the rest together.

Dharma can mean the words that the historical Buddha supposedly spoke. I say "supposedly" because we don't know what he actually said. We just have written records produced hundreds of years after he died, based on an oral tradition. We also have other words created long after Buddha died but written as if they were spoken by the historical Buddha. These are all considered dharma — although some sects of Buddhism reject the later stuff out of hand because it is even more historically dubious than the early stuff. Again, Dogen was from one of the sects of Buddhism that accepted the later stuff as authentic — although Dogen did single out a few of the later supposedly Buddhist sutras as bullshit.

That being said, there is a more cosmic meaning to the word *dharma*. The Sanskrit word *dharma* means "truth" or "law" — although even saying that is a bit misleading. It's impossible to translate the word *dharma* into any single English word. But for our purposes, "truth" or "law" is adequate.

In the more cosmic sense, the word *dharma*, then, doesn't just mean what the Buddha said but the truth that lies behind what the

Buddha said. In terms of "law" as a meaning of *dharma*, Nishijima Roshi used to use the phrase "rule of the universe" a lot. By this he meant that the universe has rules or laws — like the law of gravity, for example. You might be able to go against these laws for a time, but they'll always win in the end. You can jump real high, but gravity will pull you down.

As for sangha, it basically refers to any group of people who come together to try to practice the dharma. Such a group might call itself a sangha, or it might not. But as long as they are dedicated to honestly pursuing the truth together, they're a sangha.

Buddhism is a communal practice. If you go up on a mountain-top and practice alone, that is not Buddhism in the truest sense. Buddha's great innovation wasn't inventing meditation. Lots of people already meditated. His great innovation was turning what had been a solitary practice into something you could do with other people.

Personally, sangha is the part of Buddhism I've always hated the most. Those of you who read my books regularly can skip this part because I feel like I say it at least once in every book. I'm not a joiner. I don't like organizations. I don't trust them. Even the best organizations always seem to degenerate into systems that exist more to perpetuate their own existence than to do whatever it is they were originally created to do. Sanghas are no exception.

Even so, you don't do Buddhist practice by yourself. You do it with others. But if you want to get really Buddhist about it, there are no others. All of the universe is you. Still, you do Buddhism with others. So, Dogen says, it's important to respect and revere the group with whom you practice.

Next, we get to the life-after-death stuff, which is pretty tripped out. Let's dig into it a bit and see what Dogen is really saying and why he might be saying it.

What I'm paraphrasing as Womb Storehouse World is *taizo* (胎蔵), which is short for *taizokai* (胎蔵界). These Chinese characters literally mean "womb," "storehouse," and "world." It is the

Japanese word for the Sanskrit term *garbha-dhatu*. According to the footnotes in the Nishijima/Cross translation, this is "a term used in esoteric Buddhism to describe a world produced by the Buddha's benevolence. It is the subject of one of the two major mandalas of esoteric Buddhism."

After that we get some stuff about chanting while you're being born. Obviously, I added the line "That should surprise your next mom's obstetrician!" But otherwise I'm sticking pretty close to most of Dogen's original descriptions of what happens after you die. All I'm doing is making the language sound a bit more like contemporary, conversational English.

The term I'm paraphrasing as "some horrible, hellish world" is *akushu* (悪趣), which means something like "world of hungry ghosts." It's one of the many bad places someone can be reborn in, according to old Buddhist cosmology. A hungry ghost is a being who is hungry all the time, no matter how much it eats. I think that describes a lot of us in the age of consumerism.

The word I'm paraphrasing as "worship" when Dogen says we should worship the Buddha is *ogamu* (拝む).* It means to assume the posture of prayer. Like down on your knees with your hands together. That sort of thing.

A bit after this, Dogen did not exactly say to offer your Buddha statue a place to sit, some soda pop, and some Christmas lights. But he did say to offer it "seats of straw, sugared drinks, and lights." Which is close enough, if you ask me.

One of the key words that occurs many times in this essay appears around this part. The word is *matsuru* (祭る). In Japan you hear this word a lot in its noun form, *matsuri* (祭り), which means "festival." In the verb form the word is usually translated as "deify," "enshrine," "praise," or "worship." That's another of the things

---

* It's actually written in hiragana in Dogen's text and is part of a compound word, but that's getting really technical. I say this only for the benefit of the super-nerds out there.

you're supposed to do for the Three Treasures, and for the Buddha when you're born in his realm, and for the statue you make of Buddha.

I also added some descriptive words around the stuff Dogen says to offer to your copies of the Lotus Sutra, but otherwise it's all in the original.

Dogen really does say to put the Lotus Sutra on your head, though. The word he uses is one every first-year student of Japanese learns, *itadaku* (頂く). You generally learn the more formal version, though, which is *itadakimasu*. It's what you say when someone gives you food. The mnemonic I learned to memorize it is "eat a duck, I must." In practice it means something like "thanks for the grub, bub!" But it literally means "I receive this on top of my head." It's a way of showing humility, like the person offering you the food is of higher status than you and must therefore bend down and give you that steaming plate of yakisoba on top of your head.

In Buddhist temples you'll often see monks putting things on top of their heads, then folding their hands in prayer and chanting. The most common of these rituals takes place in the early mornings, usually after the first round of zazen. The monks all take their outer robes (*o-kesa*), which are folded up, and put them on their heads chanting, "Great robe of liberation, field beyond form and emptiness, wearing the Tathagata's (Buddha's) teachings, saving all beings." That's the standard English version in the Soto school of Zen Buddhism. There are other variations. After this chant they unfold the robes and put them on.

Finally, we get that story about the prostitute putting on a Buddhist robe as a joke and then getting reborn as a nun. Dogen cites this story more than once in *Shobogenzo*. I don't know if he took it literally. But he evidently liked the message the story conveyed, the message that any sort of Buddhist practice you do — even if you do it as a joke — has merit.

With all this stuff about rebirth, it's easy to lose sight of the point of this essay, which is the importance of having the will to the truth or the way-seeking mind. I can't blame you if you lost sight of it, since Dogen seems to lose sight of it as well. It's hard to know just what sort of audience this piece was intended for, but I'll have a guess at it anyway.

In their intro to the essay "Doshin," Nishijima and Cross speculate that it might have originally been written for laypeople. My guess is that it was intended for the kinds of folks who might have come to one of Dogen's temples to hear a lecture but who were not ready to commit to the cloistered life. These are the sorts of folks who'd be most likely to take stories about the afterlife and rebirth at face value. He seems to want to encourage these folks to stay on the path.

It also may have been intended for novice monks. To people like this, Dogen would have been a role model, a guy who started off being a monk when he was twelve and was now the master of a temple, having never strayed from the path. It is entirely possible that some of the people who first heard this sermon were as young as Dogen was when he was first ordained.

We often forget just how different things were back then. We tend to picture Dogen's monks as the kinds of idealized people we see in temples in old kung fu movies or as the upper-middle-class, college-educated sorts you see in Zen temples today. While some of Dogen's flock were probably high-born intellectuals like him, others were just country boys straight off the rice fields, barely old enough to be in middle school.

That's why I take all the stuff about the afterlife with a grain of salt. It's plain from other pieces of Dogen's writings that he was completely unconcerned with making sure his students believed the correct things about life after death. But he was willing to use the stuff they already believed as a way of encouraging them in the things he did think were important, such as having the will to the truth.

I don't know if, after we die, we spend seven days in Middle Existence and then enter the Womb Storehouse World or any of that. I don't see why it matters very much, even if it's true. But I do see the value in having a willingness to accept the truth and of having a strong reverence for what is real.

Next up, we're going to look at some more words of encouragement from Dogen about the practice of zazen.

13. A NEEDLE IN THE BUTT OF ZAZEN
Zazenshin
A Needle for Zazen

THE ORIGINAL TITLE of this essay is really "A Needle for Zazen." That doesn't refer to the kind of needle like you'd use to poke somebody in the butt as they're sitting zazen; it refers to a bamboo needle like they use in acupuncture to heal the body. In Dogen's time, short verses that were helpful were referred to as "needles" in this sense.

These days when you get instructions for doing your standard commercialized-type meditation practice, generally you'll be told a little about posture and a lot about what to do in your head. In fact, the big trend in popular meditation courses these days is not to address posture at all and only to deal with what sort of thoughts you ought to think while meditating. Zen is not like that.

In fact, Dogen's instructions for doing zazen are the complete opposite. In his little pamphlet "Fukanzazengi" or "Standard Method for Practicing Zazen," he goes into great detail about the proper posture. But when it comes to what to do with your thoughts he only tells you to "think the thought of not thinking." He then helpfully adds that this is "different from thinking."

This leaves a lot of contemporary students of Zen perplexed. The question I get more than any other goes something like this: after the questioner tells me a long, long story about what goes on inside their head when they're meditating, they ask me if this means they're doing it wrong.

I had the same question. Whenever I would bore Nishijima Roshi with a protracted account of all the things that happened in my brain while I sat zazen, he would wait patiently for me to finish and then say exactly the same thing: "That's just the content of your zazen."

This always pissed me off. It seemed completely unhelpful. I was thinking all these things! How could I get to that whole thinking-not-thinking business with so gosh darn many thoughts?

In my previous book, *Don't Be a Jerk*, I spent a page or so on a linguistic analysis of the words Dogen used when he said that stuff about not-thinking being different from thinking. I pointed out that the word that's usually translated as "thinking" actually means something closer to the English word *consideration*. So he's not asking us to cut off all mental activity, just to stop deliberately manipulating our thoughts. But even *that* is way easier said than done. It still leaves you wondering what to actually do.

This essay is Dogen's attempt to get a little more into exactly what this whole not-thinking deal is and how to do it. But if you're expecting Dogen to give you a nice, neat step-by-step guide to calming the mind and achieving inner bliss, you're going to be disappointed.

Step-by-step instructions for how to calm and center the mind are not difficult to find these days. I just googled the phrase "how to calm the mind" and came up with more than a dozen webpages with specific methods. Many of the methods for calming the mind are claimed to have originated with the Buddha himself. But although it is impossible for me to imagine that Dogen was unaware of these ancient methods, he never recommends any of them himself.

Instead of writing down what to do in a nice, orderly fashion, he denounces the whole idea of trying to attain a state of tranquillity and peace of mind. Then, rather than answering his own questions about how to think the thought of not-thinking, he gives us even more questions! What a jerk!

Still, the questions he raises are valid and, I think, point the way toward this whole not-thinking business better than any step-by-step method for calming the mind ever could.

Those of you who read *Don't Be a Jerk* may notice that in this essay Dogen talks about some of the same conversations between ancient Buddhist masters that he talked about in the essay I called "Monkeys and Mirrors and Stones."

This is a huge essay with a lot of stuff that deserves comment. So I have split it into three parts. First we'll just look at the essay itself. The commentary that follows is split into two different sections to try to make it a little easier to deal with.

One fine day Master Yakusan Igen (Ch. Yaoshan Weiyan, 745–827 CE) was sitting zazen and a monk asked him, "What are you thinking about when you sit there like a big ol' rock?"

The master said, "I'm thinking the actual state of not-thinking!"

The monk asked, "How can you think the actual state of not-thinking?"

The master said, "Well it sure ain't the same as thinking!"

If you want to know what this means you have to sit like a big ol' rock for yourself and look into it. This is what Buddhism is all about.

It includes skin, flesh, bones, and marrow as thinking and as not-thinking.

The monk asks how you can think the actual state of not-thinking. It's a good question. But, then again, when you're sitting like a big ol' rock, how could there be any thinking involved? What's there to understand or to misunderstand?

The master said, "Well it sure ain't the same as thinking!"

If you want to think the actual state of not-thinking you have to use this "ain't the same as thinking" to do it. In this "ain't the same as thinking" there is somebody, and that somebody relies on me.

Even though the *state like a big ol' rock* is me, it isn't just thinking. It's hoisting up the *state like a big ol' rock*.

Even though the *state like a big ol' rock* is the *state like a big ol' rock*, how could the *state like a big ol' rock* think the *state like a big ol' rock*?

In any case, the *state like a big ol' rock* isn't Buddha thought, isn't dharma thought, and isn't enlightenment thought. It's beyond even the very concept of understanding.

You can trace the transmission of this state all the way back to Shakyamuni Buddha. And this "ain't the same as thinking" is right here now, too.

Even so, some doofuses these days will tell you that zazen is all about reaching a state of complete mental quietness and that total tranquillity is where it's at. You can't even call such people students of Buddhism. In China you hear this crap a lot. It's a sign of how bad things have gotten.

Then there are dweebs who say that zazen is necessary for beginners or slow learners but that real Buddhist masters don't need to do it. These guys say stuff like "walking is Zen" and "talking is Zen" and "whatever you do, that's Zen, too!" Lots of people in the so-called Rinzai sect say this kind of garbage. They say it because they haven't ever been taught the truth.

I mean, come on. What's a beginner? Who is not a beginner? Where would you even look for a beginner?

Keep in mind that if you want to understand the Buddhist truth, you gotta do zazen. The best thing is to practice Buddha's practice without any desire to become a Buddha. Since practicing Buddha's practice doesn't involve becoming a Buddha, the universe is realized.

When you break through your self-made cages, you see that sitting Buddha doesn't get in the way of becoming Buddha. At this very moment you have the eternal power to enter the World of Buddha or the World of Demons. A step forward or a step backward can fill up a ditch or fill up a whole valley.

A long time ago Zen Master Baso Doitsu (Ch. Mazu Daoi, 709–788 CE) was practicing with his teacher Nangaku Ejo (Ch. Nanyue Huairang, 677–744 CE). Baso had already received dharma transmission and become a Zen master, but he still sat zazen all the time.

One day, Master Nangaku asked his student Baso, "What's your intention in doing zazen?"

Let's spend some time looking at this question in detail. Is

Nangaku asking if there's some aim that's above sitting zazen? Has there ever been a state of truth that exists somehow outside of zazen? Is he implying that we shouldn't have any intention at all? Right now, while doing zazen, what sort of intention is being realized? Really pay attention to this.

It's better to love the real Godzilla than a Godzilla action figure. Yet both the real Godzilla and a Godzilla action figure have fins that light up when they use their atomic fire breath.

Don't make a big deal out of something just because it's far away, and don't think that just because something is commonplace it's inferior. What's commonplace is just commonplace. What's far away is just far away. That's all there is to it. Don't think of what you see as being better than what you hear, or vice versa. They are what they are.

Baso answered, "I intend to become a Buddha!"

What does he mean, "become a Buddha?" Is that, like, a Buddha being made by a Buddha? Or Buddha being made into Buddha? Is it another Buddha being added to the number of Buddhas there already are? Is he gonna drop off body and mind to become a Buddha as the dropping off of body and mind? Does he mean that even though there are many ways to become a Buddha, it's still wrapped up with intention?

Baso himself said that the very act of doing zazen *is* intending to become a Buddha. To sit in zazen is always the intention to become a Buddha. Intention may come before becoming a Buddha. Intention may come after becoming a Buddha. Intention might be the very moment of becoming a Buddha.

I mean, just how many instances of becoming a Buddha are twisted up inside this intention? And even intention is twisted up inside of intention.

Hell, you can't possibly run away from intention! If you did so you'd die! But even dying is all twisted up inside of intention.

After hearing Baso's answer, Nangaku picked up a tile off the floor and started polishing it on a rock.

Baso said, "What are you doing?"

What a dopey question! He's polishing a tile, idiot. Then again, who can see what polishing a tile really is? The way to ask about this is to say, "What are you doing?" But *what* is always what you're doing, if you get my drift. In this world, or in any other world, tiles are always being polished. Your own view isn't necessarily the way things really are. No matter what's going on, it's important to learn in practice.

We see Buddha, but we don't really know Buddha or understand Buddha. Don't come to hasty conclusions about what you encounter. That's not the way to study Buddhism.

Nangaku said, "I'm polishing it to make a mirror."

Let's take a look at his words. It's pretty deep stuff. The Buddhist truth is right there in this "polishing it to make a mirror." Tiles are tiles. Mirrors are mirrors. But *polishing*? That's something else entirely! If you're aiming to know the whole truth of life, look into *polishing*.

Maybe even the "clear mirror" and the "eternal mirror" spoken of in ancient Buddhist teachings get made into mirrors by polishing a tile. If you don't know that mirrors become mirrors by polishing tiles, you don't know the first thing about Buddhist philosophy.

Baso said, "How can you make a mirror by polishing a tile?"

You gotta admit that even Iron Man couldn't polish a tile hard enough to make it into a mirror. Be that as it may, although polishing a tile is not making a mirror, mirrors appear spontaneously.

Nangaku said, "How can sitting zazen make you into a Buddha?"

Obviously, doing zazen isn't working on becoming a Buddha. Even becoming a Buddha is irrelevant to zazen.

Baso said, "Then what's right?"

It might look like Baso is just asking about this particular instance, but he's really asking about what's right everywhere and throughout time. It's like when you talk to a close friend. Their being a close friend to you is your being a close friend to them. This question is like both sides appearing at the same time.

Nangaku said, "When your car stops working, do you fix the engine or kick the tires?"*

What does he mean by saying, "When your car stops working"? What's it mean to say a car is moving or isn't moving? For example, is water flowing the same as a car moving? Is water not flowing the

---

* In the original it's more like, "When your cart won't move, do you prod the ox or prod the cart?" See the discussion that follows for more details.

same as a car moving? You could say that flowing is water not moving. Maybe the real movement of water is beyond our ideas about
"flowing."

So if you look closely at the phrase "when your car stops working," you might find there is "stops working" or you might find there
is no "stops working." The words *when your car stops working* aren't
as one-sided as you might think.

Then Nangaku says, "Do you fix the engine or kick the tires?"
Could there be both fixing the engine *and* kicking the tires? Is fixing
the engine the same as kicking the tires?*

In the regular world, there's no method for kicking the tires, at
least not one that works. But in Buddhism we could say "kick the
tires." And by that I mean that we learn in physical practice. Even so,
methods for fixing the engine are not the same as methods for kicking the tires. Pay attention, people.

Although there are methods of "fixing the engine" in the regular world, we should look into the Buddhists methods for fixing the
engine as well. How do you fix an engine? Is it fixing an engine that's
still got some hope of working again? Or is it fixing a plastic replica
of an engine? Or a statue of an engine carved out of rock?

Should you fix the engine with a wrench? Or should you use the
whole universe and the whole of the mind? Should you get your fists
involved?

There needs to be a foot kicking a foot, and an engine fixing an
engine.

Baso didn't reply. Pay attention to that, too. It's like that old story
about the Zen master who threw away a tile and got a jewel in return.
Saying nothing is the best reply Baso could have made.

Nangaku had more to say, though. He said, "Sitting zazen is
learning how to be a sitting Buddha." These are important words.
They're like the words of all the great ancient masters. We may not
know the real meaning of zazen practice, but here it's defined as

---

* Most commentators on Dogen see what I've paraphrased as "fixing the engine"
(prodding the horse) to mean something like working on the mental aspects
of practice, while what I'm giving you as "kick the tires" (prodding the cart)
means physical practice. We'll talk about this in the commentary.

"learning how to be a sitting Buddha." Only a real master can say stuff like that.

And get this. A beginner's first time sitting zazen is the first time anyone ever sat zazen. It's the first sitting of the Buddha.

Then Nangaku said, "Once you learn sitting zazen you know that zazen ain't about sitting or lying down." He means that zazen is zazen, not sitting or lying down.

Once we understand from a good teacher that sitting zazen is beyond sitting and lying down, we can truly be ourselves when sitting or lying down. Then you don't have to look for what's commonplace or for what's faraway. You don't have to worry about delusion or enlightenment. Why get caught up in intellectual stuff like that?

Nangaku kept on going. He said, "When you're sitting like Buddha, Buddha doesn't have any set form." The reason there can be more than just one Buddha is that Buddha has no set form. Because Buddha has no set form, you can't avoid sitting Buddha. In other words, you learn to be Buddha by sitting like Buddha. Doing zazen is being Buddha.

Could anybody in this real world tell who is a Buddha and who isn't a Buddha? Before you even have a thought of differentiating one from the other, a sitting Buddha is a Buddha sitting.

Nangaku wasn't finished yet. He said, "Studying sitting Buddha is just killing Buddha."

So whenever you do zazen, you're killing Buddha. And that's a good thing. If you want to know how to kill Buddha, just do zazen and see how it's done. The word *kill* that Nangaku uses is the same word everybody uses, but it doesn't mean quite the same thing.

Look into this. The very existence of Buddha could be called "killing Buddha." We also ought to see if we are killing a person when we do zazen or not killing a person when we do zazen.

"If you get hung up on the sitting form, you just don't get it." To get hung up on the sitting form is to disrespect the sitting form. When you're sitting zazen you're gonna get hung up on the sitting form, no matter what you do. That's cool. But it's also an example of not getting it. Do you feel me? If you get this, you know what I mean when I talk about "dropping body and mind."

People who've never done zazen can't even hope to get this.

It exists in the very moment of doing zazen. It exists in the person sitting. It exists in the seated Buddha. It exists in the Buddha learning sitting.

Normal sitting or lying around isn't a Buddha sitting. Even if someone seems like they're doing it, maybe they're just trying to become a Buddha. There are people who are becoming Buddhas, but not all people are becoming Buddhas. All Buddhas are not all people, because Buddhas aren't only people. Sitting Buddhas are always like this.

Baso verified how sitting Buddha becomes Buddha. Nangaku taught how to become a Buddha by sitting like a Buddha. Just keep in mind that every great Buddhist sage says that sitting zazen is the one essential thing. Those who are Buddhist sages teach this. Those who aren't sages don't have a clue in the world about it.

In India and China this is the way Buddhism has always been taught. That's because zazen is the main thing. The principle of zazen is the one thing that has been passed down all the way from the very beginning. Until you understand this, you can't understand anything else. In every single case, Buddhist masters have taught zazen.

Still, even since way back in the day, not many people have understood zazen. There are even big famous temples in China where they don't get it. They have rules that say everybody's gotta do zazen, and they all do it. But those who know what zazen is really all about are rare. They even write books about how to do zazen, but most of those books are pretty useless.

It's a shame they can spend a whole lifetime sitting and still be so clueless. They don't put any real effort into their practice. They write books about having tripped-out experiences or about stopping all thought to attain blissful states of mind. This is not what zazen is about.

There is, however, one poem about doing zazen that I can whole-heartedly recommend. It was written by a really great Chinese master named Wanshi Shogaku (Ch. Hongzhi Zhengjue, 1091–1157 CE). It's called "A Needle for Zazen," and it goes something like this:

At the heart of every Buddha
At the heart of each sage who's not dozing

Is to know without ever touching
To be awakened without opposing

To know without ever touching
Knowing is naturally refined
To be awakened without opposing
Awakening is naturally sublime

Knowing is naturally refined
There's no thought of discrimination
Awakening is naturally sublime
Not a hint of fabrication

There's no thought of discrimination
No sense of duality, it's one
Not a hint of fabrication
Awake without grasping, it's done

The water's clear all the way to the bottom
Fishes are swimming slow and lazy
The sky is wide and limitless
Birds fly far away where it's all hazy

The point of this needle — see what I did there, folks? — is that the Great Function is right here in front of us. It's super-cool style that's the finest of the fine. It's like getting a look at the time before your mama was born. It's like knowing why it's stupid to insult the masters of the past. It's like death isn't even a thing anymore. It's like if your head and your neck were as big as the Buddha's.

The "heart of every Buddha" means that Buddhas see every moment as being the most important moment there ever was or will be. You realize that by doing zazen.

The "heart of each sage" is kinda like the way some of the ancient sages spoke without using any words. Every turn of their heads and every expression that crossed their faces was a Buddhist teaching.

"To know without ever touching" means that knowing isn't the same thing as perceiving something with the senses. That's small-scale stuff. Nor is this knowing he's talking about a kind of intellectual knowing. Intellectual knowing is calculated and purposeful. And don't think of this as some kind of God-like universal knowledge, either.

It's like what Fuke said. He's the fat "happy Buddha" you see outside Chinese restaurants sometimes. He said, "When a clear mind comes, a clear mind comes. When a cloudy mind comes, a cloudy mind comes." It means to sit in the skin you were born with.

"To be awakened without opposing" doesn't mean some kind of "spiritual awakening." To be awakened means you don't oppose your real circumstances. Awakening is not something outside your real circumstances. Your real circumstances *are* your awakening.

The meaning of "without opposing" is that in the whole universe nothing is ever hidden. It's subtle and mysterious. It's not reciprocal, and it's not one-sided.

"There's no thought of discrimination, no sense of duality, it's one" means that knowledge in the form of thought doesn't depend on outside forces. It's subtle and mysterious the way mountains and rivers are subtle and mysterious. When you use this subtle and mysterious state, it's as if everything comes alive.

The old Chinese legends talk about how a fish becomes a dragon when it passes through the magical Dragon's Gate. It's sorta like that, only we don't pass through any kind of magical gate to make the change. When we stop discriminating things from each other, we sense everything directly.

However, you don't need to worry if you're still discriminating things from each other. That's fine. All the Buddhas do that, too. That is precisely their state of realization. There is no past, but the past still exists. In other words, without discriminating things from each other, you live directly in the present moment.

"Not a hint of fabrication, awake without grasping, it's done," the poem says. "Not a hint" means the entire universe. The naturally sublime awakening looks like it just appeared out of nowhere. Don't doubt what you see, but don't always believe what you hear. Awakening means seeing beyond words. To be awakened is to doubt your own awakening.

"The water's clear all the way to the bottom / Fishes are swimming slow and lazy," says Wanshi in his poem. Water as a metaphor for some kind of clear understanding isn't really as pure as we might want to believe.

When fish swim through the water they feel like water is nonexistent, the same as we feel when we move through the air. Doing zazen is like fish swimming. To them, the water seems limitless. Who can say they're wrong? Getting all the way to the bottom of things isn't like flying through the sky like a bird.

"The sky is wide and limitless, birds fly far away where it's all hazy" doesn't refer to the sky in a materialistic sense. It doesn't even refer to some kind of idealistic meaning of *sky* in the sense of all-pervading spiritual space. The sort of sky this poem refers to isn't hidden or revealed, nor is it outside or inside. When a bird flies through the sky he's flying through the immeasurable dharma as the sky. The whole universe is flying through the sky.

We can't know how far the sky goes on, so we just call it "far away." Birds and sky fly together. This is an expression of the real place you're in right now.

Anyway, that's Wanshi's "Needle for Zazen." It's the world's best poem about zazen, if you ask me. Nobody's ever gonna top it. My teacher used to say Wanshi was the greatest Buddhist master ever.

It's now March 18, 1242, so it's been around eighty years since Wanshi died. I guess it's been long enough that I can try to write my own "Needle for Zazen." So here goes:

The heart of every Buddha
The heart of each sage, so designated
Is beyond any kind of thinking
Is realization, uncomplicated

Beyond any kind of thinking
Awakening's naturally instantaneous
Realization, uncomplicated
Is a natural state and spontaneous

Awakening's naturally instantaneous
Nothing's ever been contaminated

In this state natural and spontaneous
No right or wrong can be located

Nothing's ever been contaminated
Immediate, with nothing impeding
No right or wrong can be located
With no expectation it goes on proceeding

Clear right down to the bottom
A fish, like a fish, just swims
The sky is big and wide open
A bird flies like a bird, look at him!

Wanshi's "Needle for Zazen" is perfect exactly as it is. I just thought I'd try to add a little something of my own.

The most important point is that zazen is the one great matter. Everybody who's really interested in the Buddhist truth needs to do zazen. This is the authentic teaching that has been transmitted right from the very beginning.

— Written at Kannon-dori-kosho-horin-ji Temple
on March 18, 1242; preached at Kippo-ji Temple
in Fukui Prefecture in November 1243

Okay. Let's start with that dialogue at the very beginning. In the original story, what I've paraphrased as "sit there like a big ol' rock" is *kotsu kotsu chi* (兀兀地). It's actually Chinese, but a Japanese person would likely say it something like that.

In his complete translation of *Shobogenzo* my teacher translates that as "still-still state" and says in a footnote that the expression "suggests a table-mountain, and hence something imposing and balanced." You can see the table-mountain image when you look at the Chinese characters used to express it, which are a highly stylized drawing of such a mountain. In other places Nishijima and Cross translated the same phrase as "mountain still state."

Kaz Tanahashi translates this phrase as "steadfast sitting." Carl Bielefeldt translated this essay for the Stanford Soto Zen Text

Project. He gives us "sitting so fixedly." Shasta Abbey translates it as "sitting there all still and awesome like a mountain."

That's the easy part. I just wanted you to know that I meant "big ol' rock" to sound positive rather than negative. The next bit's where it starts getting tricky.

Where I say, "thinking the actual state of not-thinking" Dogen actually has *shiryo ko fu-shiryo tei* (思量箇不思量底). Tanahashi translates this as, "Think not-thinking." Bielefeldt gives us something very similar, "I'm thinking of not thinking." Nishijima/Cross have, "Thinking the concrete state of not thinking." And Shasta Abbey's much wordier translation is, "What I was thinking about was based on not deliberately thinking about any particular thing."

The reason Nishijima/Cross and Shasta Abbey make the statement a little longer than the others, and the reason I've done so as well, is that the original Chinese says a bit more than simply "thinking (of) not-thinking." There are a couple of characters stuck in there that indicate the master is saying that this "not-thinking" he's talking about is a concrete thing. It's like the difference between asking "what the fuck?" and asking "what the actual fuck?"

After the monk asks the master how to do this not-thinking stuff, I have the master say, "Well, it sure ain't thinking!"

In the actual Chinese, the master first says *fushiryo* (不思量), which is the last part of that phrase we just looked at (minus the final Chinese character). Most people translate this as "not-thinking." When asked how to do that the master answers, *hishiryo* (非思量), which always hangs translators up.

Tanahashi translates this as "beyond thinking." Nishijima/Cross give us "non-thinking" in their complete translation, which is also the word the Bielefeldt and the Nishiyama/Stevens translations use. Although I can also recall Nishijima sometimes translating it in lectures as "utterly different from thinking." Shasta Abbey's translation has the master answer, "It is a matter of 'what I am thinking about' not being the point."

The difference is the Chinese character the master uses to modify the word *shiryo* or "consideration" (as opposed to "thinking"; see the intro to this chapter). First he uses *fu* (不), and next he uses *hi* (非, pronounced *he* as in "he and she" rather than *hi* as in "hi there"). The first prefix indicates denial, while the second indicates a much stronger level of denial. The second prefix makes it more like, "Well it sure ain't the same as thinking!"

Dogen gets into what he means by this as the essay goes on. So let's move on as well.

The phrase "skin, flesh, bones, and marrow" is an allusion to a story about Bodhidharma, the red-bearded foreign guy we met a few chapters back who brought Zen practice to China. Nobody's really sure if all the stories we now attribute to Bodhidharma are based on things that actually happened or even if they all refer back to the same guy. Be that as it may, the story goes that when he was dying, Bodhidharma asked his four closest students for their interpretation of what he'd taught them.

Daofu said, "The truth can't be affirmed or negated. It is what it is."

Bodhidharma told him, "You've got my skin."

Congchi (which is pronounced like *song-shoe*, by the way) said, "Once the truth is seen, it's never seen again."

Bodhidharma told her, "You've got my flesh."

Daoyu said, "Everything is empty. There's no dharma to be grasped."

Bodhidharma told him, "You've got my bones."

Huike (Taiso Eka in Japanese) remained silent.

Bodhidharma told him, "You've got my marrow."

Lots of people see this as Bodhidharma saying that Huike was superior to the other three. But Dogen says all four understood Bodhidharma perfectly. They just understood him in different ways. So having the "skin, flesh, bones, and marrow" is Dogen's fancy way of saying having a complete understanding.

In this case Dogen is saying that having a complete understanding doesn't mean just getting it with the mind. Rather, it's an understanding that includes all parts of your being. He says this same thing a lot of different ways throughout this essay.

A bit further on I have Dogen saying, "In this 'ain't the same as thinking,' there is somebody, and that somebody relies on me." I'm more or less following Nishijima/Cross, who give this as, "In non-thinking there is someone and [that] someone is maintaining and relying upon me." Bielefeldt's translation says, "There is someone in 'non-thinking,' and this someone maintains us." Shasta Abbey's version goes, "There is a someone involved in not deliberately trying to think about something, and that someone is maintaining and supporting an I." Nishiyama/Stevens have, "There is a 'who' in non-thinking; a 'who' that maintains the self." The Japanese original says *hishiryo ni tare ari, tare ware wo honinsu* (非思量にたれ あり、たれわれを保任す).

It's a confusing and weird line, to be sure. But it's important, which is why I'm spending some time with it. It's all about the nature of the self and its relationship with thinking.

Most of us bumble through our lives, just as most people in Dogen's day did, imagining that thinking is done by something we call our "self." Dogen is trying to get us to see things another way. He wants us to question deeply our assumption that there is any so-called self in there doing all this thinking, or non-thinking, for that matter.

The various translators all struggle with the way Dogen expresses this. He places the word *tare* (who/someone) and *ware* (me/I) side by side, which is grammatically weird in Japanese. Nishijima and Cross personalize this by making it "[that] someone is relying upon me," while the others flip it around, saying this mysterious *someone* "maintains the self." In Japanese it's deliberately ambiguous as to whether this "someone" maintains "me" or this "me" sustains "someone."

It's all part of Dogen's way of trying to shake us loose from our preconceptions about the nature of ourselves and of reality. What I call "me" may not be what I imagine it is.

After this, Dogen says some trippy stuff about how you have to use "ain't the same as thinking" to think the state that is "ain't the same as thinking." The state beyond all thought isn't faraway or exotic. It's not even hard to come by. You go beyond thought all the time. We all do. You had moments of non-thinking as you were getting ready for work today, as you were pouring whatever milk-like product you pour on your cereal, and as you were reading this book. We just don't have words for that state, so we ignore it.

Stop ignoring it. It's more important than thought.

Use those fleeting moments when thought is absent as an opportunity to see the things that thought can't encompass. Which is just about everything. Don't try to figure those fleeting thought-free moments out or make them last longer. Just see them. Enjoy them.

Next up we get a paragraph in which I've put the phrase *state like a big ol' rock* in italics. I did that to try to set it off the way the original phrase that Dogen uses (兀兀地, *kotsu kotsu chi*) is set off in Japanese. I much prefer Nishijima's phrase "mountain still state" to my clumsy "state like a big ol' rock." But I stuck with my version for the sake of making it a little funnier.

Basically all Dogen's saying here is that the actual "mountain still state" is a concrete reality. As such, no thought or phrase you could create to describe it could possibly do it justice.

After this I have Dogen say, "Some doofuses these days will tell you that zazen is all about reaching a state of complete mental quietness and that total tranquillity is where it's at." I actually didn't deviate much from the original here. Where I have Dogen say "doofuses" he's actually saying something that translates directly as "composed by Zu or To." Zu and To were famously bad poets in ancient China. It's an old-fashioned way of calling someone a doofus.

It's clear that things haven't changed much in our day in terms of what people think meditation is for. I can't tell you how many people ask me if they're doing zazen wrong because their mind doesn't go completely blank. But, as Kodo Sawaki, one of my teacher's teachers, said, "The only time your mind is a complete blank is when you're dead."

The word I've rendered as "beginner" a couple lines down from this is *shoshin* (初心). This actually means "beginner's mind." It's the same pair of kanji that appear on the cover of Shunryu Suzuki's book *Zen Mind, Beginner's Mind*. When I advertise my Zen classes I've started saying they're "for beginners only." We're all beginners.

A few lines later I have Dogen say, "Since practicing Buddha's practice doesn't involve becoming a Buddha, the universe is realized." The words I've rendered as "the universe is realized" are actually *koan genjo* (公案見成), which is very close to *genjo koan* (現成 公案), the title of one of Dogen's most famous essays. My teacher called this essay "The Realized Universe" in his translation. Kaz Tanahashi called it "Actualizing the Fundamental Point." In their respective translations of this essay, they use variations of those phrases in this sentence.

The point is that there's no sense in trying to become a Buddha. Buddha was Buddha because he discovered who he actually was. We don't try to become him. We try to become ourselves.

As Dogen says, just at this moment we have the ability to do the right thing and enter the World of Buddhas or do something that leads us into the World of Demons. That's not like going to heaven or going to hell. It's a much more concrete thing. When we work on balance, we feel like a Buddha, and when we don't, we end up feeling like crap.

I take the stuff that comes up after this about filling ditches or filling valleys to be a metaphor for making small improvements or really changing ourselves radically for the better. We have the ability to do either one at any moment. It's a pretty optimistic statement!

244 IT CAME FROM BEYOND ZEN!

The question, "What's your intention in doing zazen?" that Nangaku asks Baso gets translated a few different ways. My paraphrase follows Tanahashi's translation and uses the word *intention*. Nishijima/Cross give us, "What are you aiming at sitting zazen?" Nishiyama/Stevens give us, "What is the purpose of doing zazen?" Bielefeldt has the question as, "What are you figuring to do, sitting there in meditation?" I'm sure there are other variations.

The key word they're translating as "intention, aim, purpose," etc. in the original is *hakaru* (図る), which in contemporary Japanese means "to intend, plot, plan, attempt, devise, take aim at," etc. The Chinese character used in this word is part of the word *chizu* (地図), which means "map." So it has all those meanings, and more. I bring this up because I've found that certain types of people who read books like this one will fixate on particular words. I've even caught myself trying to explain that there's no *goal* in Zen practice but that sometimes there's an *aim*. But that's just me falling into a linguistic trap.

I also point this out because Dogen really digs into this question, so it's important to get a sense of what the question actually is.

My paraphrase of Dogen's questions about this question follows Nishijima/Cross. Tanahashi translates it a bit differently. His version has Dogen saying, "Was Nanyue [Nangaku] asking if Mazu [Baso] had the intention of going beyond zazen, if he had an intention outside of zazen, or if he had no intention at all? Was Nanyue asking what kind of intention emerges while doing zazen?"

Bielefeldt's version is, "Does it mean that there must be some 'figuring' above and beyond seated meditation? Is there not yet a path to be 'figured' outside the bounds of seated meditation? Should there be no 'figuring' at all? Or does it ask what kind of 'figuring' occurs at the very time we are practicing seated meditation?"

I'll let you look up the original Japanese for yourself. It's sort of a mash-up of all these questions.

Moving right along. Obviously Dogen did not really say, "It's better to love the real Godzilla than a Godzilla action figure. Yet both the real Godzilla and a Godzilla action figure have fins that light up when they use their atomic fire breath."* The standard version is more like, "It is important to cherish real dragons more than imitation dragons; yet know that both a real and an imitation dragon can cause clouds to form and rain to fall." That's from Nishiyama/Stevens, but other translations are almost identical.

The basis of this quote is an old story about a guy who loved to collect figures of dragons. An actual dragon heard about this guy and figured he'd enjoy meeting him. But when the dragon came to the guy's house, the guy was terrified and ran away.

Usually Dogen uses this as a metaphor for people who talk about meditation all the time but seem terrified of actually doing it. There were people like that in his day, and I'll bet there are even more of them now, since meditation has become so trendy lately.

Another aspect of this is that Dogen sometimes refers to practitioners of zazen as "dragons and elephants" (龍象, *ryuzo*). Nobody seems to know why. But it seems to be a term of affection. An "imitation dragon" — or "Godzilla action figure," if you like — is someone who likes playing at being "into meditation" but never actually meditates.

When he says that even imitation dragons can cause clouds to form and rain to fall — or even Godzilla action figures have light-up fins and atomic breath — he's saying something like what he says in an essay called "Gabyo," which means a "painting of a rice cake." In that essay Dogen examines an old saying that a painted rice cake can't cure hunger, and he says that sometimes a painted rice cake really can cure hunger.

The painted rice cake is a metaphor for written or spoken Buddhist philosophy as opposed to meditation, which is a real rice cake. Dogen points out that both aspects have an important place in actual

---

* For those sad souls who've never seen a Godzilla movie, Godzilla has fins on his back that glow whenever he uses his atomic fire breath.

practice. Here he's saying that even those who do nothing but talk about meditation and never do it are also, in their own small way, on the Buddhist path. They have light-up fins and atomic breath, too. But if you're one of those people, maybe try meditating for real sometime.

I really like the line that comes right after this about not making a big deal of things that are faraway or thinking that commonplace stuff is inferior. This is especially important to those of us who are into exotic things like Zen. We have a tendency to overvalue that which is faraway and undervalue the commonplace. That can lead us to miss the fact that the most important place in the universe is always right here.

Baso answers the question, which we talked about so long ago you've probably forgotten it, by saying that he's intending to become a Buddha. Then Dogen asks us a whole bunch of tripped-out questions about intention and about becoming a Buddha.

Zazen is often described as being a goalless practice, a practice without intention. You're not trying to make something happen. You're trying your best to stay with what actually *is happening*.

Even so, it's impossible to do zazen with no intention at all. Just plopping yourself down on your cushion for a few minutes of goalless practice requires some kind of intention. Dogen is using a series of poetic expressions to try to focus on all the ways intention is mixed up in this intentionless practice, no matter how hard you try to eliminate it.

That stuff about dropping off body and mind comes from Dogen's description of his own moment of profound understanding. Nishijima Roshi used to explain that dropping off body and mind was becoming totally balanced. Neither body (matter) nor mind (spirit) dominated him at that moment. In perfect balance, it was as if both body and mind had vanished.

After Baso asks his teacher Nangaku what he's doing when he picks up a tile and starts polishing it, I have Dogen say, "But *what* is always what you're doing, if you get my drift." He didn't really say anything equivalent to "if you get my drift." But I wanted to call attention to the way this statement reflects what he said in the essay I titled "It Came from Beyond Zen."

In that essay he uses *inmo* (恁麼), a word that we learned means "it" or "what," to emphasize how everything we encounter is, in some sense, an *it* or a *what*. We may have names for things and for people, but we don't know what they truly are. Same with actions like polishing a tile, or anything else someone might do. We can name them, but we don't really know them. Therefore, *what* is always what you're doing. See?

A little bit after this I have Dogen kind of casually remark, "Your own view isn't necessarily the way things really are." This is a summation of a much longer passage. Here is Carl Bielefeldt's translation of that part: "Not only should we avoid deciding that what we see is what we see, we should be firmly convinced that there is an essential message to be studied in all the ten thousand activities. We should know that, just as we may see the buddha without knowing or understanding him, so we may see water and yet not know water, may see mountains and yet not know mountains. The precipitate assumption that the phenomena before one's eyes offer no further passage is not the study of the buddha."

I just thought you might like to know. I took a cue from the Nishijima/Cross translation of the beginning of this section, which is, "It is not simply a matter of not fixing to our own views as our own views."

After this, we get to where Dogen starts saying some crazy stuff about how you make mirrors into mirrors by polishing tiles. In Dogen's time mirrors weren't made out of glass like they are these days. Mirrors were made by polishing metal until it was shiny. You had to maintain your mirrors by polishing them regularly. But nobody would try to make a floor tile into a mirror. You could polish forever and still never see yourself in it. That's the image Dogen is working with.

The story Dogen is telling us here was used for a long time as an example of how stupid it was to try to become a Buddha by meditating. It was as dumb as trying to polish a tile until it was a mirror.

Dogen disagreed with this interpretation. What a weirdo!

I covered that stuff about the "clear mirror" and the "eternal mirror" at length in my book *Don't Be a Jerk*. The short version is that the Buddhist ideal is for the mind to be like a mirror, reflecting everything just as it actually is. As I said in that book, the differences between the "clear mirror" and the "eternal mirror" are a bit hard to work out. I don't think they're that important. I take it as two names for the same concept: the eternal, clear mirror that reflects things just as they are.

You probably think I made up that bit that comes after this about how even Iron Man couldn't polish a tile hard enough to make it a mirror. Well — HA! Dogen really does use the word *testu-nan* (鉄漢), which literally means "iron man." So there! Eight hundred years ago Dogen predicted Iron Man!

All right. Most translators say something like "*an* iron man" or "a man with iron will." Fine. Whatever...

After the Iron Man thing I have Dogen say, "Be that as it may, although polishing a tile is not making a mirror, mirrors appear spontaneously." The Nishijima/Cross translation of this line is, "The realization of a mirror — though it is nothing other than itself — may be [described as] instantaneous." Bielefeldt has, "Even if it is 'producing a mirror,' it must be quick about it." Tanahashi gives us, "Even if making a mirror is not polishing a tile, a mirror is immediately there."

The word they're translating as "instantaneous" or "quick" or "immediate" is *sumiyaka-ni* (すみやかに), which pretty much means just that — immediately, quickly, speedily.

The point is that the so-called enlightened state isn't something you bring into being. It's always there. But we pile so much junk on top of it that we don't even remember it's at the bottom of the junk pile we've made of our minds.

After Nangaku asks how zazen can make you into a Buddha, I have Dogen say, "Obviously, doing zazen isn't working on becoming a Buddha. Even becoming a Buddha is irrelevant to zazen." This is based closely on the Nishijima/Cross translation. Tanahashi's version is, "Be clear that zazen is not working toward becoming a Buddha. The teaching that becoming a Buddha has nothing to do with zazen is evident." Bielefeldt has Dogen say, "This is clearly understood: there is a reason that sitting in meditation does not await 'making a buddha'; there is nothing obscure about the essential point that 'making a buddha' is not connected with sitting in meditation."

In all cases the translators have zazen as the subject and "working on/toward" or "awaiting" as the verb, which is how it is in Japanese. The word Dogen used actually seems to me more like "awaiting" (まつ, *matsu*, which generally means "waiting"). However, Tanahashi and Nishijima, both native speakers of Japanese, agree that "working on/toward" is better than "awaiting." So I've deferred to their greater knowledge of the older versions of their language.

Once again, the point is that zazen is a thing in and of itself. It isn't done for any outside purpose, even for the purpose of becoming a Buddha.

A little ways down I have Nangaku ask, "When your car stops working, do you fix the engine or kick the tires?" In the original it's more like, "When your cart won't move, do you prod the ox or prod the cart?" The obvious answer is you prod the ox, or, in my version, you fix the engine.

Everybody always jumps to the obvious conclusion that you prod the ox / fix the engine. But, as usual, our contrarian Mr. Dogen wants us to look at the other possibility. In this metaphor the ox/engine represents the mind, and the cart/tire represents the body.

At the beginning of Dogen's response I have him saying,

"What's it mean to say a car is moving or isn't moving? For example, is water flowing the same as a car moving? Is water not flowing the same as a car moving?" Here I've simply replaced Dogen's cart with a car. What a weird question!

Bielefeldt's translation of this line is, "For example, is water's flowing the cart's 'going,' or is water's not flowing the cart's 'going'?" The Nishijima/Cross and Tanahashi translations are more or less the same. In Japanese that's pretty much exactly what Dogen asks. I added "the same as" to try to clarify what I think he means. But Dogen doesn't actually say that. He makes them equivalent.

Also, where I have Dogen saying, "Maybe the real movement of water is beyond our ideas about 'flowing,'" the original is more cryptic and poetic. It's closer to, "There is a time when water's flowing is not-flowing." That's based on Tanahashi's translation.

Nishijima/Cross have a footnote around here that says, "If a river is running alongside a cart, or a cart is moving alongside a lake, because water and the cart are in mutual relation, it is not possible to say that one element is moving and one element is not moving." In another footnote to this paragraph they say, "Action transcends relative movement."

Bielefeldt adds a long footnote to his translation of this section that says, in part, "In this passage, Dogen is doubtless playing on the Buddhist paradox of impermanence: that, while all things are changing and hence always 'going' even when seemingly at rest, each dharma is momentary — or, as is said, 'abides in its own position' (*jû hôi*) — and hence does not 'go' through time.... There are two lines of interpretation of this cryptic remark: (a) that, whether the cart is going or not going, it is [present in] time; (b) that both going and not going are present in each time."

When Bielefeldt says "abides in its own position," he's referencing Dogen's statement in "Genjo Koan" that goes, "Firewood becomes ash; it can never go back to being firewood. Nevertheless, we should not take the view that ash is its future and firewood is its past. Remember, firewood *abides in the place* of firewood in the Dharma. It has a past and it has a future. Although it has a past and a future, the past and the future are cut off. Ash exists in the place of ash in the Dharma. It has a past and it has a future." I italicized the words *abides in the place* so you could see what I'm referring to. Sometimes certain Zen people say "abiding in a dharma position." Those people are weird because they say stuff like this without realizing the rest of the world has no idea what they're talking about.

In a footnote at the end of the whole discussion of "when your car stops working," Nishijima seems to agree with Bielefeldt. But Nishijima puts it a little more straightforwardly. He says, "Time is a series of instants. In each instant there is no movement, but the progression from instant to instant is continuous movement."

I like Nishijima's way of making this stuff a whole lot less convoluted than most commentators do. But it's still kind of a freaky idea.

Nishijima liked to describe the movement of time as being like frames of a film. Each frame of a film is a still photo, but when projected, all together they give the illusion of movement. He said that actual time is like that. Buddhists have had similar ideas since long before the invention of film.

Go use the bathroom or something, and we'll do the rest of the commentary when you get back.

◆

Feeling better? Good. Let's keep going with the commentary on Dogen's "Needle in the Butt of Zazen."

A couple more lines down I have Dogen say, "In the regular world, there's no method for kicking the tires, at least not one that works. But in Buddhism we could say 'kick the tires.' And by that I mean that we learn in physical practice." In the original it says that in

Buddhism we have methods for "prodding the cart." I added "physical practice" to make it clearer what I think he meant.

In a footnote in the Nishijima/Cross translation it says, "A method of prodding the cart means a method of regulating the physical state, for example, zazen." Another footnote says, "A method for prodding the ox means a method for motivating the mind, for example, the offering of rewards."

Carl Bielefeldt again appears to agree, saying in his footnotes, "'Beating the cart' here is most often interpreted to refer to the physical practice of zazen, and 'beating the ox' to the mental process of 'making a buddha.'"

Where I have Dogen asking about engines that might be fixable, as opposed to plastic engines or statues of engines, the original has a living ox, an iron ox, and an ox made out of clay.

Nishijima sees the thing about an ox made out of clay as a reference to an old story in which Zen Master Ryuzan said, "I saw two oxen made out of clay. They fought and entered the sea. There's been no news of them since." Which is interesting but still leaves me scratching my head. At least Nishijima says that much about this section. Other translations offer nothing.

My feeling is that Dogen is asking us to do real work on ourselves. I take the reference to iron and clay oxen to mean the way some people get off on superficial practice. They like the look of being "into Zen" or whatever it is they're into, and they might even practice a little. But sometimes in practice you hit up against a part of yourself that's pretty hard and inflexible. Being willing to work on that would be like prodding a living ox or working on an engine that at least has some hope of running again — as opposed to pretending to work on an object that really can't be made to work in the form of doing your practice in a half-assed way.

I then have Dogen say, "There needs to be a foot kicking a foot, and an engine fixing an engine." In the original it's more like "fist hitting fist (拳打拳) and ox hitting ox (牛打牛)."

The character that acts as the verb in these phrases is *utsu* (打, also pronounced *ta* or *da*, depending on context). This same character appears as the third Chinese character in one of Dogen's favorite words, *shikantaza* (只管打坐), which means "just sitting." *Utsu* or *ta* is the "just" in "just sitting." It's Dogen's way of describing zazen practice as the practice of doing nothing but sitting rather than trying to make something happen by sitting, such as trying to become a Buddha. In zazen you do nothing else but *strike* the very moment of sitting. Whap!

So "foot kicking a foot and engine fixing engine" means to do your practice with full commitment and engagement.

Baso doesn't say anything in response to the question about the engine and the tires. Dogen praises this reply. Sometimes saying nothing is the best response.

In my paraphrase, Nangaku winds things up by saying, "Sitting zazen is learning how to be a sitting Buddha." Other translations of this line are, "If you practice sitting Zen, you practice sitting Buddha" (Tanahashi), "Your learning sitting dhyana is learning sitting Buddha" (Nishijima/Cross), and "Are you studying seated meditation or are you studying seated buddha?" (Bielefeldt). I'm not sure why Bielefeldt turns it into a question. Although the original quotation is in Chinese rather than Japanese, it sure looks like a statement to me rather than a question.

The point is, that in doing zazen practice, we are doing the actual activity of a Buddha. At that moment, no matter what's going on in our noggins or why we have decided to meditate, we are exactly like Buddha. Even if the resemblance ends as soon as we stand up again, that still means a lot.

After this I have Dogen say, "A beginner's first time sitting zazen is the first time anyone ever sat zazen. It's the first sitting of the Buddha." The original line is *shoshin no zazen wa saisho no zazen nari, saisho no zazen wa saisho no za-butsu nari* (初心の坐禅は最初の坐禅なり、最初の坐禅は最初の坐仏なり). Other translations have "a beginner's zazen is the first zazen; and the first zazen is the first sitting Buddha" (Nishijima/Cross), "beginners' zazen is initial zazen and...initial zazen is the initial sitting Buddha" (Nishiyama/ Stevens), "Know that the zazen of a beginner's mind is the beginning of zazen. The beginning of zazen is the beginning of sitting Buddha" (Tanahashi), and "the first seated meditation is the first seated buddha" (Bielefeldt).

This echoes what Dogen said earlier. In fact, he uses that phrase we saw meaning "beginner's mind" as the first word in the sentence. So another way to translate the first part could be, "Sitting zazen with a beginner's mind is the first zazen."

Everybody knows that as you do some practice over time, you get better at it. But zazen is a little different. There's no improvement to be had, no matter how long you do it. Oh, sure, you'll mature in your practice and you'll probably start noticing the benefits as you continue. But that doesn't mean the practice itself has improved. Each sitting is its own unique, never-to-be-repeated event.

I have Dogen saying, "Once we understand from a good teacher that sitting zazen is beyond sitting and lying down, we can truly be ourselves when sitting or lying down. Then you don't have to look for what's commonplace or for what's faraway. You don't have to worry about delusion or enlightenment. Why get caught up in intellectual stuff like that?"

My paraphrase follows Nishijima/Cross. Bielefeldt has a similar take on it, saying, "Why should we inquire about close or distant familial lines? How could we discuss delusion and awakening? Who would seek wisdom and eradication?"

However, Tanahashi sees this line differently. He has Dogen say, "When you reflect on your life activities are they intimate with zazen or remote from it? Is there enlightenment in zazen or is there delusion? Is there one whose wisdom penetrates zazen?"

To me the point Dogen is making here is that zazen is something special. My teacher used to say that there were a lot of ways to enter what he called the "balanced state." Zazen was one, but he also believed you could enter this state through activities like sports and art, as well as other activities where concentration on the moment was required. Still, zazen is zazen, as Dogen says. It is its own unique thing.

Nishijima Roshi would always say that even though you could enter the state of balance through other activities, "zazen is the easiest way." It's easy because it requires almost no preparation or rehearsal, it doesn't demand that you have any particular talent, it resists being turned into a kind of competition the way sports and even art can become, and almost anyone can do it. Even those who can't do the traditional postures can find other ways of doing zazen that work for them.

Once you become familiar with zazen, you start to find ways to enter the balanced state in the midst of almost any other activity. Or, as Dogen puts it, "We can truly be ourselves when sitting or lying down."

The next paragraph begins with Nangaku saying, "When you're sitting like Buddha, Buddha doesn't have any set form." This paragraph is a doozy. Nobody translates it quite the same way. The key phrase in Nangaku's statement is "set form." That's how Nishijima/Cross translate it. The actual word Dogen uses is *joso* (定相). Other translators give this as "fixed form" (Tanahashi, Nishiyama/Stevens). Bielefeldt translates it as "fixed mark" and sees it as a reference to a discussion of the thirty-two marks of a Buddha in the Diamond Sutra. But even he agrees that "fixed form" would be the more colloquial translation.

I chose to go with the Nishijima/Cross translation of "set form" because the same first character appears in the very common Japanese word *teishoku* (定食), which is usually translated as "set menu." Small restaurants in Japan often serve only one specific meal each day. You don't get a choice or a menu. If you come on a Tuesday, you get what they have on Tuesdays.

That's the easy part. The more common translation of the next line is, "That the 'seated buddha' is like one or two buddhas is because he has adorned himself with 'no fixed mark.'" That's Bielefeldt's version, but other translations are similar. It's easy to get tripped up on that "one or two buddhas" (一仏二仏, *ichi-butsu ni-butsu*) business. But it's just Dogen's way of saying that there can be more than just one Buddha.

This is an important doctrine in Buddhism. In Christianity, there is just one Christ. He might return someday, but there's still only one of him. The Muslims believe that Muhammad was God's final prophet. There aren't gonna be any more final prophets. In Hinduism, Vishnu shows up in various incarnations, but he's always Vishnu, not somebody else.

Buddha, on the other hand, isn't just the historical Buddha, known also as Siddhartha or Gautama or Shakyamuni — the guy had a lot of names. We are all Buddhas. It's just that only a few of us notice it, and even fewer of us ever really manifest our Buddha-ness in our lives. So Buddhism is not the worship of a guy named Buddha; it's learning to manifest your unique inner Buddha.

Here Dogen is saying that Buddha has no set form. He's not necessarily from India. He doesn't necessarily have curly hair like he does in all the statues. He's not even necessarily a man. Buddha could be a woman. Buddha could be a child. Buddha could be your Uncle Melvin with the bad toupee. Buddha could be the guy who cut you off on the highway last week. You never know.

But Dogen won't let even Buddha get away with not practicing seated meditation. He says that *because* Buddha has no set form, a Buddha can't avoid seated meditation. That's the one thing all Buddhas have in common. They all do seated meditation.

The next paragraph is just two sentences. In my version it's, "Could anybody in this real world tell who is a Buddha and who isn't a Buddha? Before you even have a thought of differentiating one from the other, a sitting Buddha is a Buddha sitting." The phrase I've given as "in this real world" is *muju-ho* (無住法), and most people translate that as something like "nonabiding dharma." In a footnote Nishijima and Cross explain this as "reality which exists only at the moment of the present." In other words, right here and now.

The next sentence is there to remind us that the real world is exactly as it is before we come along and define it. Most of us spend much of our lives getting that ass-backward.

Next up we get to some stuff about killing Buddha. I'm sure a lot of you have heard the phrase "If you see the Buddha on the road, kill him." This is an old Zen saying, usually attributed to Master Rinzai (Ch. Lin-chi), that is generally explained as meaning that any Buddha you see as something outside yourself is not Buddha. So you need to get rid of that idea; you need to kill it.

Here Dogen tells us that the way to kill Buddha in the sense I just talked about is to do zazen. That way we destroy any romantic fantasies we might have about the real activity of Buddha (i.e., getting to work on oneself through meditation). In this way we might also "kill a person" in the sense that we cease to see ourselves merely as individuals and begin to identify with the entire universe as our self.

The next paragraph starts off, "If you get hung up on the sitting form, you just don't get it." The key word here is *sho* (執), which I'm paraphrasing as "hung up." In Buddhist contexts this word is usually translated as "attachment." It can also mean "clinging to," "identifying with," or "grasping at." It's been translated all these ways by people who have tackled this essay.

I chose "get hung up on" because I find the word *attachment* to be a big stumbling block for lots of people trying to understand Buddhism and, indeed, a lot of other philosophies that have come out of India. Those old Indian smart guys were always warning us against *attachment* to various things. But this leaves lots of us who are half a world and a few centuries away just plain confused.

To me it simply means getting hung up on something. If you're hung up on something, you're thinking you "got this." In this case it would mean thinking that sitting zazen and only sitting zazen is the way, the truth, and the life and that no one comes unto the Buddha except through sitting zazen, to paraphrase the Gospel according to John. It also means thinking you understand this whole zazen business and are now ready to move on to more advanced things. Kobun Chino Roshi was asked if he was a Zen master. He said, "Nobody masters Zen!"

In the next paragraph I have the lines, "It exists in the very moment of doing zazen. It exists in the person sitting. It exists in the seated Buddha. It exists in the Buddha learning sitting." In the original this is much shorter. It's *utsuza-toki ni ari, utsuza-hito ni ari, utsuza-butsu ni ari, gakuza-butsu ni ari* (打坐時にあり、打坐人にあり、打坐仏にあり、学坐仏にあり). In my paraphrase I say "it" exists, but in the original no subject is stated. Different translators choose different subjects. I am trying to preserve the nebulous nature of Dogen's original by just saying "it."

To me the word *it* suggests the unnameable something that is the universe and is us. We recognize this in zazen. Or we don't. But in either case, it's there. As it always is. But in zazen there's a quietness that allows us to be a little more open to it.

Once again we get the character *utsu* (打, also pronounced *ta*) that usually means "to strike" or "to hit," which appears in the word *shikantaza* (只管打坐), or "just sitting."

Dogen uses it here to indicate a very direct experience — the direct experience of sitting, of being a person who is sitting, of being a Buddha who is sitting, of being a Buddha who is learning to sit.

Further along I have Dogen say, "Baso verified how sitting Buddha becomes Buddha. Nangaku taught how to become a Buddha by sitting like a Buddha." The original says *za-butsu no sa-butsu wo sho suru, Kozei kore nari. Sa-butsu no tame ni za-butsu wo shimesu, Nangaku kore nari* (坐仏の作仏を証する、江西これなり。作仏のために坐仏をしめす、南嶽これなり。).

Nishijima/Cross give us, "Sitting buddha realizes the experience of becoming Buddha: this is Kosei's case. For the benefit of becoming buddha, sitting Buddha is demonstrated: this is Nangaku's case." Bielefeldt's version is, "Jiangxii [Kosei] is the one who verifies that the 'seated buddha' is 'making a buddha'; Nanyue [Nangaku] is the one who points out the 'seated buddha' for 'making a buddha.'" Tanahashi's translation is, "Mazu [Baso] realized sitting Buddha as becoming buddha, and Nanyue [Nangaku] taught becoming buddha as sitting buddha."

I give the prize to Tanahashi this time.

We're back to the original dialogue about polishing the tile. You don't sit zazen in order to become a Buddha. Yet the only way to become a Buddha is by sitting zazen.

Next up we get a poem. Apart from making it rhyme and adding "who's not dozing" to rhyme with "opposing," I tried to stay close to the original. My paraphrase is closest to the Nishijima/Cross translation, but the differences among the other versions are pretty minor.

After the poem there's that part where Dogen tells you how great the poem is by comparing it to other stuff. I took some liberties here — obviously he didn't actually say "super-cool style that's the finest of the fine" — because the actual list of reasons for the poem's greatness he gives would require tons of explanation.

The Nishijima/Cross translation of this list is pretty close to most of the others. It goes, "The point of this needle for zazen is that 'the Great Function is already manifest before us,' is 'the dignified behavior that is ascendant to sound and form,' is a glimpse of 'the time before our parents were born,' is that 'not to insult the Buddhist patriarchs is good,' is 'never to have avoided losing body and life,' and is 'the head being three feet long and the neck being two inches.'"

All the things they put in quotation marks are quotations Dogen draws from ancient Buddhist sources. In the Nishijima/Cross translation all these are footnoted and explained. I used those footnotes as a guide for my paraphrase. I'll let you look at the Nishijima/Cross footnotes for yourself.

Then Dogen explains some of the verses of the poem. In one of his explanations, Dogen uses the phrase *kanmen* (換面). It literally means "change face." To me it's perfectly obvious that this means to change your facial expression. So that's how I paraphrased it. Another phrase, *kaito* (回頭), appears in the same verse. It literally means "turn head." I don't think there's any ambiguity there, either. But some translators love to make these sound mysterious and Oriental, such as "turning faces and exchanging heads" (Tanahashi) or "turn the head and reverse the face" (Bielefeldt). Whatever.

I had a dickens of a time with the phrase I finally paraphrased as "some kind of God-like universal knowledge." What Dogen actually wrote was *henchi* (遍知). Nishijima and Cross translate this as "universal awareness." Both Bielefeldt and Nishiyama/Stevens have "universal knowledge." Tanahashi has "all-inclusive knowledge." Shasta Abbey takes a different approach and translates it as "something everybody knows."

I added "God-like" because this is what it sometimes feels like when you reach a certain point in your meditation practice. You feel like God Almighty His Very Self. Almost everyone who does enough meditation practice gets to this point. Some meditation systems are specifically designed to make this happen. Those systems are terribly dangerous. Luckily, they're in the minority. Dogen, like all good Zen teachers, cautions against getting too seduced by this kind of thing.

Shasta Abbey's translation seems, on the surface, like a valid interpretation of the original word, if you were just to consider the two Chinese characters individually. But in Buddhist contexts this character combination generally means "complete knowledge." The Japanese word for "common knowledge" (i.e., something everybody knows) is *shochi* (周知).

The word I paraphrased as "spiritual awakening" is *reisho* (靈照), which literally means "spiritual illumination." Throughout the poem I translated this same character for "illumination" as "awakening." I did this because in new age circles *awakening* seems to be the preferred term these days for this sort of thing.

Tanahashi translates this as "illuminating with brilliance." Most every other translator goes with some variation on "spiritual illumination." This discrepancy is what made me want to go track the word down in the original text. The first character in the word *reisho* is *rei* (霊, also pronounced *tama*) and it means "spirit, soul, or ghost." So Tanahashi is just plain wrong here — although he is usually very reliable.

The phrase I've given as, "It's not reciprocal, and it's not one-sided" is actually *ego fu-ego* (回互不回互). It's not a character combination found in contemporary Japanese or Chinese. The translators all have their own interpretations, such as "complicated or uncomplicated" (Nishijima), "changeable or interchangeable" (Tanahashi), "interacting without interacting" (Bielefeldt), "interdependent or independent" (Shasta Abbey), or "harmonious and interrelated" (Nishiyama/Stevens).

I don't really like my "not reciprocal or one-sided" much. But it's the best I could do. Bielefeldt adds a footnote in which he explains that this term is "usually interpreted to mean that subject and object are both independent and interdependent." As you can see, Shasta Abbey just went with that as their translation.

I take this as a reference to the way we are both independent individuals with our own minds and our own wills and yet we are not. Much of what we think of as our own minds has been shaped by society and by outside circumstances. Much of what we think of as our own will is just us doing what we've been conditioned to do.

Some people think it has to be one or the other. Either we have free will or everything is predestined and conditioned. Dogen liked to have it both ways — of course. Nishijima Roshi used to say that when you look at things according to linear time moving from the past, through the present, and into the future, it seems like everything is predetermined, but in the present moment we are free to do whatever we like, within the circumstances our past has created.

The part where Dogen explains the meaning of the line "There's no thought of discrimination, no sense of duality, it's one" is translated in a variety of ways. I'll leave it to you to look at them all. They're mostly kind of confusing. My paraphrase is mainly based on the Nishijima/Cross translation and its footnotes.

The whole Dragon's Gate business refers to the common idea that Buddhist enlightenment is sort of like crossing through a magical barrier, after which you emerge a completely new sort of creature. Dogen criticizes that view throughout *Shobogenzo*.

He then talks about the state in which you no longer discriminate things from each other. But he also says not to worry if you feel like you haven't reached that rarified state, because even the Buddhas discriminate things from each other.

The human brain is basically a discrimination machine. Its job is to enable you to tell binoculars from bicycles and shit from Shinola®. You need that function in order to survive.

And yet the universe is also an all-inclusive whole in which nothing is separate or independent from everything else. That's harder to see because you have to take a step outside your own brain to notice it. Sometimes drugs can get you out of your brain, and in the stupor they induce you might get a little glimpse of that interdependent all-inclusive oneness. But such glimpses aren't very useful because they're accompanied by a lot of confusion and surprise, and sometimes even fear. It's much better to steadily work on seeing this through meditation, so that when you finally do get a little glimpse it's not all muddled up.

A little ways down I finished a paragraph with the sentence, "To be awakened is to doubt your own awakening." The Nishijima/ Cross version of this is, "While having dwelled in and retained this state as 'singularity' and having maintained and relied upon it as 'completeness,' [those descriptions] I still doubt." Bielefeldt gives us,

"This has been preserved as 'rare' and maintained as 'comprehending,' but 'I have my doubts.'"

So Bielefeldt takes Dogen's statement of his own doubt as a quotation from another source, while Nishijima/Cross see it as Dogen's expression of his personal doubts. Tanahashi and Nishiyama/Stevens hedge their bets. Tanahashi's version says, "To maintain illumination is extraordinary and to accept it as complete is no other than doubting it thoroughly." The Nishiyama/Stevens translation says, "Even if we can grasp and maintain the essence our 'doubt' remains." I've tried to steer a middle course, although I favor the Nishijima/Cross interpretation.

Bielefeldt includes a footnote that says, "Dōgen's 'doubts' (疑著, *gijaku*) here are usually taken in the sense, 'there is more to this than meets the eye.'" I like that. But I also see the word *ware* (我), which means "my." So I think it's reasonable to read this as Dogen's expression of his own doubts.

In his essay "Genjo Koan," which I wrote about in my books *Don't Be a Jerk* and *Sit Down and Shut Up*, Dogen says, "When dharma does not fill your whole body and mind, you think it is already sufficient. When dharma fills your body and mind, you understand that something is missing." That's the Tanahashi translation, but others are pretty much the same. To me this expresses the idea that a certain degree of doubt is actually part of the awakened state of a Buddha. Anyone who lacks all doubt cannot be said to be truly awakened.

I also took some liberties with Dogen's interpretation of the line, "The water's clear all the way to the bottom / Fishes are swimming slow and lazy." The various translations aren't all that different from each other. It's just that Dogen gets really metaphorical here. The original is pretty long, so I'm not going to quote one of the standard versions here. I'll let you check those for yourself. My interpretation is based mainly on the footnotes in the Nishijima/Cross and Bielefeldt translations.

At the end of the explanation of this line I have Dogen say, "Getting all the way to the bottom of things isn't like flying through the sky like a bird." The Nishijima/Cross translation has a footnote after this that says, "The way of birds generally suggests the transcendent state, but in this case Master Dōgen contrasted it with the concrete state on the ground."

I take this as yet another warning by Dogen not to get too caught up in the so-called spiritual or heightened states of consciousness one often encounters in meditation. This is a recurring theme in Dogen's work, as we've seen. It's also a recurring theme in Buddhism in general. Often statues depicting the Buddha's moment of enlightenment show him touching the ground. This symbolizes that his enlightened state included a firm grounding in this reality instead of serving as an escape from it.

And, as you've come to expect by now, I also took some liberties with Dogen's explanation of the line, "The sky is wide and limitless, birds fly far away where it's all hazy." And, once again, you'll have to look up the standard translations on your own, I'm afraid. They're kind of long. My interpretation is based mostly on the Nishijima/Cross footnotes, as usual. And, as in the other cases, they're based on my own experiences with zazen practice.

Dogen also uses this metaphor of skies and birds, and fish and water in "Genjo Koan." There he says, "When fish move through water, however they move, there is no end to the water. When birds fly through the sky, however they fly, there is no end to the sky." That's the Nishijima/Cross translation. It's pretty standard.

I made the bird a "he." Dogen didn't do that. I just did it for the sake of my forced rhyme at the end of the poem that comes after.

And speaking of that poem, I highly recommend looking up one of the more standard translations. My version isn't miles off the mark, though.

Phew! That was a marathon! Let's look at a shorter essay next.

14. Talking to the Trees about Reality
Mujo Seppo
The Insentient Preach the Dharma

The Japanese title of this chapter is "Mujo Seppo" (無情説法). Kaz Tanahashi translates that as "Insentient Beings Speak Dharma." Carl Bielefeldt translates it as "The Insentient Preach the Dharma." Nishiyama and Stevens translate it as "The Proclamation of the Law by Inanimate Beings." The Shasta Abbey translation has "On the Dharma That Non-Sentient Beings Express." You're probably seeing a pattern here.

My own teacher, Gudo Nishijima, and his co-translator, Chodo Mike Cross, chose to be different. Their title is "The Non-Emotional Preaches the Dharma." I think that's worth commenting on since it's a very crucial point in the essay that follows.

You'll first note that the word *beings*, which several translators add to their titles of the chapter, is not in the original. The reason it's not there could be that Dogen generally preferred to title his *Shobogenzo* essays with two- or four-character phrases. He doesn't always do this, but he seems to do it whenever he can. However, I think there's another reason he doesn't say "beings." I believe he wanted the title to have a certain ambiguity.

See, in Buddhist philosophy there is a strong belief that nothing is ever just one way. To say "insentient beings" would be to imply that there are certain beings who are forever and always insentient.

265

But when you say "the nonemotional" or even "the insentient" you're indicating a condition that comes and goes, just like everything else comes and goes.

The character that Nishijima and Cross translate as "nonemotional" and others tend to translate as "insentient" or "inanimate" is *mujo* (無情). If you look up the word *mujo* in a contemporary Japanese-English dictionary, you will find words like *heartlessness*, *cruelty*, or *ruthlessness*. That's clearly not what Dogen was getting at. The meaning of the word has changed over time.

The first character, *mu* (無), means "no," "nothing," or "without." It's the famous *mu* that people often shout when solving their first koan at a Rinzai-style Zen training center. It's the *mu* that answers the question, "Does a dog have Buddha nature?" And, by the way, that's also a little joke. Because in Chinese this same character can be pronounced *wu*, which is the Chinese way of making the sound of a barking dog.

The second character, *jo* (情), means "emotion" or "feeling." Depending on context it can also mean "compassion" or even something like "the actual situation."

In classical Japanese, especially in Buddhist contexts, *mujo* is almost always translated as "insentient." In his notes on his translation of this essay Bielefeldt says, "The term *mujō* 無情 ('the insentient') refers to inanimate, or unconscious, objects — i.e., things, both vegetable and mineral, other than (a) the 'living,' or 'animate,' beings (shujō 衆生; sattva) subject to rebirth in the five (or six) states of saṃsāra and (b) the transcendent buddhas and advanced bodhisattvas."

Even so, the English word *insentient* is not quite the same as the word *mujo*, and I believe that's why Nishijima/Cross decided to translate it differently. Here's what they say in their footnotes: "*Mu* means 'not having' or 'without.' Conventionally, opposed to 'sentient beings,' *mujō* means 'insentient things' or 'the insentient'; that is, trees, rocks, fences, walls, etc. At the same time, in this chapter it also means 'the non-emotional'; that is, the state without emotion, or reality, which is beyond emotion."

If you look up the English word *insentient* in a dictionary one of the first definitions you'll often get is "lifeless." You may also get "lacking perception" or "lacking consciousness." However, in Buddhist terms nothing is ever truly lifeless. Also, everything is said to be composed of the five aggregates, two of which are perception and consciousness. So the very definition of the word *insentient*, which shows up a whole lot in English language writings about Buddhism, is actually a concept that Buddhism rejects.

The concept of an "insentient *being*" is even harder to defend from a Buddhist point of view. It seems to imply that certain beings or animals are lifeless or at least that they lack consciousness. There has been a running debate in the West for many centuries as to whether animals are sentient beings. In contrast, most Indian philosophers have held for a very long time that animals are sentient. The Buddha certainly viewed all animals as sentient beings.

When it comes to plants and rocks and things like that, it gets a little bit trickier. When you read this essay you can see that these are some of the kinds of things Dogen is referring to as *mujo* — insentient or nonemotional. But there is also another layer of meaning.

Perhaps when we, our sentient selves, become *mujo*, that is the only time when we can preach the dharma. In their introduction Nishijima and Cross say, "Master Dōgen insisted that even inanimate things can preach the Dharma, and at the same time he insisted that human beings can preach the Dharma when they are not emotional."

This, I believe, is why Nishijima and Cross chose their unorthodox way of translating the title of this essay. They wanted to make sure readers had a chance to get this point.

My paraphrase is prejudiced toward the Nishijima/Cross reading. Even so, I have tended to use the standard translation of "insentient" for the word *mujo*, mostly because "nonemotional" sounds a little forced and clunky to me. I'll try to note all the important differences between the Nishijima/Cross interpretation and other interpretations in the commentary at the end. See you there!

How do you truly proclaim the dharma when "proclaiming the dharma"? This is the most essential thing that Buddhist teachers transmit to Buddhist teachers. This is how the dharma explains the dharma.

This preaching of the dharma isn't sentient or insentient. It doesn't have a purpose, but it's not without purpose. It doesn't depend on circumstances. It doesn't just follow along the way birds follow a flock. And it's something we who teach Buddhism give to those who listen.

When the truth is fully realized, the dharma is fully explained. When you explain it to someone else, the dharma is kept alive. A long time ago Buddha held up a flower, thus symbolizing that his student Mahakashyapa was to be his successor. That was also an example of explaining the dharma. This is why, since the distant past, all the Buddhist masters have explained the dharma.

Don't think this explaining of the dharma is just something the Buddhist masters make happen. Explaining the dharma makes Buddhist masters happen.

Explaining the dharma doesn't just mean explaining the vast number of sutras and whatnot that exist. It's every way anyone ever tries to explain the dharma.

Former Buddhas do not return as later Buddhas. It's the same with explaining the dharma. Former explanations are not used again. That's why Shakyamuni Buddha said, "I explain the dharma exactly the way every Buddha explained it. The dharma is always the same."

So Buddhas explain the dharma the way they explain the dharma. That's how the dharma is authentically transmitted. Thus, what's been transmitted from the ancient past is the insentient explaining the dharma. That's why there are Buddhas and Buddhist teachers. It's a long-standing tradition, not just some kind of an old-timey cliché.

One time a master called Nanyo Echu (Ch. Nanyang Huizhong, c. 675-775 CE) was asked by a monk, "Can the insentient really understand and explain the dharma?"

Echu said, "They explain it all the time!"

The monk said, "Then how come I can't hear it?"

Echu said, "Just because you don't hear it doesn't mean nobody can."

The monk asked, "What kind of person hears it?"

Echu said, "The great saints can."

The monk said, "Do you hear it?"

Echu said, "Nope. I don't hear it."

The monk said, "If you don't hear it how do you know they explain it?"

Echu said, "It's a good thing I don't hear it. If I did, I'd be a great saint and you wouldn't be able to hear me explain the dharma."

The monk asked, "Does that mean living beings like people can't understand it?"

Echu said, "I explain it to people, not saints."

The monk asked, "What are people like after they hear it?"

Echu said, "When that happens they're not living beings."

Whether you're just starting out doing zazen or you've been doing it for ages, you can learn a lot from this dialogue.

Echu says the insentient explain the dharma all the time. "All the time" means they actually explain it at every real moment. There's no break in their explanation. Real explanations always happen without any break.

We ought to look into how they explain the dharma. The insentient don't necessarily explain it the same way the sentient do. If you think the insentient would have to explain it the same way as the sentient, you're not giving the insentient the credit they deserve. That's not Buddhism.

The insentient don't necessarily explain with sounds the way we do. I think it's good to ask what we mean by *sentient* and *insentient*. In order to do so, we need to look at how the insentient explain the dharma.

Some doofuses think that the rustling of the leaves in the trees or the opening of flowers is how the insentient explain the dharma. That's because they don't get what Buddhism is about. I mean, if that were so, everybody would be hearing the dharma all the time.

Let's just think for a minute about this rustling leaves stuff and whatnot explaining the dharma. In the world of the insentient, do they think about things in terms of "trees" and "leaves" and "forests?" By that I'm asking if the views and ideas of the world of sentient things like us somehow break into the world of what we call the insentient. I don't think they do.

On the other hand, to think of grass or trees or rocks and pebbles as insentient doesn't really get at it, either. Nor does seeing insentience as synonymous with grass and trees and rocks and pebbles.

When seen by human eyes, we might be able to discuss grass and trees and other such stuff as insentient. But, really, they're beyond any such designations. By that I mean you can't possibly conceive of what they really are. No one can.

Let's just take grasses and trees as examples. There are huge differences among real grasses and real trees in the actual world. And what about plants very much like grasses and trees that grow under the ocean? What about the trees in *Lord of the Rings* that talk really slow? We don't know if such trees are sentient or insentient. We don't doubt what we see with our eyes, but isn't it hard to explain even what we know to be real?

The master says, "Great saints can hear it."

That means that saints pay attention so they can hear what the insentient have to say. It also means that both the saints and the insentient emerge together with both hearing and explaining.

So the insentient do explain the dharma. But is it a saintly thing, or is it an everyday thing? What I'm saying is, after you learn to hear stuff the way saints hear it, you'll experience stuff the way they do. Once you get to that point you'll understand things the way saints understand them. And you'll understand in ways that can't be defined as saintly or common.

The master says, "Nope. I don't hear it."

You shouldn't think this is just an easy-peasy little statement. Why doesn't he hear? Is it because he's beyond all things saintly or common? Or is it because he totally smashes up the very idea of there being anything saintly or common, much like a punk rock band wrecking their instruments at the end of a show? Make some effort, and you'll get it.

Then the master says, "It's a good thing I don't hear it. If I did,

I'd be a great saint and you wouldn't be able to hear me explain the dharma."

This isn't just some kind of trick he's playing. He's speaking directly to the monk in a way the monk can understand. The master is a person who is beyond saintly or common. So what he hears might not be what saints hear.

Look into the master's words, "If I did, I'd be a great saint and you wouldn't be able to hear me explain the dharma." What he means is that when the insentient explain the dharma, saints can hear it, and when the master explains the dharma, that monk he was actually talking to could hear it.

I want to ask the master something myself: I don't care what living beings are like after they hear this stuff. I want to know what living beings are like at exactly the moment you explain it.

Here's another story. One time, great master Tozan Ryokai (Ch. Dongshan Liangjie, 807–869 CE, one of the founders of the Soto school of Zen) was practicing with his teacher Ungan Donjo (Ch. Yunyan Tansheng, 780–841 CE). Tozan asked his teacher, "Who can hear the insentient explain the dharma?"

His teacher, Ungan, said, "The insentient can hear the insentient explain the dharma."

Tozan asked his teacher, "So do you hear it or not?"

Ungan said, "If I heard it then you couldn't hear me when I explained it."

Tozan said to his teacher, "In that case, I'd rather not hear you!"

Ungan said, "You don't even hear *me* explaining the dharma. How are you gonna be able to hear the insentient explain it?"

Then Tozan recited a little poem that went like this:

It's nice, it's nice, it's so very nice
The insentient say what's mysteriously wise
The ears never hear their good advice
It can only be heard with the eyes

You have to really, really investigate the question, "Who can hear the insentient explain the dharma?" It's not just a statement. It's an assertion. Like, "*Who* can hear the insentient explain the dharma."

As an assertion it's super-powerful. It's the great truth of everything expressed in a single statement. How could the dumb-asses of today expect to understand it after just a few months of practice?

Tozan already heard from his teacher that the insentient explain the dharma. So now he's asking who hears this. Is he agreeing with his teacher or not? If he doesn't agree, then how could he ask such a thing? Yet if he did agree you also have to wonder how he could ask such a thing.

Ungan said, "The insentient can hear the insentient explain the dharma."

If you get this, then your body and mind both drop away. It's like saying that Buddhas can hear other Buddhas explain the dharma. When a bunch of people listen to the insentient explain the dharma, the only ones who hear it are those who are themselves insentient, meaning nonemotional — whether we think of them as sentient or insentient. Thus it is the nonemotional hearing the nonemotional.

If you understand this, you'll know how to tell true teaching from false. Even if some supposedly great master came directly from India, we shouldn't be awed by him or her unless his or her teaching is true.

Nowadays the authentic teaching is all over the place, so it ought to be easy to tell what's true from what's not. Upon hearing a simple phrase like "living beings can explain the dharma to living beings," we should get it immediately.

When the nonemotional (insentient) express themselves in non-emotional (insentient) ways, that in itself is the ultimate truth. Their very lack of emotion (insentience) is an expression of the ultimate truth.

Tozan said to his teacher, "In that case, I'd rather not hear you!"

The words *in that case* are important. They refer to Ungan's statement that the insentient explain the dharma. When he says "I'd rather not hear you," he's saying it's beyond hearing. He's showing that he really does get what his teacher is saying. He experiences directly that which transcends being heard and not being heard.

We don't just hear the dharma with our ears. We hear the dharma with our whole body and our whole mind. We hear it from the limitless past to the limitless future.

There is even benefit to hearing the dharma without understanding it. If you're so dog-tired you think you can't go on, you can still get some benefit from hearing the dharma. Even if you're too busy to think about this stuff, it can still help you. It's like planting a seed that grows later.

Dumb-bunnies think that if they don't understand the dharma or memorize it, then there's no benefit to even hearing it. They think that the best thing is to pursue knowledge and that if they forget what they've learned they might as well not have learned it at all. They think this way because they haven't met a good teacher, one who has received face-to-face transmission in an authentic lineage.

Sure. It's good to be able to remember the dharma. That's when it penetrates your whole being. That's when you enact what you've learned.

But it's not easy to recognize the benefit of simply hearing the dharma. Even so, if you do just that much it will be a good influence and guide to you. Everywhere you go, the dharma will go with you.

Even so, you shouldn't just throw away what you've learned. Just don't see this kind of intellectual learning as the main thing. Those who practice know this is true. Tozan, the guy in the story we just looked at, also knew this.

Ungan said, "You don't even hear *me* explaining the dharma. How are you gonna be able to hear the insentient explain it?"

Ungan lays it all out to Tozan here. He's saying, "Even if I explain, you are beyond hearing." He's paying Tozan a big compliment. He's saying that you don't need to be smart to get this stuff. This is truly not saintly teaching or common teaching.

So Tozan answers with a poem. He starts off saying, "It's nice, it's nice, it's so very nice." He's not just saying it's nice. He then says that the way the insentient explain the dharma is totally mysterious. That means it's not the kind of thing you'll ever understand intellectually. It's such a mystery that nobody — not common people and not even saints — can ever understand it intellectually. Even the gods don't understand it that way. Human beings don't have a chance.

In the poem he says, "The ears never hear their good advice."

No kind of ear can understand it, not even the universal ears that spread through all time and space.

It's not that it's impossible to listen to it with the ears. But even if you worked at it for bazillions of years you'd never understand it intellectually. When the insentient explain the dharma, it's a formless and soundless and undivided truth that doesn't even come near being saintly or common.

Tozan ends his poem by saying, "It can only be heard with the eyes."

Sometimes people make the mistake of thinking this means that looking at the beauty of nature is somehow an example of "hearing through the eyes." That's not the Buddhist way of understanding.

He means literally hearing with your eyes. We need to understand eyes thoroughly. Hearing with the eyes is just like hearing with the ears. And for this reason it's totally different from hearing with the ears.

We shouldn't think it means there are ears in our eyes or eyes in our ears. It doesn't mean that there is sound in our eyes.

An ancient master said, "The whole universe in all directions is one eye of a monk."

There are thousands of eyeballs on your fingertips. There are a thousand eyeballs of the dharma. There are a thousand eyeballs in your ears. There are a thousand eyeballs on the tip of your tongue. There are a thousand eyeballs in your mind. There are a thousand eyeballs throughout your body and mind.

There are a thousand eyeballs in life and a thousand eyeballs in death. There are a thousand eyeballs on the end of a stick. There are a thousand eyeballs in the moment that came just before this one. There are a thousand eyeballs in the mind you had a second ago. There are a thousand eyeballs of death in death, and a thousand eyeballs of life in life.

There are a thousand eyeballs of the self. There are a thousand eyeballs of the outside world. There are a thousand eyeballs on the tops of a thousand eyeballs. There are a thousand eyeballs of learning and practice. There are a thousand vertical eyeballs and a thousand horizontal eyeballs.

So we should know that the entire universe is eyeballs. But even knowing that doesn't mean you really understand what eyes are. Use your eyeballs right now to study what the insentient explaining the dharma means.

Tozan's point was that the ears can't understand the insentient explaining the dharma. Eyes hear sounds. Furthermore, sometimes the whole body hears sound. Even if we never really get this, we need to master it, and we need to get free of this whole "insentient hear the insentient explain the dharma" deal. That's what I've been trying to tell you this whole time.

My teacher back in China said, "A gourd is tangled up in a gourd."

This is an example of the nonemotional (insentient) explanation of the dharma. In fact, all dharma comes from this nonemotional (insentient) place.

What do we call "insentient"? Remember, those who listen to the insentient get it. What do we call "explaining the dharma"? Remember that when you don't know yourself to be insentient, that's exactly it.

When he was asked what the insentient explaining the dharma was, an old master named Tosu Daido (Ch. Touzi Datong, 819–914 CE) said, "Don't be such a potty mouth!"

That's the eternal Buddhist truth right there. That's the insentient explaining the dharma. It's "Don't be a potty mouth." Only real practitioners of the truth devote themselves to trying to comprehend it.

— Preached to the congregation at Kippo-ji Temple
in Fukui Prefecture on October 10, 1243

Okay. This chapter is weird right from the very first words, which I paraphrased as, "How do you truly proclaim the dharma when 'proclaiming the dharma'?" The weird words are *seppo o seppo* (説法於説法). Every translator has a heck of a time with this. The *seppo* (説法) part is easy enough. It means "explaining/expounding/proclaiming/preaching (the) dharma." The other character *o* (於), the one between the two *seppo*s, means something like "at," "in," "on," or "as for."

Tanahashi uses the phrase, "Speaking dharma by means of

speaking dharma." Bielefeldt and Nishijima/Cross render it the same way, "Preaching the dharma in preaching the dharma." Nishiyama/Stevens just ignore the repeated phrase and give us, "The act of proclaiming the dharma."

I decided that Dogen probably meant really explaining the dharma as opposed to engaging in a ritual activity called "explaining the dharma." He often makes that kind of distinction. That's why I paraphrased it, "How do you truly proclaim the dharma when 'proclaiming the dharma'?"

The phrase I've given as "the most essential thing" in the sentence, "This is the most essential thing that Buddhist teachers transmit to Buddhist teachers," is actually Dogen's pet phrase *genjo koan* (現成公案). We've seen this phrase a lot in this book. In this case I feel like "the most essential thing" is probably a reasonable enough way to put it. Other translators generally try to reuse whatever phrase they used to begin with to translate *genjo koan*.

When Dogen says it's how the dharma explains the dharma, he's not just being goofy. In his view, it's not that people explain the dharma to other people. His view is that the dharma is embodied by people and by other things, and that the dharma then explains itself to other embodiments of the dharma. Weird, huh?

Moving right along, in the next sentence he says, "This preaching of the dharma isn't sentient or insentient." In this case, even Nishijima and Cross use the word *insentient*, as does everyone else. In Japanese the key words are *ujo* (有情) or "sentient" and *mujo* (無情) or "insentient." Just FYI.

The terms I've paraphrased as "(have a) purpose" and "without purpose" in the sentence, "It doesn't have a purpose, but it's not without purpose" are *ui* (有爲) and *mui* (無爲). Nishijima and Cross make these "intentional doing" and "non-doing." Bielefeldt gives us "constructed" and "unconstructed." Tanahashi has "creating" and "not creating."

In conventional contemporary Japanese the character *i* (爲) is now written like this — 為. It is often pronounced *tame*. It's a very common word that indicates the reason, purpose, or intention for doing something. That's why I give you "purpose" and "without purpose."

Then I have Dogen say, "It doesn't just follow along the way birds follow a flock." Bielefeldt sees this as reference to a certain dialogue between an ancient Zen master and his student. In that dialogue "following the way of birds" symbolizes both following one's natural inclinations and just going along with what everybody else does. Dogen appears to be saying that explaining the dharma isn't one or the other of these things.

On the one hand, explaining the dharma is expressing one's truest and most natural understanding. On the other, in order to express that understanding we often rely on the ways others before us have expressed it. So we quote our teachers, or we write books paraphrasing old-timey Zen guys nobody much cared about for centuries. So it's not "following the way of birds" in either of the senses I mentioned above, because it's both using what's been said before and expressing something true.

I have Dogen say, "When you explain it to someone else, the dharma is kept alive." A more standard translation of this line would be, "When the dharma treasury is entrusted, speaking dharma is entrusted." That's Tanahashi's version. The other translations are very similar.

I feel like Dogen is saying, well, what I have him say. Remember that according to Buddhist theory, this living universe is just one thing. Individual people are manifestations of something much, much bigger than themselves. If an individual comes to some understanding, she or he must express that understanding in order for that understanding to remain alive within this living universe. Those to whom the dharma has been explained are then able to embody and teach it.

After this I have Dogen say, "Don't think this explaining of the dharma is just something the Buddhist masters make happen. Explaining the dharma makes Buddhist masters happen." I'll let you look up alternate translations. I think mine is fairly standard.

If this line is confusing, keep in mind that in Buddhist theory action is more fundamental than beings who do actions. We usually think that we exist and that, because we exist, we do things. In Buddhist theory, action exists first and because action happens, the people and things that do that action appear. It's weird, I know. But picture creating a couple of little whirlpools in a bucket. The whirlpools might collide or interact with each other as if they were individual beings. But you can see they're just disturbances in the water and have no existence apart from it, even if the whirlpools themselves imagine they do. It's sorta like that.

Next, Dogen tells us that former explanations of the dharma aren't used again and proves this by having Shakyamuni say precisely the opposite. You can look up other translations if you want — I encourage you to! But they're all just as contradictory. So it's exactly the same, but it's not the same.

I remember having a conversation about this idea with my first Zen teacher, Tim McCarthy. I was asking Tim about the answers to koans, those weird questions like, "What's the sound of one hand clapping?" I assumed that everyone would have a different answer to such a question. I mean, how could it be otherwise? Tim said the right answer was always the same, even if it was a different answer. Six of one, half dozen of the other? Maybe. But not really. I'm not going to try to explain what Tim said. I'll just leave it for you to ponder it the way I had to ponder it.

Where I have Dogen say that it's a "long-standing tradition, not some kind of an old-timey cliché," the actual words Dogen uses for "old-timey cliché" translate to "an old nest in a demon's cave." About this, Bielefeldt provides a footnote that says, "'Old den' (or 'nest,' or 'burrow') is regularly used in Chan [*Chan* is the Chinese pronunciation of the character that Japanese people pronounce as

Zen] literature for old or habitual ways of thinking, 'tired' concepts or clichés. 'The demon's cave' is used in reference to the dark confines of fixed positions, either intellectual or spiritual, as in the common Chan expression 'the demon cave at the Black Mountains' (*kokusan ge kikutsu*, 黒山下鬼窟)." Those of you who read *Don't Be a Jerk* may recall a reference in there to that same demon's cave in those same Black Mountains.

Then there's the story about Master Echu and the monk. I have the monk ask, "Can the insentient really understand and explain the dharma?"

Nishijima/Cross and Bielefeldt have the monk asking if the insentient can explain the dharma. Tanahashi and Nishiyama/Stevens have the monk ask if the insentient understand the dharma when it's spoken. The actual line contains a couple of funny old-fashioned Chinese characters (還解) that don't translate well. Individually they mean "return" and "understand." But it also uses the phrase *seppo* (説法), which, as we saw, means "explain the dharma." So I cheated and went with both.

There are little differences in the ways people translate the rest of the dialogue, but they're not really critical. So I'll let you look them up for yourself if you want.

When I have Dogen say that the insentient actually explain the dharma at every real moment without a break, that's my way of dealing with the phrase *tsune wa, shoji no ippun-ji nari* (常は、諸時の一分時なり). Nishijima and Cross see this as a philosophical statement on the nature of time: "*Always* is a concrete time of many instants." Other translators see it more like Bielefeldt, whose translation says, "Constantly is one time among all times" or Tanahashi, whose version is, "Always is a part of all time." In a footnote Bielefeldt calls the phrase ambiguous and says it "suggest[s] perhaps that each time somehow incorporates or expresses all times." It's an interesting phrase and deserves a close look. I invite you to give it one.

After this I have Dogen say, "The insentient don't necessarily explain it the same way the sentient do." Nishijima and Cross provide a footnote to this that says, "Because the state of the sentient (*ujo*) is sometimes emotional, but the state of the insentient (*mujo*) is always non-emotional, that is, balanced — in this part, Master Dōgen distinguishes between the two states."

In their footnote about the insentient not necessarily explaining the dharma with sounds like we do, Nishijima and Cross say, "Just as a Buddhist lecture is not only sound but also has meaning, so a mountain stream not only produces sound but also expounds Buddhist teaching."

In my paraphrase Dogen refers to the slow-talking trees in *Lord of the Rings*. Of course neither the movies nor the books they're based on existed in Dogen's time. What he actually wrote is translated by Nishijima/Cross as, "Still more, there are trees that grow in space and there are trees that grow in clouds. Among the hundred weeds and myriad trees that sprout and grow amid wind, fire, and so on, there are generally those that can be understood as sentient, those that are not recognized as insentient, and those weeds and trees which seem to be humans and animals."

He's talking about what we today would call fictional trees. He's referencing old stories that nobody remembers anymore but that his audience probably knew. So I substituted the trees from *Lord of the Rings*. You're welcome.

In Dogen's commentary on the master saying that great saints can hear the insentient explain the dharma, I have Dogen say, "It also means that both the saints and the insentient emerge together with both hearing and explaining." This is close enough to the original Japanese. It's yet another reference to the Buddhist idea of how the universe comes into being. So let's look at that for a sec.

The universe didn't pop into being billions of years ago — or even six thousand years ago, according to adherents to "creation science." It didn't chug along existing for all those years, after which we showed up and started asking about it. Not according to those whack-a-doodle Buddhists! Rather, we and the universe come into existence together in this very instant. You are not sitting somewhere in the universe reading a confusing book about a weird Japanese monk. The fact of you reading the book and the fact of the universe existing at all so that there can be a you and a book for you to read, these emerge together. It's some tripped-out stuff!

After this I inserted a reference to punk rock bands smashing their instruments. In the original it's more like, "Does he 'not hear it' having transcended the commoner and surpassed the sage? Or does he not hear it because he breaks down the dens and caves of 'commoner and sage'?" That's the Bielefeldt version. The others are pretty much the same. Just thought you might like to know.

After the master says it's a good thing he doesn't hear the insentient explain the dharma or he wouldn't be able to explain it, I have Dogen say, "This isn't just some kind of trick he's playing. He's speaking directly to the monk in a way the monk can understand." In the original this is much shorter. Tanahashi, for example, has this line as, "This presentation is not one or two phrases."

In a footnote Nishijima and Cross explain this cryptic line as meaning, "It is an expression of the whole truth of the National Master, who lived not by hard and fast rules but by freely changing his behavior to suit circumstances — he kept his teaching at a level that could be understood by the listener." So that's how I paraphrased it.

Just FYI, Bielefeldt sees it differently. His footnote about the same phrase says it's, "Generally taken to mean 'not simply a few [ordinary] words.'"

Then we get that conversation between Tozan and his teacher, Ungan. As usual I slaughtered the little poem at the end. The Nishiyama/Stevens translation goes, "Marvelous! Marvelous! The proclamation of inanimate beings is incredibly wonderful! If you try to hear it through the ear, you would not get it. Listen to it through the eye and you will have it."

In a footnote to that poem, Nishijima and Cross say, "In

general, ears represent intellectual understanding whereas eyes represent intuitive understanding, or the viewpoint of real experience." Sounds good to me.

Then I have Dogen say that the question, "Who can hear the insentient explain the dharma" is also a statement. In the original he just leaves it at that. I added in Dogen changing the question to a statement. The word I paraphrased as "who" is *shimo-nin* (麼人). It's a variation on Dogen's pet word *inmo* (恁麼). It could also be understood as "a *what* person." You'll recall from chapter 1 that it expresses the unnameable something that is you and is the universe.

After that I have Dogen ask, "How could the dumb-asses of today expect to understand it after just a few months of practice?" In the original he says something more like "three or four months of practice."

In a footnote Bielefeldt speculates on whether this might actually be a way of saying "three or four years," for reasons that are linguistically complex. Then he says the phrase isn't common and doesn't appear elsewhere in Dogen's writings.

My guess is that people in Dogen's time weren't all that different from us. We imagine we invented the idea of wanting things to happen quickly somewhere in the American Midwest sometime around 1956 when the first drive-through burger stand appeared. I doubt that's true. I think even eight hundred years ago Dogen probably had monks who wanted their understanding to happen fast. Three or four months would have been a standard training period. I believe that's what Dogen's going for here.

After this part, Dogen asks how Tozan could ask that question, whether or not he agreed with his teacher. About this, Nishijima and Cross provide two footnotes. The first is, "Because Master Tōzan completely affirms the National Master, he wants to investigate further the National Master's words that the saints are able to hear the non-emotional preaching the Dharma." The second footnote says, "Because Master Tōzan completely affirms the National Master, he absorbs the National Master's words without trying to understand them intellectually."

After this I have Dogen say, "If you get this, then your body and mind both drop away." Dogen is using another of his pet phrases here. This time it's *shin jin datsu raku* (身心脱落), or "dropping off body and mind." As I've indicated before, my teacher Nishijima Roshi always explained this phrase as referring to times when our bodily experience and our mental experience are so perfectly in balance that both seem to vanish.

Next I gave you a two-sentence paragraph that says, "When the nonemotional (insentient) express themselves in nonemotional (insentient) ways, that in itself is the ultimate truth. Their very lack of emotion (insentience) is an expression of the ultimate truth."

This is a distillation of a longer section that gets very twisty-turny in the original. I'll let you look up a standard translation on your own. I read a bunch of them and came up with that short version. As always, you're welcome.

After this I have Dogen say something that might resonate with you, dear reader, just about now. He says, "There is even benefit to hearing the dharma without understanding it." The Nishijima/ Cross translation of that is, "Never say that there is no benefit in hearing the Dharma without the involvement of mind-consciousness." That's a pretty standard translation. I mostly just eliminated the confusing double negative — the Japanese love to express things in double negatives. Or is it a triple negative here? They love those, too.

I appreciate this line because it describes my initial experience with reading *Shobogenzo*. The first few times I read it I didn't know what the hell it was saying. And yet somehow I absorbed it, and later on it started making very good sense. In fact, it went from sounding like utter gibberish to sounding like the most sensible thing I'd ever read. The worldview Dogen expressed has helped me immensely in ways I can't begin to describe.

Next up, there is a series of paragraphs, the first of which starts with, "Dumb-bunnies think that if they don't understand the dharma or memorize it, then there's no benefit to even hearing it." I did a lot of work on these paragraphs to make them shorter and more straightforward. I don't think my paraphrase strays too far from the intention of the original. If you want a more convoluted version of the same idea, go check out one of the standard translations.

When I then have Dogen point out how Tozan said the way the insentient explain the dharma is totally mysterious, he actually uses the word *fushigi* (不思議). It's a very common Japanese word usually translated as "mysterious." Nishijima and Cross give us a nice footnote about this. It says, "As a compound these three characters mean mystery, wonder, miracle, marvel, etc. Individually, *fu* means 'not' or 'beyond,' *shi* means 'think,' and *gi* means 'discuss,' 'deliberate,' or 'consider intellectually.'" I must have used that word a few thousand times. I didn't know its deeper meaning.

After this, the ending gets pretty crazy, what with all that stuff about the thousands of eyeballs everywhere and all that. What you get in my paraphrase is a mash-up of the existing translations, with a couple of references back to my own interpretation of certain words in the original Japanese. I'm not going to go through and list all that stuff. I think if you check the standard translations, you'll see that they're all pretty crazy sounding.

A lot of the eyeballs stuff refers back to what Dogen said about the thousands of eyes of the Bodhisattva of Compassion. And the character Dogen uses for "eyes" is *manako* (眼), which is more like "eyeballs," as opposed to the word *me* (目), which is usually translated as "eyes." *Manako* can also mean something like "insight" in certain circumstances. I also see a few other layers to it beyond that.

This is a tough little passage. It reminds me of the *Rick and Morty* episode "Auto Erotic Assimilation," in which a being called Unity takes over an entire planet and therefore can see through everyone's eyes all at once. It could also be like the old fifties sci-fi film *The Beast with a Million Eyes*. In that movie an alien entity, which disappointingly has only two eyes, invades the brains of a whole bunch of earthlings and therefore can see through a million eyes at once. Actually, in the movie it's not really shown that the alien takes over five hundred thousand people, but I guess we're supposed to assume it did.

What Dogen is talking about isn't exactly like that, but there may be a connection, albeit a very tenuous one. He's addressing the idea that what we call "consciousness" is not limited to those beings we call "sentient." In Buddhism all things in the universe share this thing we call "consciousness." It's just that sentient and insentient beings express consciousness in vastly different ways. Or maybe when matter gets organized in a very specific way, it starts to think for itself — or at least it *thinks* that it thinks for itself. Maybe that's the real difference between the sentient and the insentient.

Finally, we get the story of the Zen master who replied, "Don't be such a potty mouth" when asked about the idea of the insentient preaching the dharma. The phrase I've given as "Don't be such a potty mouth" is actually *nai aku kuchi* (莫悪口). Nishijima and Cross translate this as, "No abusive language" in the text and as "not bad mouth" in their footnote. The latter is a literal translation of the Chinese characters.

I think this part is pretty easy to understand. The master is saying that even to call something "insentient" is a way of insulting that thing. Ultimately there is no such thing as "insentience," even though in conventional terms there is. But that conventional understanding is just the way we human beings see things, not the whole truth of the matter.

Okay. I hope your brain isn't too stretched out by that one! The next chapter looks at the question of whether or not everything in the universe is just in our minds.

15. IT'S ALL IN THE MIND, OR IS IT?
San Gai Yui Shin
The Three Worlds Are Only the Mind

A LOT OF people describe Buddhism as an "idealistic philosophy." It is not. But many of those folks would cite essays like this one from Dogen as evidence. So let's talk about that.

When I first started hearing Buddhism being called "idealistic," I thought of the word *idealistic* as a synonym for *optimistic*. In fact, I just now used my word processing program to look up synonyms and got words like *naive, impractical, principled, committed,* and so on. So I wasn't alone in being unaware of the philosophical meaning of the word *idealism.*

In philosophical terms an idealistic philosophy is one that insists reality is all in the mind. There are different types of idealistic philosophies. Some say that the material world doesn't really exist at all. Some say that the material world does exist but that its existence is based on the mind, so it's a secondary thing.

Religions are generally idealistic in the sense that they tend to insist on the belief in nonmaterial or spiritual forces that create and control the material world.

These days a lot of folks who are into Eastern religions get super-excited over the idealistic outlook. Guru-to-the-stars Deepak Chopra famously offered the Amazing Randi, an outspoken atheist magician who debunks claims of the paranormal, a million dollars to

286

prove the universe was not all in the mind. Or something. I reread Deepak's challenge for the purpose of writing this introduction, and I'm still not exactly sure what he's asking the Amazing Randi to prove.

Here's part of it. Deepak says, "You don't realize that everything we experience as the physical world is actually a perception. And that perception is the result of an experience in consciousness. And we have no idea how that happens. If I ask you to imagine a sunset on the ocean right now and you have the experience somewhere then explain to me where that picture is."

The opposite of idealism is materialism. That doesn't mean materialism in the sense of that old Madonna song where she says the boy with cold hard cash is always Mr. Right. It's a philosophy that insists the only real thing in the universe is matter. Consciousness only exists because of material forces. Madonna-style materialism sometimes seems like the only sensible response to philosophical materialism, but they're still different things.

Nishijima Roshi used to say that the entire history of the human race can be understood in terms of a battle between materialistic and idealistic philosophies. It's a constant back-and-forth, with one side winning for a while and then the other side taking over for a time.

During the Middle Ages, Nishijima would say, people were highly idealistic and deeply religious. I was traveling through Europe last year and had to change trains in Cologne, Germany. I had about an hour to wait for my train, so I decided to take a walk around the station.

Right next to the station is a massive cathedral, so huge it dwarfs everything around it. Parts of the cathedral date back to the ninth century. Standing in front of it, I was struck by the realization that the people who built it must have really believed in God in ways that people today who claim to believe in God can't possibly comprehend. Not only was that church immense, it was much harder centuries ago to build things on such a grand scale. All those gigantic slabs of stone were carved and then hoisted into place by human power alone. You don't do that kind of work just to make a pretty building. You do it because you *believe*.

Then, Nishijima said, when the Renaissance happened, "people discovered they had human bodies." It was a strikingly odd way to put it, but he always described it this way. I think he was right. It almost seems like humanity collectively discovered the material world and was shocked to learn that they were not living in the world of the mind. Materialism began to take hold.

The nineteenth and twentieth centuries saw materialism take the lead in a big way. Many believed that soon all our problems would be solved by the rational application of science. Religions faded into the background. A guy who lived in Cologne told me there's still a small congregation at the cathedral but that most of the folks you see inside are tourists.

Unfortunately, materialism did not solve humanity's problems. Along with the miracles of television, flush toilets, and pocket-size computers more powerful than the ones NASA used to get to the moon, we also got atomic bombs, high-tech concentration camps, and runaway climate change.

So now we have people like Deepak Chopra who'd like us to turn back to idealism. The problem is that idealism already failed us hundreds of years ago, which is why the materialistic outlook became so powerful in the first place.

Even so, a lot of people searching for an idealistic philosophy to return to look to Buddhism because it says stuff like "the triple world is only mind," which is the standard translation of the original title of this essay by Dogen (*sangai yui shin*, 三界唯心).

The triple world — or "three worlds," if you prefer — is variously defined in Buddhism. Sometimes it means "volition, matter, and nonmatter." Sometimes it means "past, present, and future." Sometimes it's "desire, form, and formlessness." But in all these cases it means the entire universe — everything. So another perfectly legit way to translate the title of this essay might be "Everything in the Universe Is Only Mind," although nobody translates it that way.

Obviously, then, Dogen was a prime example of an idealistic Buddhist.

You didn't think it was gonna be that easy, now did you? Nothing with Dogen is ever that easy. In this essay he examines the more profound meaning of the old Buddhist insistence that the world is mind-only. Let's see what he has to say.

In the Garland Sutra, Shakyamuni Buddha said, "The three worlds are mind only. Outside of mind, nothing else exists. The mind, Buddha, and living beings are not three different things." The Buddha's whole lifelong effort is poured right into this one quote.

When he says "three worlds" he means the entire universe. But he is not saying that the entire universe is the same as the mind. The universe is still the universe. If you think there's something outside the universe, that's just plain impossible.

Inside or outside, beginning, middle, or end, it's all the "three worlds." Whatever our opinions or definitions of it are, the universe is exactly what it is. Every opinion you might have is an opinion about the universe.

That's why the Buddha also said, "You'd best see the universe as the universe."

He's totally right. The universe is just like he says it is. It hasn't been around forever. But it didn't appear just now. It isn't brand-new. But it isn't the result of something else. It has no beginning, middle, or end.

Old sutras have stuff about escaping the universe, or they say that the universe is here and now. This is like a moment of awakening meeting a moment of awakening, and it's like getting tangled up in confusion that's already tangled up and confused.

When you're present in the here and now of the universe, you can see the universe here and now. What you see is the universe.

When you see the universe as the universe, that's when you experience realization. That's how you make the universe meditate, and that's how you have the experience of knowing that the whole universe belongs to you.

This is why in the Lotus Sutra the Buddha says, "The whole universe here and now belongs to me. Every living thing is my child."

The universe belongs to Buddha, and that's why the universe is the universe. When he says "here and now" he means past, present, and future. The past, present, and future don't interfere with here and now. Here and now blocks off past, present, and future.

When he says it "belongs to me" he means that the whole universe in all directions is one single human body. And it means the whole universe is a monk's eyeball.

When he says "every living thing" he means that living things are the body of the universe in all directions. Because each living being is alive and there are lots of them, that's why we call them living beings.

When he says they're all his children, he's talking about how everything in the universe is a manifestation of the underlying functioning of the universe. It's like how a child inherits her hair color and skin tone and all that from her parents without somehow removing those things from her parents. This is how a child realizes herself as a child.

In this case it's not like the parents existed before the child. It's beyond that. It's also beyond the child existing first and the parents coming along after. It's also beyond both parents and child appearing at the exact same time. That's the truth of what the Buddha means when he says "my children."

Without anything being given, you receive it. Without stealing anything, you make it your own. It's not coming or going. It's not large or small. It has nothing to do with being old or young.

It's like the way the Lotus Sutra talks about the concepts of old and young. It says sometimes a parent is younger than his child, other times both parent and child are old, and other times they're both young.

Children who pretend to be adults aren't being children. But you don't get to be an adult without first being a child. Pay close attention to the oldness and youngness of children and adults.

Sometimes the relationships between parents and children

suddenly become clear to both of them at the same time. Sometimes those relationships suddenly end all at once. Sometimes they figure it out at different times from each other. And sometimes they fail to figure it out at all.

A child can be realized without hampering anything about a compassionate parent. And a parent becomes realized without impeding anything about a child.

There are beings who are conscious and there are beings who are not conscious. There are children who know they're children and children who don't. All those who the Buddha called "my children" as well as those who understand themselves to be "me who is a child," they're all the heirs of Buddha and his understanding.

Everyone who ever lived or ever will live is, was, or will be a Buddha. They are Buddhas as children of Buddha and Buddhas as parents of everyone.

Because this is the case, the flowers and fruits of everything are Buddha's possessions. Forests and fields are, too.

And also please take note that even though the Buddha said all beings are his children, he never said anything about him being their father.

In the Prajna Paramita Sutra on Benevolent Kings, Shakyamuni Buddha also said, "Even when the Buddhas take on different bodies to teach beings in other realms, they don't leave this universe. There are no beings outside the universe, so who could they possibly teach? That's why I say that anyone who says there's another universe outside of this one is full of it."

Whatever bodies the Buddhas manifest in, all those are in this universe. They *are* this universe. The universe doesn't have any outside. Buddha also has no outside. Walls and fences have no outside. In the same way that the universe has no outside, we living beings also don't have an outside.

The Buddha asked, "There are no beings outside the universe, so who could they possibly teach?" The Buddhas always teach living beings. Remember that he said the idea that there is something other than this universe or that there are living beings outside the universe is bull.

"Mind-only" isn't like saying "only" in the sense of being one as opposed to two or three or whatever. It's not the universe and it's not outside the universe. You can't doubt its existence. It has thought, knowledge, attention, and realization and it's free from thought, knowledge, attention, and realization. It's any material thing you can imagine. It's any spiritual thing you can imagine.

When the Buddha picked up a flower and smiled at his student Mahakashyapa, thus making him the new leader of the Buddhist order, that too was mind-only. Mind can be conscious or unconscious. Sometimes mind has a body and sometimes it doesn't. There was mind in the moment just before this one, and there is mind in the moment just after this one.

According to the old Buddhist tradition, bodies can be born from a womb, from eggs, from moisture, and from transformation. Same with the mind. It can be born in all those ways.

Colors are mind. Sizes are mind. Shapes are mind. Living and dying, appearing and disappearing are also mind. Time is mind. Dreams are mind.

Water, foam, and flame are mind. Flowers in the spring and the moon in the autumn are also mind.

Each moment is mind. And yet mind can never be destroyed. That's why everything that's real is mind, and the Buddhas along with other Buddhas are mind.

Master Gensa Shibi (Ch. Xuansha Shibei, 835–907 CE) said to Master Rakan Keichin (Ch. Luohan Guichen, 867–928 CE), who was his successor, "Buddha said the whole universe is mind-only. How do you understand this teaching?"

Rakan pointed to a bass and said, "Master, what do you call this thing?"

Gensa said, "A Fender Precision electric bass guitar."*

Rakan said, "Then, my teacher, you don't understand what *the whole universe is mind-only* means."

---

* Okay. He actually says, "A chair." But that's boring! He also describes it as a thing made out of wood and nails. I have him say the bass is made *mostly* out of wood and screws. I added the word *mostly* because there are other parts of a bass, like the pickups, the tuning keys, the strings, etc. The word *mostly* is not in the original. So don't get hung up on it and think he's indicating other mysterious unnamed things.

Gensa said, "I call it something made mostly out of wood and screws. What do you call it?"

Rakan said, "I also call it something made mostly out of wood and screws."

Gensa said, "You could search everywhere in the world and still not find someone who understands Buddhism!"

First let's look at the initial question. Both understanding and not understanding are part of the universe, are part of the very thing Buddha said was "mind-alone." Which means the universe is not understood.

So Rakan points at a Fender P-bass and asks his teacher what it's called. He is answering the question about how he understands by stating, "*What* do you call this thing." In other words, the bass might be called a bass, but it's also beyond any name we could give it, as is everything else in the universe.

When Gensa says "a Fender Precision electric bass guitar," do those words represent an understanding of the universe, or not? Are the words themselves the universe? Are they beyond the universe? Do they express the bass, or do they express Gensa?

My teacher in China used to say, "Try to say something for yourself." We should look at Gensa's answer in terms of this question. We should understand them in terms of this question. We should try to say something for ourselves in terms of our real experience.

Rakan said, "Then, my teacher, you don't understand what *the whole universe is mind-only* means."

This is like when Master Joshu Jushin (Ch. Zhaozhou Congshen, 778–897 CE) was asked where he lived and he said, "The front door and the back door." But there might also be side doors on the east and west. Joshu's name was also the name of the city where he lived. So imagine his name was Cleveland. He could say he lives in east Cleveland and west Cleveland.

Even if you get the whole *universe is mind-only* deal, you should also try to fully understand the nonunderstanding of that idea. Hell, mind-alone is beyond understanding and nonunderstanding!

Gensa said, "I call it something made mostly out of wood and screws."

We should really dig into this statement. We need to completely understand it both before it becomes words and after it's spoken. It's an expression that was never heard before and hasn't been heard since.

"I call it something made mostly out of wood and screws," he says. Before he described it, what was it? Has it always been mostly wood and screws?

By calling it wood and screws is he also saying the universe is mind-only? Or is he avoiding saying that?

When you say the universe is mind-only in the morning, maybe it's a bass guitar. Or maybe it's mind-only. Or maybe it's the universe.

But when you say the universe is mind-only in the evening we might hear it as, "I call it something made mostly out of wood and screws."

Rakan said, "I also call it something made mostly out of wood and screws."

Keep in mind that this is a conversation between a great master and his advanced student. They have studied this stuff together a whole lot already.

Still, we should ask whether Gensa is saying, "I call it something made mostly out of wood and screws" is the same as Rakan saying, "I also call it something made mostly out of wood and screws." And we should ask whether or not these statements really get to the point.

Gensa said, "You could search everywhere in the world and still not find someone who understands Buddhism!"

We should also take a hard look at this statement. Remember, both Gensa and Rakan said it was wood and screws. They never understand what *the universe is mind-only* means and yet they never deny that the universe is mind-only. Nor did they go beyond the expression "the universe is mind-only."

Still, I wish I could say to Gensa, "You say you could search everywhere in the world and still not find someone who understands Buddhism, but I got a question I want to see if you can answer. What would you call the whole Earth?"

You should investigate the unnameable this way.

— Preached to the assembly at Mount Yoshimine
in Fukui Prefecture on July 1, 1243

This one sounds weird right from the get-go. Most translations of the final part of the quote from the Garland Sutra say something like "Mind, Buddha, and sentient beings are not divided" (Tanahashi) or "The mind, buddha, and living beings — The three are without distinction" (Nishijima/Cross). But I prefer the Nishiyama/Stevens version, which says, "Mind, Buddha, and sentient beings are not three different things." The original line is in Chinese, but the Japanese pronunciation indicated in some versions of the text would be *kokoro (to) hotoke oyobi shujo (to) ʒe (no) san (wa) nashi (to ni) sabetsu* (心仏及衆生是三無差別, in the original Chinese). "The three are without distinction" wins for best literal translation, but Nishiyama/Stevens get the prize for making it sound like real English.

Dogen attributes this quote to Shakyamuni, the historical Buddha who started the whole thing off 2,500 years ago. But the Garland Sutra (a.k.a. Avatamsaka Sutra in Sanskrit) was written at least five hundred years after Buddha's death. It's possible that the historical Buddha said this and it just wasn't written down until much later. But I seriously doubt it.

It's quite likely that Dogen was aware that the sutra was composed long after the Buddha died. This isn't something people just recently discovered. Dogen was a thorough scholar of such matters and criticizes other sutras of late origin as being historically suspect. But if he knew this about the Garland Sutra, he clearly did not care. He still believed it accurately expressed the essential philosophical outlook of the Buddha. A lot of Mahayana Buddhists take this approach to the late-period sutras. They know these sutras are historically suspect, but they accept what they say based on the merit of the words themselves and not who said them.

Throughout my paraphrase of this essay I alternated between saying "three worlds" and "the universe." Dogen consistently just says *sangai* (三界), which means "three worlds" or "the triple world." Since he told us already this is just another way of saying "everything," I alternated terms in my paraphrase. This is because the term *three worlds* tends to sound a bit spooky and esoteric to us today.

Where I have Dogen say that whatever your opinion is about the universe, the universe is what it is, Dogen doesn't actually say "opinion." What he says translates more directly as "old nests" (*kyusu*, 旧巣) and "new buds" (*shinjo*, 新条). Those are just poetic ways of saying "views and opinions." Nishijima and Cross have a footnote about this that says, "While living in reality, we are constantly getting rid of views and opinions of reality, and at the same time, at every moment we are looking at reality directly."

Nishiyama and Stevens see "old nests" as meaning delusional viewpoints and "new buds" as meaning enlightened ones. They have Dogen say, "The three worlds are seen as both delusion and enlightenment." Which is interesting.

I then have Dogen quote the Buddha as saying, "You'd best see the universe as the universe." That's based on the Nishijima/Cross translation, only they say "triple world" instead of "universe." Tanahashi has Buddha say, "Nothing sees the three realms better than the three realms." Which is an interesting alternate reading. Nishiyama and Stevens, though, read it very differently. They have Buddha say, "The three worlds I see are not like the three worlds of ordinary people."

What it actually says is in Chinese, but an approximate Japanese pronunciation would be *fu-nyo sangai ken yo sangai* (不如三界見於三界). Google Translate agrees with the Nishijima/Cross translation, for whatever that's worth.* I can also see why Tanahashi translated it the way he did. I'm not sure how Nishiyama and Stevens came up with their version (obviously).

The stuff that comes after this about the universe not having been around forever or appearing just now, not being brand-new but

---

* I do not rely on Google Translate at all, but sometimes I'll run things through it to see what it gives me.

not the result of something else, and so on has a bunch of different translations. You can look up the variations. But I think the differences between them are not terribly important.

Basically, all Dogen is doing here is refuting common lines of thinking about the origin of the universe that were popular in his time. If he were speaking today he might say that the universe isn't the result of the Big Bang, it's not vibrating super-strings, God didn't make it in seven days, and so on, refuting our common ways of explaining the origin of the universe. I could probably have done this in my paraphrase, but I thought it might be too distracting.

After this Dogen quotes the Buddha from the Lotus Sutra again. Like the Garland Sutra, the Lotus Sutra was written long after Buddha was dead. Dogen probably knew this but again clearly did not care.

Then we see him referring to the same Lotus Sutra passage that he references in the chapter we just looked at about the insentient speaking the dharma. That chapter was actually written about three months after this one, just in case you're keeping track. Anyhow, it's that part about everything being a monk's eyeball. He also talks here of "living beings" (*shujo*, 衆生), as he did in that chapter. So keep in mind that he's not distinguishing living things from nonliving things. To Dogen, everything was alive.

Then I have Dogen say, "When he [Buddha] says they're all his children, he's talking about how everything in the universe is a manifestation of the underlying functioning of the universe." I'm being interpretive here. Tanahashi's translation says, "My children is the total actualization of children." Nishiyama and Stevens give us, "'All my children' is the principle of the emergence of the total activity of children."

My paraphrase is my own reading of these translations, along with the original Japanese mixed in with what I know about Dogen's basic outlook. To me he's saying that when Buddha calls all living things his children, he's not saying he's God and that he created them. He's taking the standpoint of the universe expressing itself as a single entity. The people and the things in the universe — you and me included — function as if we were the children of the greater thing that encompasses us all (the universe). Or something like that.

Then we get some stuff about the parents not necessarily coming along before the child and vice versa and about both appearing at the same time. Dogen's really just trying to get us to see beyond our preconceptions. We all have a basic assumption about the nature of time. Parents come first and children come later. There's no way to reverse that. Yet here Dogen is saying we have to put aside even such completely common-sense ideas in order to see things as they really are.

The paragraph that starts out, "Sometimes the relationships between parents and children suddenly become clear to both of them at the same time" was tricky. The translations here are all different, and the original Japanese is hard to follow.

Kaz Tanahashi's translation talks about parents and children being born at the same time, dying at the same time, being born at different times, and dying at different times. Nishiyama and Stevens see this discussion as a metaphor for the relationship between Buddhas and patriarchs (male and female teachers who follow in the Buddhist lineage; these days, many people prefer the nongendered term *ancestors*). In the Nishijima/Cross version it's also about their mutual relationships, but between each other rather than as Buddhas and patriarchs/ancestors. The Shasta Abbey translation takes it the same way. I followed Nishijima and Cross here.

Next we get those two lines that say, "A child can be realized without hampering anything about a compassionate parent. And a parent becomes realized without impeding anything about a child." I did my best with those. Let's look at this paragraph for a bit.

The word I've paraphrased as "realized" is Dogen's old standby, *genjo* (現成). We've seen this word a lot already and, as I've mentioned before, I wrote extensively about this word in my discussion of Dogen's famous essay "Genjo Koan" in my book *Don't Be a Jerk*. Basically, it's a word that only Buddhists use, and it tends to get translated as "realize."

A bit further along, I have Dogen say, "There are beings who are conscious and there are beings who are not conscious." The word I'm paraphrasing as "conscious" is *yushin* (有心) and what I'm paraphrasing as "not conscious" is *mushin* (無心). Both words still exist in Japanese but have different meanings now. Nowadays, the first one means "discrimination" and the second one means "innocence," although it can also mean "insentient" or "inanimate."

Both Tanahashi and Nishiyama/Stevens translate these words as "with mind" and "without mind." That's a literal reading of the Chinese characters used to write the words. Nishijima and Cross translate them as "mindful" and "unmindful." I feel like "mindful" has become somewhat of a brand name these days, so I avoid it. Besides, the usual word translated as "mindful" is *nen* (念), which just means "attention" in common usage. I'm not really happy with any of the translations, including my own. But there you go.

The other weird part in this section is where I have Dogen say, "All those who the Buddha called 'my children' as well as those who understand themselves to be 'me who is a child,' they're all the heirs of Buddha and his understanding." This part always gives translators problems. Nishiyama and Stevens have "my children" and "children as me." Tanahashi has "these children — my children — are all Shakyamuni Buddha's heirs." Nishijima and Cross give us "my children" and "childlike 'me's."

The phrase they're struggling with is *goko kogo* (吾子子吾). It's another one of Dogen's many weird turns of phrase. It literally means "me-child, child-me." In context it means "my-child, child-me." Since there are no true plurals in Japanese, "child" could be replaced with "children."

A little after this I have Dogen say, "Because this is the case, the flowers and fruits of everything are Buddha's possessions." To me this means it's not just material stuff that Buddha is saying are metaphorically his children, it's all activities (fruits and flowers) in the whole universe, too. He is taking full responsibility for absolutely everything.

At the end of this section I have Dogen say, "And also please take note that even though the Buddha said all beings are his children, he never said anything about him being their father." That's a pretty standard way of putting it into English. I think he's trying to say what I said at the outset, that Buddha is not to be viewed as some kind of God or creator. I put some interesting stuff I discovered about Buddhist notions of God as creator in my book *There Is No God and He Is Always with You*, in case you want to have a look.

After this we get another quote from the Buddha, "Even when the Buddhas take on different bodies to teach beings in other realms, they don't leave this universe. There are no beings outside the universe, so who could they possibly teach? That's why I say that anyone who says there's another universe outside of this one is full of it." In the original he doesn't quite say that those who postulate a universe other than this one are "full of it."

Nishijima and Cross translate what he actually says as, "I say the doctrine that there is another world of living beings outside the triple world is a doctrine in the non-Buddhist Scripture of the Great Existence, and not the preaching of the Seven Buddhas." The Seven Buddhas are the historical Buddha and the six mythical Buddhas who supposedly preceded him. As for the Scripture of Great Existence, even Nishijima and Cross don't know exactly what that was. And if they don't know, I doubt anyone else does. The upshot is that the Buddha said the idea of there being another universe apart from this one was wack.

Once again this is a quote from yet another sutra written ages after Buddha died, which means it's historically dubious. And once again, Dogen didn't care.

If you're a fan of *Rick and Morty*, you may want to argue with

Dogen here and say that there are scientific theories postulating the existence of an infinite number of alternate universes. I'm not sure I buy in to those theories. They always sound to me like what happens when you invent a way of explaining something and then start extrapolating from your invented explanation.

But I'm no scientist, so I have to say that there's a possibility they're right. Yet even if there are an infinite number of alternate realities full of Abradolf Linclers, robotically enhanced dogs, and intelligent singing farts, these are still part of a single universe. And that's the universe Dogen is talking about. The idea Dogen is reacting against here is that there's some sort of spiritual realm that exists entirely outside the universe — even the alternate ones, if they exist.

In the next paragraph I have Dogen say that whatever bodies the Buddhas manifest in, they are in this universe and they *are* this universe. Tanahashi's translation says they're *in* the triple world (a.k.a. the universe) while Nishijima/Cross say they *are* the triple world. Nishiyama and Stevens say they *form* the triple world. The original Japanese is *minna kore sangai nari* (みんなこれ三界なり) and is ambiguous. It could be taken all these ways, though it sounds to me more like the Nishijima/Cross translation.

In case you're wondering, although the original text doesn't specify what bodies the Buddha transforms himself into, the Nishiyama/Stevens translation lists them as the "Dharma-body," the "Bliss-body," and the "Nirvana-body." A bunch of ancient Buddhist sources list various bodies of the Buddha. Maybe this is the version Dogen had in mind. He doesn't say.

Even if that's so, the specifics don't really matter much. The basic idea is that the Buddha can manifest himself in different bodies to teach different types of beings. A more contemporary version might have him incarnating on different planets in forms suitable to that planet, or as different races and nationalities here on Earth. This doesn't mean that some eternal spiritual being called Buddha descends into different realms. It just means that the grounded and realistic philosophy the Buddha taught can be independently discovered and enacted by different types of beings.

Dogen then says the universe has no outside. The word he uses is *muge* (無外), which means "no outside." He's playing a little word game here. The Chinese source for the quotation from the Buddha has these characters in reverse (*gemu*, 外無). The Buddha says, "There are no (*mu*, 無) beings outside (*ge*, 外, also pronounced *gai*) the universe." The word order in the original is such that you get the compound *gemu* (外無). Nishijima and Cross say in their footnotes, "Master Dōgen reversed the order of the characters in the sutra in order to suggest the state in which there is no object separate from the subject."

Where I have Dogen say it both has and is free from thought, knowledge, attention, and realization, the string of characters Dogen uses is *ryo chi nen kaku* (慮知念覚). Nishijima and Cross translate this as "thinking, sensing, mindfulness, and realization." Nishiyama and Stevens give us "thought, knowledge, cognition, and awakening." Tanahashi turns the whole shebang into a single word, "consciousness." My version is based on the current dictionary definitions of these characters. This character string appears a few times in *Shobogenzo* as an enumeration of the major aspects of the mind. So maybe one could say that mind both has mind and is free from mind. Whoa.

Where I have Dogen say it's any material or spiritual thing you can imagine, what he actually says is more like, "It is fences, walls, tiles, and pebbles and it is mountains, rivers, and the earth. The mind itself is skin, flesh, bones, and marrow." That's the Nishijima/Cross version. The other translations are pretty much the same.

The first list (fences through the earth) is of material objects. The second list (skin through marrow) is a reference to the various types of realization attained by the students of the great teacher

Bodhidharma, who is said to have brought Zen to China from India. We talked about that earlier.

There aren't any huge variations in the way the rest of the essay is usually translated. The only big difference between mine and the usual translations is that the others try to preserve some of Dogen's poetic ways of expression, whereas I just barrel right over all that. I also added a few lines of explanation here and there. I suggest you look at some of the legit translations if you want to get a real sense of what the original is like.

The only major change I made is in the final line. I have Dogen say, "You should investigate the unnameable this way." Tanahashi just has, "Thoroughly investigate in this way." The other translations are similar.

However, I noticed that our old friend, Dogen's pet word *inmo* (恁麼), which we looked at way back in chapter 1, once again appears here. It seems odd to me that even Nishijima and Cross didn't put their usual translation of that word, "the ineffable," in their version of the final line of this essay. I decided to indicate it by having Dogen tell us to investigate the unnameable.

I like this chapter a lot. It's possible to read it as championing an idealistic view of the universe, but it's really not. Dogen accepts the Buddhist assertion that the universe is "mind-only," but he doesn't take that to mean that the material aspect of the universe is illusory or secondary. Rather, matter and mind are different aspects of a universe that is neither purely mind nor purely matter.

It's important to understand that Dogen didn't just read a lot of stuff, think deeply about it, and then draw his conclusions. He did all that, too. But he also had a meditation practice that he worked at every day of his life, beginning in early adolescence, if not before. He's not just telling us his thoughts and ideas, or the thoughts and ideas of great people of the past. He's also telling us what he has directly experienced in his practice. He has seen for himself that something he calls "mind" is a fundamental component of everything in the universe.

In the final essay we're going to look at, we'll see Dogen examining whether the entire universe might be a dream. Let's see what he has to say about that.

16. ALL YOU HAVE TO DO IS DREAM
Mu-chu Setsu-mu
Explaining a Dream within a Dream

THE TITLE TO this chapter is a mindblower: "Explaining a Dream within a Dream." It's almost like Dogen is breaking the fourth wall, to put it in movie lingo. That's when a character in a movie or TV show speaks directly to the audience, acknowledging that she or he is in a movie. Here Dogen describes his own efforts in writing his books as "preaching a dream within a dream." It's almost as if he's winking to us from across the ages and miles that separate us.

In many of his essays in *Shobogenzo*, Dogen attempts to articulate his answer to the question of what is real. The one we're about to look at is one of the strangest and most compelling.

The Japanese title is *mu-chu setsu-mu* (夢中説夢). The first and last characters are the same and mean "dream." This character can also be pronounced *yume*. The second character means "within" and can also be pronounced *naka*. The third character is pronounced *setsu* and means "explain," "express," or "manifest." Dogen makes use of all these meanings in the essay.

Nishijima and Cross's introduction to this chapter says, "In Buddhist philosophy there is an idea that our life is a kind of dream, because in everyday life we cannot recognize our life itself. In other words, our actual life is just a moment here and now, and we cannot grasp such a moment."

We can't recognize our life as an item apart from ourselves. We can't step out of our own life and objectively examine it. People talk a lot about "being in the moment." And, of course, that's an improvement over spending all your time obsessing over the past or dreaming of the future. However, we can't objectively observe this moment because we are completely embedded within this moment and fused to everything that exists. By extension, we are fused to everything that has ever come before this moment and everything that will come after.

So if we cannot separate ourselves from our lives any more than we can extract ourselves from a dream — even a lucid one — then we're stuck explaining a dream within a dream.

This is one of Dogen's most difficult essays. I have simplified and condensed it a lot (you're welcome), but even so it remains pretty weird. My suggestion is to just read through it. I'll see you again at the end and try to explain some of what I think it means.

Catch you on the flip side!

The path of the Buddhas and ancestors, and the truth they manifest, existed before the universe even existed. So you can't talk about it in conventional terms. That's because this teaching is even bigger than the Buddhas. It's timeless. There isn't any ordinary way to judge it.

The Wheel of Dharma was set into motion before the dawn of all creation. It's like a giant light-up billboard for virtue that's too great to describe. So to talk about it is to describe a dream within a dream. Because it is verification seen within verification, it is a dream explaining a dream.

This dream state is explained in the realm of the Buddhist ancestors. If you wanna know what the Buddha-lands are and what the Buddhist ancestors are, they are verification seen within verification and a dream explained within a dream. When you hear talk like this, don't think it's anything else.

Because it's the great turning of the Wheel of Dharma, it includes and embodies the whole universe and is the reason for the existence of everything. This is the dream explained within the dream that's existed since before any other dream.

Everything you can possibly think of and everything you can't even imagine is this dream. Even the experience of doubting this is so, or being confused about it, is the dream as well.

At this very moment it is the mental side of reality, and it's the physical side of reality, and it's also any discussion of the nature of reality, and it's even more than that. Plants and leaves, fruits and flowers, light and color, all are part of the dream. But this Great Dream should not be confused with just being dreamy.

People who don't like Buddhism hear the phrase "explaining a dream within a dream" and imagine it's about creating stuff that doesn't even exist or adding hallucinations to existing hallucinations. No way, José.

Even when we're hallucinating about hallucinations we need to learn the clarity of the phrase "hallucinating about hallucinations." It's like that line in the Lotus Sutra about riding the precious go-cart of Buddhism across the finish line of truth.

The Wheel of the Dharma turns the entire universe and turns the tiniest atom. Whatever you got, the Dharma Wheel turns it. Even the bitterest haters smile at each other when the Dharma Wheel turns. It's free as the breezes and goes wherever it pleases.

The whole universe is undeniable cause and effect. Everything you encounter is a teaching of the dharma. Don't even try to figure out the limits of this. It's all happening right here and right now. Whatever stuff you find yourself tangled up in, that right there is the Supreme Truth. As much as delusions are limitless, enlightenment is just as limitless.

An old-timey Zen master once said, "The truth of the universe will beat the crap out of you." That's another way of explaining the dream within the dream. So a hipster who hates lattes, an American city without a McDonald's, a reality TV show that's actually real, and other such impossible things are also the actualization of explaining a dream within a dream. It's beyond anything any human being or even any of the gods could possibly explain, and it's beyond anything regular folks could even conceive of.

How can you doubt this dream? It's not even doubtable. How

could you validate it, either? It doesn't care if you validate it or not. The Supreme Truth is just the Supreme Truth, that's why we call it the Supreme Truth. So a dream is called a dream. Duh!

There are all kinds of different dreams. There are times when you "have a dream" like Martin Luther King did or, like, where you dream of growing up to be a rock star. There are times when you tell somebody the dream you just woke up from. There's the explanation you give of that dream, which isn't the same as the dream itself. And there are times when you're right there in a dream without knowing it's a dream.

But without being in a dream you can't explain (manifest) a dream. And without explaining (manifesting) a dream, there's no being in one. And without explaining the dream, and without being within the dream, there aren't any Buddhas. And without any Buddhas, who would turn the Wheel of Dharma? The Wheel of Dharma is Buddhas alone together with Buddhas. The only reason all the Buddhas and ancestors exist at all is in explaining (manifesting) a dream within a dream.

This explaining a dream within a dream stuff goes way beyond even the whole universe. You can't be attached to your own head or your own body or even your own brain. When you're not attached to anything, that's when subject and object become one, like sellers of French fries becoming buyers of French fries.

In China the Zen guys used to describe doing something that was uselessly dreamy as being like putting another head on top of your own head. Well, this is like putting your own head right where it belongs.

Both regular folks and sages can get this, if they want. It starts off in the past and progresses into the present. Let me see if I can explain.

Yesterday explaining a dream within a dream was recognized as explaining a dream within a dream. Today explaining a dream within a dream is experienced as explaining a dream within a dream. That's how you meet the Buddha directly. See?

It's a shame that, even though this is totally obvious, so many people fail to get it at all. You guys should study it yourselves. All right?

This truth of explaining a dream within a dream is itself a

manifestation of Buddha and of the Supreme Truth. Dream causes and dream effects are not hard to see.

Remember when I said, "You might ask, How do I know I'm a person who is *it*? You know you're a person who is *it* because you want to understand what *it* is and align yourself with *it*"? This whole explaining a dream within a dream stuff is kinda like that. Plus, it's also like matters that are not *it* and people who are not *it*.

Every Buddha there ever was just explained a dream within a dream. In the old story in which Buddha picks up a flower and winks at his student Mahakashyapa, thus indicating that Mahakashyapa was to be his successor, that was also explaining a dream within a dream. When Bodhidharma told his successor, Huike, he'd gotten his marrow, that again was explaining a dream within a dream.

Whether or not you know it, it's all explaining a dream within a dream. Whether you hold it back or let it go, it's all explaining a dream within a dream.

Even the very fact of your own bodily existence is explaining (manifesting) a dream within a dream.

Dig me. When you hold back or let go you need to study it like on a balancing scale. When you understand it, the ounces and pounds — or kilos and grams or whatever — will explain the dream within the dream. When you get balanced yourself, that's when you'll understand what being balanced really is. Before you get balanced, you're not gonna be able to get that.

Balance is like the great weighing scale of universal truth. It doesn't depend on anything but itself. It's like the scale is floating in empty space or something. Whether it's material objects or non-material things, the dream is the world and the world is in balance. Everything is liberated in this explaining of a dream within a dream. Even all your thoughts about it are just a matter of getting it together right inside this dream within a dream.

In the Lotus Sutra Shakyamuni Buddha said:

All Buddhas have bodies colored golden
With happiness they beam
Preaching the dharma since times of olden
They live in a pleasant dream

In the dream they act as kings
Giving up their palaces, they're free
Not attached to any things
They sit under the Bodhi tree

On the lion's seat sitting for seven days
Attaining the wisdom that's truly profound
Having understood the Buddha Way
They turn the Dharma Wheel around and around

Preaching the dharma to everyone
For thousands and millions of years
The flawless dharma they preach by the ton
Freeing all beings from their fears

After that they enter nirvana
Like a lamp going out when it's spent
In future ages, if to preach this you wanna
You'll attain virtue that's magnificent

You should pay close attention to this little poem. The stuff about living in a pleasant dream is not just some kind of metaphor. The amazingly awesome dharma is "Buddhas alone together with Buddhas." Whether in dreams or awake, all dharmas are real form. It's just like it says in the Lotus Sutra, "Buddhas alone together with Buddhas are directly able to perfectly realize that all dharmas are real form."

When you're awake you establish the will, do training, get enlightened, and reach nirvana. When you're dreaming, you also establish the will, do training, get enlightened, and reach nirvana. Dreaming and awakening are both real. One is not superior to the other. They are beyond any of that noise.

When people read that part where it says "they act as kings" sometimes they think it means that somehow some kinda magic or something will make their dreams come true. If you think that's what it means, you don't know anything about Buddhism!

Waking and dreaming are both real. The Buddhist teachings

might be metaphors, but they're also true. But this dream that the poem is talking about, that's not a metaphor. That's the Buddhist truth.

Shakyamuni, like every other Buddha, establishes the will, undergoes training, and gets enlightened to reality within a dream. Since that's so, the Buddha's entire lifework in the human world is action taking place in a dream.

In the poem it talks about sitting for seven days. Then it says Buddha preaches the dharma and frees beings for thousands and millions of years. That's because in a dream you never really know how fast or how slow something actually happens. It's not definable in normal terms.

The poem says, "All Buddhas have bodies colored golden / With happiness they beam / Preaching the dharma since times of olden / They live in a pleasant dream."

This "pleasant dream" is the same as "all Buddhas." When they manifest themselves in bodily form, that's how they preach for others. To hear the dharma means hearing with the eyes and hearing with the mind. It's letting the sound of the dharma penetrate deeply into you. It's to hear sound long, long before even the universe itself came into being.

The poem says the Buddhas' bodies are golden and beam with happiness. This means that the "pleasant dream" is the very bodies of the Buddhas. It means not doubting that you exist in the here and now anymore.

It's an established principle that the Buddha's instructions in the awakened state never cease. It's also an established principle that the actual realization of all the ancestors is dream-action that happens inside a dream.

As Buddhists we take a vow never to abuse or insult the Three Treasures: Buddha, dharma, and sangha. When we learn the truth of this vow in actual practice, the truth that the Buddha has spoken is instantly realized and enacted.

— Presented to the assembly at
Kannon-dori-kosho-horin-ji Temple on September 21, 1242

Dogen says a lot of stuff in this chapter about how reality is all a dream and yet is still absolutely real. I'm going to leave the discussion of what I think that aspect means till near the end of this commentary. So don't worry if I seem like I'm ignoring the weirdest part. I'll get there. First some technical stuff.

The phrase I have given as "verification seen within verification" is *sho-chu ken sho* (証中見証). Nishijima and Cross translate this as "realization of experience in experience." Tanahashi gives us "awakening is seen within awakening." The Nishiyama/Stevens version has "seeing enlightenment within enlightenment."

The character everyone is translating differently ("verification," "experience," "awakening," "enlightenment") is *sho* (証, also pronounced *akashi*). In contemporary Japanese it means "to prove or verify." The ID card I carried as a resident alien when I lived in Japan was called a *gaikokujin toroku shomeisho* (外国人登録証明書), which means something like "registered foreigner proof of identity card." The *sho* that begins the third word of that compound, a.k.a. the third character from the end of that long string, is the same one Dogen uses here. In regular terms it just means "proof," as in "proof of identity." In Buddhist usage this character tends to refer to verifying for oneself what is real and true. So "awakening," "enlightenment," and "experience" are all valid translations. I'm going with the word *verification* because it's the most common meaning of the word.

What Dogen is saying here when he says, "Because it is verification seen within verification, it is a dream explaining a dream" strikes me as one of his many deliberate contradictions. *It* is both realer than the realest real thing and *it* is a dream. Like all translators into English, I've had to state a subject ("it," which is the subject most translations use). Dogen was writing in Japanese, in which you don't have to state the subject of a sentence. But I feel the unstated subject is the same unnameable "it" he refers to in the chapter I've retitled "It Came from Beyond Zen!"

I paraphrased a line that comes up soon after this as, "Because it's the great turning of the Wheel of Dharma, it includes and embodies the whole universe and is the reason for the existence of everything." I took a lot of liberties here. The original is much longer and includes references to "the ten directions and eight facets of a clear crystal," "the Great Ocean," "the legendary Mount Sumeru," and some other stuff. All that seemed unnecessary to me, so I truncated it into "the whole universe."

It's the verb at the end of this sentence (Japanese verbs are usually at the end) that gave me real trouble. Dogen once again uses his favorite word, *genjo* (現成), here. The way he uses it here functions almost like the English word *is*. So it's a very malleable little word!

In this case I made it into something like "the reason for the existence of everything." Nishijima/Cross have "all dharmas are realized in the here and now." Tanahashi has that list of stuff I told you about, followed by "are actualized." Nishiyama/Stevens have the same list, followed by "emerge." My paraphrase is how I interpret what I think Dogen is saying.

The next paragraph in my version starts off with, "Everything you can possibly think of and everything you can't even imagine is this dream." Tanahashi offers a more literal translation involving dewdrops and "the clarity of the hundred grasses." Nishijima and Cross turn Dogen's poetic device about dewdrops and grasses into "the pervasive disclosure of the entire universe." Their footnote tells us that "clear-clear hundred grasses" is an old Buddhist way of indicating individual concrete things. For my paraphrase I chose an approach that's different from either of these translations and that feels to me like it expresses the same idea. I hope you enjoyed it.

I love the line I've given you next as, "Even the experience of doubting this is so, or being confused about it, is the dream as well." I first heard it in the Nishijima/Cross translation as, "The dream state is just the clear-clear hundred things — and is the very moment in which we doubt this is so; it is the very moment of confusion." It was one of those phrases that got etched into my memory.

Tanahashi's translation of this same line is, "This dream is the glowing clarity of the hundred grasses. What requires questioning is this very point. What is confusing is this very point." I'm sorry, but I don't like that version much. If I'd only seen it translated that way, I would've passed right over that point, just confused and questioning.

Having said that, I'll admit that Tanahashi's translation is a bit more literally what Dogen wrote in Japanese, and Nishijima and Cross are being a little more interpretive here. As I've already noted, usually Nishijima/Cross is so close to a literal translation it's almost annoying, while Tanahashi is often highly interpretive. Even so, Nishijima and Cross make this particular phrase much more meaningful to me. Even when you doubt this is a dream, that very doubting is still part of the dream. Or, to put it another way, even if you doubt this is real, even your doubt is part of the reality you're doubting.

But let's keep moving along anyway, shall we?

Because it's right after this that Dogen starts getting really interesting. Up till now you might have mistaken his philosophy for a kind of solipsism or a kind of "life is but a dream" thing. But then he says this Great Dream (大夢, omu or maybe o-yume, the pronunciation isn't indicated) is not to be confused with "being dreamy." The word I'm paraphrasing as "being dreamy" is bozen (夢然), which literally means "dream-nature" or, in more colloquial terms, "dreamy."

Here is where Dogen starts getting into how this reality is a dream but how that doesn't mean that it's unreality.

Nishijima and Cross add a footnote in this section that says, "Master Dogen understood delusion practically as a momentary state that we should clarify by our effort." This is their explanation of why Dogen says the line I paraphrased as, "Even when we're hallucinating about hallucinations we need to learn the clarity of the phrase 'hallucinating about hallucinations.'" We use our understanding that we are in the dream state to clarify the dream state while realizing we can't leave the dream state and peer into it from outside.

Then I have Dogen refer to go-carts in the Lotus Sutra. Of course the actual Lotus Sutra doesn't say anything about go-carts.

What it does say translates to something like "ride in the treasure boat to the place of truth." I'm from Akron, Ohio, where they have go-cart races, not treasure boats. I don't think the Lotus Sutra would have used a metaphor about finishing lines because Buddhist practice doesn't have a finishing line after which you're all done. But, then again, neither does go-cart racing. You're not done even after you cross the finish line. There's always another go-cart race. Or there's the trip to Strickland's ice cream stand across from the go-cart stadium after the race. In any case, even finishing lines aren't the end.

The next paragraph in my version ends, "It's free as the breezes and goes wherever it pleases." Tanahashi's translation of this line is, "Wherever such a dharma is turned, it freely circulates like the flowing breezes." I like my Muhammad Ali–style version better. Anyway, this paragraph is my distillation of a longer section that uses the word *inmoji* (恁麼事) as the subject of several consecutive sentences. Let's talk about that for a sec.

Sharp-eyed observers will recognize the first part of this compound as the word in *inmo*, which Dogen uses as the subject of the essay I retitled "It Came from Beyond Zen!" mentioned earlier in this commentary. It means "it" or, as Nishijima/Cross footnote it in this section, "ineffable something." So the "it" that's free as the breezes is the "ineffable something" that is the universe and is you.

In the next paragraph I have Dogen say, "The whole universe is undeniable cause and effect." The phrase Dogen uses here is *fumai no inga* (不昧の因果), which basically means "not unclear cause and effect." It's a very important concept to him. We already looked at an entire essay he wrote just about this one idea.

To review what we saw in that earlier chapter, for Dogen nothing escapes the rule of cause and effect. There are no miracles. There may be causes and effects we are incapable of ever fully comprehending, and sometimes that makes stuff seem miraculous. That doesn't mean even such things are uncaused and have no effects. It just means that sometimes we can't see how cause and effect operates. But everything is interrelated in a universal web of causes and effects.

Moving along, I gave you one line as, "Whatever stuff you find yourself tangled up in, that right there is the Supreme Truth." In the original, this line is all about arrowroot and wisteria. We talked about this a few chapters ago where I told you that arrowroot and wisteria are vines that tend to get tangled up on other things. It's an image Dogen often uses for the complications we all encounter in life.

This whole passage is important. When people get into meditation practice they're often looking for an escape from the entanglements of real life. Dogen constantly points out that we do not need to escape our actual lives to find the truth — however much people who run expensive getaway-type retreats insist that we do. What we are living through right now is the Supreme Truth. Which is not to say that retreats are a bad thing. I lead a lot of them myself. It's just that they should never be seen as an escape from life's entanglements.

The line a little after this, where I have Dogen quote an old-timey Zen master as saying, "The truth of the universe will beat the crap out of you," is usually translated as something like, "The actualization of the fundamental point shall grant you thirty blows." In the original the "actualization of the fundamental point" bit is yet another reference back to Dogen's favorite word, *genjo* (see discussion above).

That thing about hipsters who hate lattes and the rest was originally a tree without roots, the land beyond yin and yang, and the valley that does not echo a cry. Just in case you wondered. Basically things that don't exist. I tried to update it a little.

After this, when I have Dogen list the various types of dreams, such as MLK's dream and so on, he doesn't actually go into the kind of detail I did in the paraphrase. Instead, he does this thing he does a lot in *Shobogenzo* where he takes a few Chinese characters and rearranges them in different orders to make new compounds. In this case it's the title of the chapter, *mu-chu setsu-mu* (夢中説夢). He rear-ranges these characters as follows: *chu-mu* (中夢, a dream within), *mu-setsu* (夢説, a dream explained), *setsu-mu* (説夢, explaining a dream) and *mu-chu* (夢中, within a dream). My expansions in the paraphrase are very loosely based on the footnotes in the Nishijima/Cross translation in which they give their own explanations of what these different renderings of the title phrase mean.

Right after this I have Dogen say, "The Wheel of Dharma is Buddhas alone together with Buddhas." The original phrase Dogen uses here is another one of his favorite catchphrases, *yui-butsu yo-butsu* (唯仏与仏). A direct translation of this would be "Buddhas alone together with Buddhas" or "only a Buddha along with a Bud-dha." Remember that Japanese does not have plurals.

Carl Bielefeldt wrote about this phrase in his notes to his translation of a Dogen essay called "Jippo" (The Ten Directions), "[This phrase is] probably to be understood simply as 'the buddhas'; Dogen uses here a famous phrase from the *Miaofa lianhua jing*: 佛所成就第一希有難解之法、唯佛與佛乃究盡諸法實相。'The prime, rare, difficult to understand dharmas perfected by the buddha — only a buddha and a buddha can exhaust the real mark of these dharmas.'"

The Chinese quotation above uses an alternate set of Chinese characters to express the phrase *yui-butsu yo-butsu* (唯佛與佛). But they mean the same thing.

And just by the way, *Miaofa lianhua jing* is the Chinese name of the Lotus Sutra. The good professor is being a little pretentious here by insisting on giving the Chinese title of the Lotus Sutra when there's already a perfectly good English translation that he could have used so I wouldn't have been forced to waste several minutes looking up what the hell that meant. But that's how academia works. Every little thing has got to be in some kind of super-secret code. It's annoying as hell. The only purpose it serves is to make difficult stuff even more difficult. Be happy that I'm dealing with it so you don't have to. You're welcome. End of rant.

Let's move along and dig into this *Buddhas alone together with Buddhas* thing a little deeper.

Neither Nishijima/Cross nor Tanahashi see this phrase as meaning simply "the Buddhas." Nishijima and Cross translate it as I did above, while Tanahashi prefers "only a buddha together with a buddha." Dogen wrote an entire essay about this phrase, which I didn't include in this volume. It's one of those bonus track essays that were not included in the earliest versions of *Shobogenzo*. We know it from a copy made around thirty-five years after Dogen died by a latter-day student in his lineage. The original is lost.

That essay is the source of some of my favorite Dogen quotes. He says, "Delusion, remember, is something that does not exist. Realization, remember, is something that does not exist" (Nishijima/ Cross). He says, "When you realize Buddha Dharma you do not think, 'This is realization, just as I expected.' Even if you think so, realization inevitably differs from your expectation" (Tanahashi). He says, "The colors of the mind excited by a flower or the moon should not be seen as self at all, but we think of them as our self. If we consider what is not our self to be our self, even that can be left as it is, but when we illuminate [the state in which] there is no possibility of either repellent colors or attractive ones being tainted, then action that naturally exists in the truth is the unconcealed original features" (Nishijima/Cross again). I wrote a whole chapter of my book *Sit Down and Shut Up* about that quotation, along with other parts of the essay it comes from. The chapter is called "The Colors of the Mind."

As you've probably come to expect from the inscrutable Mr. Dogen, he never just gives a straight explanation of what the phrase means to him in a nice, quotable little sound bite.

However, near the end of that essay he comes close, using a bunch of metaphors about fish and birds:

There is a saying from ancient times that none other than fish knows the mind of fish, and none other than birds can follow the traces of birds....Fish together with fish always know each other's mind. They are never ignorant [of each other] as human beings are. When they are going to swim upstream through the Dragon's Gate [an old timey way of describing swimming upstream to spawn], this is known to all, and together they make their mind one....None other than fish know this [mind].

Again, when birds are flying through the sky, walking creatures never imagine even in a dream the knowing of these tracks or the seeing and the following of these traces....Birds, however, can see in many ways that hundreds or thousands of small birds have flocked together and flown away, or that these are the traces of big birds that have gone south or flown north in so many lines. [To birds, those traces] are more evident than wheel tracks in a lane, or a horse's hoof prints visible in the grass....This principle also applies to buddhas. They suppose how many ages buddhas have spent in practice, and they know small buddhas and great buddhas, even among those who have gone uncounted. These are things that, when we are not buddha we never know at all....If, with [our own] eyes we can see these traces, we may be in the presence of buddhas and we may be able to compare their footprints....To realize these traces may be called the Buddha-Dharma. (Nishijima/Cross)

Dogen would not have known the science of this, but there is now evidence that birds do know the traces of other birds flying through the sky. Nobody's certain exactly how they do this. There's speculation that it may have to do with the positions of the sun and stars, a keen sense of smell, or even the ability to follow the Earth's magnetic field. In any case, as Dogen says, it's something that birds know but human beings don't. So there are things that Buddhas know, which the rest of us cannot see any more than we can see the tracks of birds in the sky or of fish in the water.

I've always liked this little turn of phrase: Buddhas alone together with Buddhas. It expresses the great mystery of being. We are all Buddhas. We are all supremely alone. And yet there are billions of us on just this one planet. There must be an uncountable number of Buddhas in the universe. Each one is alone. Each one is you. Together we realize the universe. Together we realize ourselves. And when we do that, we're not alone anymore.

Let's get back to the essay at hand, shall we? Later I have Dogen say, "When you're not attached to anything, that's when subject and object become one, like sellers of French fries becoming buyers of French fries." I'm paraphrasing a line that actually goes something like, "In nonattachment sellers of gold become buyers of gold." In their footnotes Nishijima and Cross say that this phrase refers to the balance of subject and object. That makes perfect sense to me. But since I would have missed the metaphor I decided to make it clearer. I also changed gold to French fries just to be funny. French fries are more valuable than gold, if you ask me.

The stuff that comes up after this about replacing your head is much longer as well as being very convoluted and tricky in the original. There's a reference to the crown of Vairocana Buddha and yet another reference to the clear-clear hundred grasses. I boiled it down as I did, based on the footnotes Nishijima and Cross provide. Again, you are very much welcome.

Then I have Dogen say, "Yesterday explaining a dream within a dream was recognized as explaining a dream within a dream. Today explaining a dream within a dream is experienced as explaining a dream within a dream. That's how you meet the Buddha directly. See?"

In the original, this part is a real brain twister. I'll let you look it up for yourself. It's really long and really confusing. But I read it through several times and came up with that paraphrase. To me it sounds like something Dogen says a few times in *Shobogenzo* about the relationship between ancient teachings and our experience in actual practice. Let me see if I can explain.

In my book *Don't Be a Jerk* there's a chapter I titled "Hearing Weird Stuff Late at Night." It's my retitling of a Dogen essay, whose actual title is more like "River Voices and Mountain Sounds." In that chapter there's a story about how a guy hears the sounds of a river and gets enlightened. Dogen says he does so because the words of his teacher had prepared him for that experience. His experience is real, but he might not have recognized it had he not learned from his teacher how to recognize it.

To me Dogen seems to be saying something very similar here, only with reference to the more ancient written teachings. The Buddha, as well as the other teachers of the past, had their own life experiences and explained them to their contemporaries or wrote about them. When we read those explanations, we can recognize the same experiences in our own lives here and now. In that way we can be said to meet those ancient teachers.

Just after this, Dogen again refers to that chapter I retitled "It Came from Beyond Zen!" In the original he just references the essay without being quite as direct as I have him being in my version. The Tanahashi translation gives the word I just translate as "it" as "a thing beyond suchness." It's our old friend *inmo* (恁麼) once again.

A little later I have Dogen say, "Even the very fact of your own bodily existence is explaining (manifesting) a dream within a dream." The Nishijima/Cross translation has, "There is preaching a dream in a dream as manifestation of the body." Tanahashi has, "The manifesting body is the expression of a dream within a dream."

I feel like Dogen's getting real trippy here. He's saying that our existence in bodily form is also an example of a dream explaining a dream to itself, or of a dream manifesting within a dream. We ourselves, in concrete form, are like symbols in a dream. That's heavy stuff. But if you think about it, that's kind of what other people amount to when we see them and what we must amount to when we're seen by others. In Dogen's view, the entire universe sees itself through all of us by means of our eyes. Whoa.

After this comes a lot of stuff about balance. The translators all agree (for once) that the passage refers to balance by using the metaphor of a scale. Remember that scales in Dogen's time required you to balance things against little metal weights. You couldn't just step on one and get your weight digitally.

Balance was one of Nishijima Roshi's favorite metaphors for what other people call "enlightenment" or "awakening" or what have you. He believed that real enlightenment occurs when the human nervous system gets into proper balance so that all parts are functioning at equal strength. Some of the scientific research now being done on meditation seems to suggest that he was onto something there.

Then we get another poem. This one wasn't too hard to make rhymes out of without changing the meaning a whole lot. Tanahashi, Nishijima/Cross, and Shasta Abbey all translate this in verses, while Nishiyama and Stevens turn it into prose. In any case, though, they all say kinda the same thing as I did, but without the rhymes. The original can be found in the Lotus Sutra chapter titled "Anrakugyo" ("Peaceful and Joyful Practice"), LS 2.282. Since my version doesn't stray too much from the standard ones, I'll let you look it up instead of reproducing one of those versions.

After the poem Dogen talks about establishing the will, doing training, getting enlightened, and reaching nirvana. It's a formula he uses a lot. In the original it goes *hasshin, shugyo, bodai, nehan* (発心、修行、菩提、涅槃). These are the four major steps in the life of a Buddhist practitioner.

We've already looked at the first one. It can also be translated as "arousing the mind." I prefer "establishing the will (to the truth)," which is how Nishijima phrased it. As I mentioned earlier in this book, it means not only establishing the will to undergo training but also establishing the willingness to accept how your training turns out. It isn't always what you want, and it's never what you expect, as Dogen pointed out in his essay about Buddhas alone together with Buddhas. Doing training mostly means getting down to the real work of actually meditating rather than just talking and thinking about it.

The third and fourth phases are much harder to define. People write whole books on the meaning of *bodai* (a.k.a. *bodhi* or enlightenment). This is not some kind of a finishing line after which you're permanently enlightened. But it is a major turning point. You'll know it when it happens. Or maybe you won't.

Nirvana is even more impossible to define. *Nirvana* literally means "extinction." It means you stop manifesting as an individual at all and merge at last into everything. But then again, you never really left that state in the first place. You just got confused and thought you did.

A little ways down, there's a paragraph that starts, "When people read that part where it says 'they act as kings' sometimes they think it means that somehow some kinda magic or something will make their dreams come true." This one was tricky.

Tanahashi translates this line as, "However, on hearing the words of the passage 'in the dream you are made a king' people of the past and the present mistakenly think that, thanks to the power of 'expounding this foremost dharma,' mere night dreams may become like this dream of Buddha."

The line it refers back to is also tricky. In Tanahashi's translation it's "in the dream you are made a king," while in Nishijima/Cross it's "in dream-action as kings of nations." Nishiyama and Stevens translate it totally differently. Their version is, "Its proclamation to all people is their continual good dream." No mention of kings at all.

The original line is Chinese and it's *you meng zuo guowang* (又夢作国王). According to Google Translate it means, "I wish to be king." I don't read Chinese myself and don't put too much stock in Google Translate's ability to deal with classical Buddhist poetry.

So I defer to the professionals I've cited above here. I do know the meaning of the individual characters, though. They mean "again," "dream," "make," "nation," and "king," in that order. For whatever that's worth.

Nishijima/Cross provide a footnote that says, "*Yū-musa-koku-ō* [the Japanese pronunciation of the Chinese characters], as usually read in Japanese, *mata yume[muraku] koku-o to na[rite]*, means, 'Again, [the dreamer] dreams of becoming the king of a nation'— thus according to the Lotus Sutra: 'Again he will dream he is a king...' However, *sa* (作) means both 'to become' and 'to act,' and Master Dōgen in his commentary emphasizes that, even in the sutra, *musa* (夢) means not 'to dream of becoming,' but rather 'dream-action.'" The ellipses are in the original, by the way.

And if you find that convoluted, welcome to my world!

So I just did what I could with it and paraphrased it the way I did. My feeling is that Dogen was reacting to a phenomenon that still exists today. People have always imagined that there must be magic spells or whatever that would enable them to realize their dreams and wishes. In recent times the book and video series *The Secret* sold millions of copies based on its promise of pretty much the same thing.

This is nothing new. But it's always been bullshit and always will be. I see Dogen here as pointing that out. That's my take on it, anyway.

Then we have the ending. What I've done in my paraphrase is to mix and match the Nishijima/Cross and Tanahashi translations with a couple of nods to the Nishiyama/Stevens version. I also took a long look at the ending in the Japanese original just to be clear about a few concepts. What I came up with is what you see.

All the translations have some differences in their interpretations of the end of this chapter, but they're all pretty close. And they're all also pretty tough to follow. As always, I encourage you to take a look at the standard translations for yourself. The ending I've given you is what I think Dogen means.

Let me see if I can break my version down a little for you.

Dogen says, "Waking and dreaming are both real...Shakyamuni, like every other Buddha, establishes the will, undergoes training, and gets enlightened to reality within a dream. Since that's so, the Buddha's entire lifework in the human world is action taking place in a dream."

In my book *Don't Be a Jerk*, I wrote about a certain line in Dogen's essay "The Certificate of Succession" (which I retitled "Buddhist Paperwork"). The line goes, "Maybe the state in a dream and the state in waking consciousness are equally real." I wrote about the ambiguity of this line and how it may refer to the specific dream Dogen had just been talking about, or how it may refer to dreams in general. I mentioned that my teacher's translation seemed to favor the idea that the line was about dreams in general, while Kaz Tanahashi took it to be a reference to one specific dream of Dogen's. I explained why, after looking at the original Japanese line, I'd come to the conclusion it was referring to dreams in general.

Here we have a similar observation about the nature of dreams. Tanahashi's reading of this passage goes in part, "All dharmas awakened in the dream are genuine forms." Nishijima and Cross translate this as, "The dream state and the awakened state are each real form." A few lines later Tanahashi has Dogen say, "Awakening and dreaming are from the beginning one suchness, the genuine reality." Nishijima and Cross translate this as, "The dream state and the waking state originally are oneness and are real form."

Dogen knew there was a big difference between dreaming in the conventional sense and being awake. One of his favorite ways of dissing someone was to say they haven't even dreamed about whatever it is they think they know thoroughly. But he also regarded the dream state as a different way of perceiving reality rather than as something removed from reality.

It's a trippy idea. I have to say I was kinda freaked out when I first came across these passages. It's taken some time to get comfortable with the notion. It's not entirely different from some of the ways that certain Australian aboriginal cultures conceive of dreaming. They also see dreams as a different way of perceiving reality.

I think Dogen says everything he wants to say about this in his essay. It is significant that he says this stuff but doesn't get too far into it. He doesn't, for example, come up with a whole theory of dream interpretation or dedicate his life to pondering the nature of dreaming. He seems content to allow dreams to speak for themselves. He just points out that they often have something to tell us.

It's also possible to see the references to dreaming here as metaphors for delusion. If you read it that way, then Dogen can be seen as saying that delusion and enlightenment are fundamentally the same, that samsara and nirvana are the same. If you ask me, he is indicating both ideas.

Moving along. In my version, Dogen says, "Buddha preaches the dharma and frees beings for thousands and millions of years. That's because in a dream you never really know how fast or how slow something actually happens. It's not definable in normal terms."

The Nishijima/Cross translation of this is, "'Seven days' expresses a length of time for 'attaining the buddha-wisdom.' 'Turning the wheel of Dharma' and 'saving living beings,' [however,] have been called 'for thousands of myriads of koṭis of kalpas' — because the situation in the dream-state is indefinable." Other translations are similar. You can see I've cut this down considerably.

The parts in quotes in the Nishijima/Cross translation are from the poem I butchered in my version. I think you're smart and can work out how they correspond. This gets into Dogen's notion of time. He believed that time was subjective. He didn't think that an hour spent doing something you love and an hour spent waiting in line at the Department of Motor Vehicles were of the same length, even if clocks and hourglasses measured them as equal. Same with dreams. Maybe that weird dream you had that seemed to go on for years really did, in some sense, go on for years.

Moving along some more. In my version, Dogen says, "To hear the dharma means hearing with the eyes and hearing with the mind. It's letting the sound of the dharma penetrate deeply into you. It's to hear sound long, long before even the universe itself came into being."

What I paraphrase as "before even the universe itself came into being" is more like "prior to the kalpa of emptiness." A kalpa is an incredibly long time. Basically, this phrase means before the universe came into being.

Zen Buddhists say weird stuff like this a lot. One of the standard koans in Rinzai Zen is, "Show me the face you had before your parents were born." Dogen also references this idea, though he never asked his students to demonstrate that face to him.

It's another super-trippy notion. We think we came into being a few decades ago, arriving in a universe that was already immensely old. But Dogen disagrees. He believes that what we fundamentally are may be even older than the universe.

Let's keep going. In my version, Dogen says, "It's an established principle that the Buddha's instructions in the awakened state never cease. It's also an established principle that the actual realization of all the ancestors is dream-action that happens inside a dream."

Again, we have a line in which the word *dreams* could mean actual nighttime dreams or could mean the deluded state. It could also be taken to mean that this waking reality, when viewed from a less deluded state, can be regarded as a kind of dream. So everything the enlightened ones did or said can also be thought of as having taken place in a dream. Whoa.

And finally, in my version Dogen says, "As Buddhists we take a vow never to abuse or insult the Three Treasures: Buddha, dharma, and sangha. When we learn the truth of this vow in actual practice, the truth that the Buddha has spoken is instantly realized and enacted."

This is one of Dogen's key points, that we should never disparage the Three Treasures. As I've said, Buddha is the Buddha, dharma is his teachings as well as reality as a whole, and sangha are those who try their best to follow the Buddhist Way. Dogen deeply believed that we need all three. He did not think it was possible to go it alone, to understand and align with the fundamental nature of reality simply by relying on our own abilities.

In an ultimate sense there is no self or other. The entire universe is one thing, and that thing is you. And yet here we are, me writing this book and you reading it, Dogen dead for eight hundred years and us still alive and watching cat videos on our phones, you living in a crummy apartment in Fort Lee, New Jersey, and Tom Cruise living in a Bel Air mansion. We are all one, and yet we are each as different as can be.

The truth includes these contradictions. And so we need a support system, we need help. That's what the Three Treasures are for. That's why we should never disparage them.

Phew! That was a bear of a chapter! But rejoice and be glad, dear reader. You and I are finished with Dogen, at least until I try to write another book about him. I promise the final chapter of this book will be less of a brain twister.

17. IN CONCLUSION

I'VE HAD A great time writing this book. Many mornings when I sat down at my laptop to begin work I actually giggled with delight. I'm not kidding. It's useful, sometimes, to live alone.

There is still a lot of Dogen that I haven't worked on. To take just one example, I was unable to find room or time in this volume to get to one of my favorite Dogen pieces, one called "Katto," which literally means "Arrowroot and Wisteria" but is more commonly called something like "Tangled Vines." I've referred to this phrase a couple of times in this book. My teacher's translation calls this essay "The Complicated."

Bielefeldt also did a translation of "Katto," and his translation contains a great version of my favorite line from that essay. In his version the line goes, "We should realize that there is, 'you've got me'; there is, 'I've got you'; there is, 'got my you'; there is, 'got your me.'" My teacher's version goes, "Remember, there are cases of 'you have got me' and there are cases of 'I have got you.' There are cases in which 'getting me' is 'you' and there are cases in which 'getting you' is 'me.'" Both translations are pretty trippy.

The idea is that the "Brad Warner" that exists in your mind is not quite the same as the "Brad Warner" that exists in my mind, and neither one of these is the real Brad Warner. Even *I* can't know the real Brad Warner much better than you because I can't step outside of Brad Warner in order to be both in and out of myself at the same time, which is what would be required (at the very least) to ever be able to know Brad Warner. Substitute your own name, and read that again to get the full effect.*

Suffice it to say, there's a whole lot more Dogen where this came from!

I had fun putting in jokes here and there and making silly rhymes out of Dogen's poetry. I hope not too many people will be offended or see this as my doing violence to Dogen's work. I figure if it encourages a few more people to read Dogen, it's worth it.

I sometimes wonder if I really *get* Dogen. I do try to. I'm sure some people will argue with my interpretations of his work. But I have tried to give you alternative readings for the parts I took the most liberties with. Plus, I think my take on Dogen is actually fairly orthodox in spite of the jokes and the Godzilla references. That stuff is just window dressing.

One thing that struck me hard while writing this book is the Buddhist idea that there is no God. So I'd like to talk about that for a little bit.

This idea of the absence of God is nothing new for me. I wrote a whole book about Buddhist ideas of God called *There Is No God and He Is Always with You.*†

In that book I contended that, although Buddhism does not believe in a God who created the universe and exists apart from it, the word *God* can still be used in a Buddhist context. This is particularly evident in Dogen's work in the essay called "Inmo," which I included in this volume, retitled "It Came from Beyond Zen!" which is also the overall title of this book.

---

* Five times fast!

† I made God a "he" only because that's the convention in English. Using *she* or *it* or any of those newfangled words like *ʒhe* or *ʒhim* or whatever just served to call attention to those words.

I still believe that. I still think it's not quite right to say that Buddhism has no concept of God, even when you're talking about Zen, which is possibly the most atheistic of all Buddhist sects. Yet it was the other side of that coin that kept smacking me on the head as I wrote this book. There may be a God in Zen Buddhism, but there is also no God.

In his book *A Universe from Nothing*, Lawrence Krauss says, "The universe is the way it is, whether we like it or not. The existence or nonexistence of a creator is independent of our desires. A world without God or purpose may seem harsh or pointless, but that alone doesn't require God to actually exist." I agree completely.

One of the problems that I as a Westerner have when approaching religious works is that I tend to try to sneak God in there through the back door. For example, when reading Dogen, I have always had this sly little notion lurking in the back of my mind that Dogen had some kind of special knowledge and that, therefore, one could not argue with him. It's the way Christians tend to look at the Bible. They view the Bible as the perfect word of God. The Bible is always right, even when our interpretations of it may be incorrect. I've always had a tendency to view Dogen that way, too. I don't do this consciously. But subconsciously this view still persists.

Working closely with the texts, as I've been doing for the past year or so in preparing this book, and for another year or so before that when working on *Don't Be a Jerk*, I feel like I've been coming face-to-face with Dogen more than I ever have before. I've been looking into the actual words Dogen originally used to express himself in his own language as well as the ways various Dogen scholars have interpreted those words. It has made Dogen appear far more fallible and less God-like.

It was eye-opening to discover places where none of the translators could agree on what Dogen meant, and then to trace back the original words and see for myself why that was. There are places where everyone, from the most learned Dogen scholars right down to dipshits like me, can't do anything but just take our best guesses. This doesn't happen a lot. The translations agree much more often than they disagree. But there are places where nobody knows what the hell Dogen was trying to say. And until we can build a time machine and go ask him what he meant, it looks like we never will. I began to wrestle with the idea that it was entirely possible even Dogen didn't quite know what he was saying sometimes. Just like I don't and you don't.

The idea that there is no God has far-reaching implications. And I think Dogen knew this and tried to emphasize it in his works. There is no ultimate arbiter of right or wrong. In the whole vast universe, there is nobody who knows what you should do in any given situation any better than you do — not your mom and dad, not your best friend Alice, not the president or the pope, and certainly not God.

This idea is kind of like the basic premise underlying existentialism. Existentialism was a reaction to essentialism. Essentialism said that our essence — which you can think of as something akin to our true purpose in life — comes first. Existentialists said that, no, first we exist, and then we figure out what we ought to do. That's a very short version of the argument, but I think it's sufficient.

What impresses me about Buddhism, and about Eastern philosophy in general, is that folks in the West only came up with existentialism a few hundred years ago. But Buddha came up with pretty much that same idea hundreds of years before Christ was born. I don't think this means Indians are better than Westerners. We're all the same species. But as a set of cultures, those of India, China, Japan, and elsewhere have had a lot more time to deal with this idea and with what it implies.

It's one thing to say that we have to find our own purpose, but I find it's a different matter altogether to live it. Buddhists deal with it, in a large part, through meditation. In meditation we try to uncover our true direction in life, completely apart from what we think we want and what we think we are. Our real desires may, in fact, be entirely different from or even opposed to what we think we want. This is something that you can start to see for yourself if you practice being very, very silent and still for long periods of time. You can also start to see some other stuff, which helps in the effort to find the best way to live.

One of the things that becomes clear to most of us who meditate is that we exist in a universe that is conscious and alive, in which all things, living or nonliving, are intimately connected. Forces like gravity and electromagnetism are living things as much as human emotions like love and sorrow. They're not exactly the same, but they have a common source. And yet, behind it all, there is no controller. Not God. Not even you.

This means we are really and truly on our own. There is no force of good out there in the universe who knows the right thing to do, and no force of evil out there compelling us to be bad. We have no excuses for our bad behavior and no one but ourselves to thank if we do the right thing. If we mess up this planet, God is not gonna burst out of the clouds to bail us out like the cavalry galloping in to save the good guy at the end of an old-time cowboy movie. He can't. Because he is you and me.

Sometimes I think that maybe even God wonders where he came from. Maybe God wonders who created him.

Lots of us search for perfect sources of knowledge. Lots of people claim they've found them. The Bible, the Koran, the Bhagavad Gita, and even Dogen's writings have all been claimed by some to be sources of perfect knowledge.

But they aren't.

These books were written by people. You may say, of your chosen book, that it was inspired by God, even if you agree that God didn't actually open up his holy MacBook and type it out himself. And I might even be willing to concede that, given my rather unorthodox idea of God. But if, by saying God inspired the book, you mean that somewhere up in heaven a super-being pointed at some scribe and said, "Write!," well, I can't accept that.

If these books were inspired by God, maybe they were inspired by God's wondering where he came from and what he is. Maybe our wondering about God is the same as God wondering about God. Maybe the answers God comes up with aren't any more final than the answers the rest of us put forth. I think Dogen might have said something like that if he'd ever encountered the Judeo-Christian idea of God.

My first Zen teacher writes poetry. I used part of one of his poems in another of my books. But I like it so much, I'll use it again here. It goes like this:

> God, she said over soup,
> cannot add or subtract from who He is.
> You believe in God, then??
> He doesn't want me to,
> knowing, as He does,
> that God does not exist.
> All fingers grasp the edge
> of this cliff. All other moments are absent.

Did Jesus believe in God? Or did he just *want* so desperately to believe in God that he was willing to suffer and die to find out? I wonder if it was worth it.

And yet here we are.

God cannot add or subtract from who he is. Maybe we can't, either. But we feel as if we are subtracted — or separated — from God and from the rest of creation. Maybe that's why God created us. Maybe, having and being everything, all God could possibly want was to find out what it was like to want something.

I often wonder what Dogen would have made of the Judeo-Christian-Islamic idea of God. I wonder what Dogen would have been like as a Christian rather than a Buddhist. Having said that, I think Christianity has had its share of Dogens. It's just that mainstream Christianity has been as baffled by them as mainstream Buddhism is by Dogen. Perhaps, just as Dogen had to wait seven hundred years to be discovered, there are Christian Dogens out there that few Christians have ever even heard of. At least not yet.

The foundation offered by Buddhism, in the form of its highly developed meditation practices, allowed Dogen to penetrate deeper into the meaning and purpose of life, the universe, and everything than we've been able to so far in the West. Here on our side of the world, in our century, we have sophisticated technology for looking outward, away from ourselves. But we are unable to look inside. Dogen was provided with the means to do so. The sad circumstances of his early life (losing his parents at a young age) gave him the push to be braver than most in actually taking that look.

Dogen was one of the world's most brilliant writers and thinkers. He dug deeper into himself than most people are willing to go, and he made a heroic effort to communicate what he found. I'm honored that I am able to take some small part in making what he wrote available to a wider and more diverse audience than has ever been able to appreciate it.

I hope you've enjoyed reading this book. I liked writing it. I look forward to continuing this journey.

BIBLIOGRAPHY

THE BOOK YOU'VE been reading is a nonscholarly book about Dogen and his work, written by a nonscholar for other nonscholars. Unfortunately, as such, it is an anomaly. Most books in English about Dogen are written by and for people with PhDs in Asian studies, philosophy, or other such fields. So they can be quite challenging to read if you don't know all the specific jargon of those fields.

I've adapted the following bibliography from the one I included in the back of my book *Don't Be a Jerk*. I've added a few books, and I've also added some commentary about the books I've listed to try to help you figure out if they might be useful or interesting to you.

Complete English Translations of *Shōbōgenzō* (in Order of Personal Preference)

Nishijima, Gudo, and Chodo Cross. *Master Dōgen's Shōbōgenzō*, 4 vols. Guildford, UK: Windbell, 1994–1999 (now available as print-on-demand from BookSurge). This is the translation done by my ordaining teacher and his student Mike Cross (Chodo is his dharma name). It is the closest you'll find in English to a literal translation of the original. It is also available for free online. It's hard to read, but it's so close to the original it's like someone gave you a magic pair of glasses that allows you to instantly read medieval Japanese. It also has extensive footnotes that are very useful.

Tanahashi, Kazuaki, and the San Francisco Zen Center. *Treasury of the True*

Dharma Eye: Zen Master Dōgen's Shobo Genzo, 2 vols. Boston: Shambhala, 2013. Kaz Tanahashi translated *Shobogenzo*, with a group of teachers from San Francisco Zen Center acting as co-translators. A different person worked on each chapter. This version isn't as fastidiously true to the original Japanese as the one by Nishijima and Cross, but it is a little easier to read. It doesn't have footnotes, though, so you never really know when Tanahashi et al. have taken liberties with the original text. Fortunately, they don't stray too far from it very often.

Nishiyama, Kosen, and John Stevens. *Shōbōgenzō: The Eye and Treasury of the True Law*, 4 vols. Tokyo: Japan Publications, 1975–1983. This was the standard English edition for a long time but has since gone out of print and can be hard to find. It's more of a paraphrase than a translation but is closer to the original than this book or my book *Don't Be a Jerk*.

Nearman, the Reverend Master Hubert. *Shōbōgenzō: The Treasure House of the Eye of the True Teaching*, 4 vols. Mount Shasta, CA: Shasta Abbey Press, 1996. This is the official edition used by Shasta Abbey, which was founded by Reverend Master Jiyu-Kennett. This is a mostly reliable translation, if you can get past the author's habit of trying to make it sound like the King James Bible. It has a few footnotes, which helps. Available for free online. Good luck trying to find a printed copy. Maybe try eBay?

Shōbōgenzō in Japanese

Nishijima, Wafu. *Gendaigo-yaku Shōbōgenzō*, 12 vols. Yokohama, Japan: Kanazawa Bunko, 1978. This is Nishijima Roshi's complete translation of *Shobogenzo* into contemporary Japanese, which also contains the entire original thirteenth-century text, based on the 1815 edition compiled by Hangyo Kozen (which was reprinted in 1906, with previously missing chapters added). *Wafu* is the alternate pronunciation of Nishijima Roshi's given name, Kazuo, and is part of his dharma name. When writing in English he went by Gudo, the other part of his dharma name, meaning "the Way of Stupidity."

There are many other translations of *Shobogenzo* into modern Japanese, and the thirteenth-century text in Japanese is pretty easy to find, too.

Partial Translations of *Shōbōgenzō*
(in Alphabetical Order by Author/Editor/Translator)

Cleary, Thomas, trans. *Shōbōgenzō: Zen Essays by Dōgen*. Honolulu: University of Hawaii Press, 1992. Contains thirteen chapters of *Shobogenzo*.

Dogen is not Cleary's specialty, nor is Soto-style Zen Buddhism. Cleary treats Dogen as a Japanese author whose work he enjoys. That's not a bad thing. But I tend to prefer translations by people who specialize in Dogen.

————. *Rational Zen: The Mind of Dōgen Zenji*. Boston: Shambhala, 2001. More translations of Dogen by Mr. Cleary.

Cook, Francis Dojun, with a foreword by Taizen Maezumi. *How to Raise an Ox: Zen Practice as Taught in Master Dōgen's Shōbōgenzō*. Somerville, MA: Wisdom Publications, 1999. Contains ten translated chapters of *Shobogenzo*, along with other material. I don't refer to these translations very often myself, but I keep the book around anyhow. It ain't bad.

Soto Zen Text Translation Project. *Shōbōgenzō: Treasury of the True Dharma Eye*. Several translated chapters are available online from Stanford University. These are excellent translations, and I refer to them a lot. Unfortunately, only a few of them are available from the website where they now live, while the rest are nowhere to be found (as far as I've been able to track down, anyhow). I have begun to doubt this project will ever be finished or published in its entirety.

Tanahashi, Kazuaki, ed. *Moon in a Dewdrop: Writings of Zen Master Dōgen*. New York: North Point Press, 1995.

————. *Enlightenment Unfolds: The Essential Teachings of Zen Master Dōgen*. Boston: Shambhala, 2000.

————. *The Essential Dōgen: Writings of the Great Zen Master*. Boston: Shambhala, 2013. The various chapters and excerpts from *Shobogenzo* and Dogen's other writings in these books by Tanahashi were gathered into the complete translation listed above.

Waddell, Norman, and Masao Abe, trans. *The Heart of Dōgen's Shōbōgenzō*. Albany: State University of New York Press, 2002. Contains nine chapters. Not bad translations. I don't refer to them often myself, though.

Books about Dogen and/or *Shōbōgenzō*
(in Alphabetical Order by Author/Editor/Translator)

Bein, Steve. *Purifying Zen: Watsuji Tetsurō's Shamon Dōgen*. Honolulu: University of Hawaii Press, 2011. This is a translation of the book that first brought a lot of popular attention to Dogen in Japan in the 1920s. As such, it's probably mostly of interest to·those doing very deep Dogen studies.

Bielefeldt, Carl. *Dōgen's Manuals of Zen Meditation*. Berkeley and Los Angeles: University of California Press, 1990. This is a very detailed examination of Dogen's famous manual on how to do zazen, "Fukanzazengi." More than you would ever want or need to know about that little book! I find it fascinating, but I'm a nerd for this kind of stuff. Probably not for beginners.

Bodiford, William. *Soto Zen in Medieval Japan.* Honolulu: University of Hawaii Press, 2008. A very scholarly history not only of Dogen but of the lineage he founded. Again, this is mostly for people really into nerding out about Dogen and the history of the movement he started.

Bokusan, Nishiari, Shohaku Okumura, Shunryu Suzuki, and Mel Weitsman. *Dōgen's Genjo Koan: Three Commentaries.* Berkeley, CA: Counterpoint, 2013. Interesting commentaries on Dogen's most famous essay. These are mostly pretty readable but could get confusing if you're not used to the way Zen teachers talk about stuff.

Cook, Francis. *Sounds of Valley Streams: Enlightenment in Dōgen's Zen.* Albany: State University of New York Press, 1989. I occasionally used this book for reference, but I must admit I haven't read it all the way through.

Heine, Steven. *Dōgen and the Koan Tradition.* Albany: State University of New York Press, 1994. This one is a super-scholarly book about Dogen's use of the Chinese koan tradition.

———. *Shifting Shape, Shaping Text: Philosophy and Folklore in the Fox Koan.* Honolulu: University of Hawaii Press, 1999. This book is all about the famous koan Hyakujo's Fox, with a chapter about Dogen's two very different commentaries on it. Very deeply nerdy.

———. *Did Dōgen Go to China?: What He Wrote and When He Wrote It.* New York: Oxford University Press, 2006. Spoiler alert: He did. This book examines Dogen's writings about his journey to China in great detail. Probably more for nerds than regular people.

———, ed. *Dōgen: Textual and Historical Studies.* New York: Oxford University Press, 2012. Essays about Dogen from scholars and practitioners.

———. *Dōgen and Soto Zen.* New York: Oxford University Press, 2015. More nerdy essays about Dogen. Another one for the super Dogen fans.

Kim, Hee-Jin. *Eihei Dōgen: Mystical Realist.* Somerville, MA: Wisdom Publications, 2000. Originally published in 1975, for a long time this was just about the only book about Dogen in English you could find. It's a bit dated nowadays but still very useful. None of the stuff that's now dated would matter much to anyone but really finicky scholars. A good intro to Dogen but kind of dense and difficult.

Kodera, Takashi James. *Dōgen's Formative Years in China: An Historical Study and Annotated Translation of the Hokyo-ki.* Boulder, CO: Routledge & Kegan Paul, 1980. More about Dogen's trip to China and what he wrote about it. This one is way nerdy.

LaFleur, William R. *Dōgen Studies*. Honolulu: University of Hawaii Press, 1985. Another book of scholarly essays about Dogen.

Leighton, Taigen Dan. *Visions of Awakening Space and Time: Dōgen and the Lotus Sutra*. New York: Oxford University Press, 2007. A super-scholarly, super-detailed look at Dogen's writings about the Lotus Sutra. Nerdy as all get-out.

Leighton, Taigen, and Shohaku Okumura, trans. *Dōgen's Pure Standards for the Zen Community*. Albany: State University of New York Press, 1995. A translation of *Eihei Shingi*, Dogen's written works about monastic rules, including the famous "Instructions for the Cook." This one is fairly readable but it's mostly about monastic rules and regulations. Casual readers would probably only want to read the translation of "Instructions for the Cook."

Nishijima, Gudo Wafu, trans. *Master Dōgen's Shinji Shōbōgenzō*. Guildford, UK: Windbell, 2003. This is my teacher's translation of the book of three hundred traditional Chinese koans that Dogen copied in China and used as the practical basis for *Shobogenzo*. Nishijima provides a short commentary about each koan, so that helps.

Okumura, Shohaku, ed. *Dōgen Zen and Its Relevance for Our Time*. San Francisco: Soto Zen Buddhism International Center, 2003. Another book of deeply nerdy essays about Dogen. It's incredibly expensive these days.

———. *Realizing Genjokoan: The Key to Dōgen's Shōbōgenzō*. Somerville, MA: Wisdom, 2010. An absolutely wonderful book about Dogen's most famous essay. Written in very accessible plain English, not the scholarly doublespeak so common to books of this nature. Get it.

———, trans. *The Wholehearted Way: Translation of Eihei Dōgen's Bendowa, with Commentary by Kosho Uchiyama Roshi*. North Clarendon, VT: Tuttle, 2011. A very thorough examination of one of Dogen's most famous essays. Not too scholarly.

———. *Living by Vow: A Practical Introduction to Eight Essential Zen Chants and Texts*. Somerville, MA: Wisdom, 2012. Another incredibly good, very easy-to-read book by Shohaku Okumura. Get this one, too.

Suzuki, Shunryu. *Zen Mind, Beginner's Mind*. Boston: Shambhala, 2011. This is one of the best introductions to Dogen's style of Zen. A collection of lectures by Shunryu Suzuki, founder of the San Francisco Zen Center, it's not the least bit scholarly. Although it's not really about Dogen per se, it was so deeply influenced by Dogen's work that I have included it here. You need this book. Along these same lines, I also highly recommend any of Dainin Katagiri's books. They're also not scholarly works about Dogen but are good examples of how to put Dogen's philosophy into practice.

Uchiyama, Kosho. *How to Cook Your Life: From the Zen Kitchen to Enlightenment.* Boulder, CO: Shambhala, 2015. A very useful translation of Dogen's famous "Instructions for the Cook," along with a commentary by one of Japan's leading teachers of Soto-style Zen. Easy to read. Not too scholarly.

Warner, Jisho, Shohaku Okumura, John McRae, and Taigen Dan Leighton. *Nothing Is Hidden: Essays on Zen Master Dōgen's Instructions for the Cook.* Boulder, CO: Weatherhill, 2001. This book is exactly what its title says it is! Very useful and not terribly scholarly or difficult.

Yokoi, Yuho. *Zen Master Dōgen: An Introduction with Selected Writings.* Boston: Weatherhill, 1976. My teacher, Gudo Nishijima Roshi, did not think very highly of Professor Yokoi's translations of Dogen. But Yokoi was one of Japan's most respected scholars of Dogen, and one of the few Japanese Dogen scholars whose work is available in English. Probably more useful for nerds than for normal people.

About the Author

BRAD WARNER WAS born in Ohio, grew up in Africa, and lived in Japan for eleven years, where he got ordained as a Zen monk. He now resides in the Hipsterville part of Los Angeles. He began sitting zazen when he was eighteen years old under the instruction of Tim McCarthy and was made a dharma heir of Gudo Nishijima Roshi in the futuristic year 2000. He used to work for a company that made movies about giant radioactive lizards eating Tokyo, and now he writes books like this one.

He also travels the world showing people how to sit down and shut up. He has given talks and led Zen meditation retreats in the United States, Canada, England, Scotland, Northern Ireland, Finland, the Netherlands, Germany, France, Poland, Israel, Belgium, Spain, and Japan. His books have been translated into fewer languages than those of anyone you've ever seen on the cover of a meditation magazine, but there are editions in Finnish, Polish, German, and Greek. And supposedly there's one in Hebrew, but he's never seen a copy. Or maybe he has but doesn't know it because he can't read Hebrew. He wishes someone would point it out to him somewhere if the book actually exists.

He plays bass guitar in the hardcore punk band Zero Defex

(oDFx).* He has had major roles in several movies, including *Zombie Bounty Hunter M.D.* and *Shoplifting from American Apparel*. He also wrote, produced, and directed his own film, *Cleveland's Screaming*. Plus, he made five albums for Midnight Records under the semi-fictional band name Dimentia 13.

When he's not doing zazen, Brad can be found at record stores all over the world searching for obscure psychedelia and songs to add to his incredible cheesy seventies playlist. He enjoys bad science fiction movies and cats, though dogs are okay too. He's a vegetarian but tries not to be a total pain in the ass about it.

---

* Did you ever wonder where NOFX got their name? We were around well before them.